Bad Boys, Bad Times

Mike + Michelle

Hopefully one of these years we will get to see a World Series game!

Best,

[signature]

BAD BOYS, BAD TIMES

The Cleveland Indians
and Baseball in the
Prewar Years, 1937–1941

Scott H. Longert

Ohio University Press   Athens

Ohio University Press, Athens, Ohio 45701
ohioswallow.com
© 2019 by Scott H. Longert
All rights reserved

Printed in the United States of America
Ohio University Press books are printed on acid-free paper ⊗ ™

29 28 27 26 25 24 23 22 21 20 19   5 4 3 2 1

Library of Congress Cataloging-in-Publication Data
Names: Longert, Scott, author.
Title: Bad boys, bad times : the Cleveland Indians and baseball in the prewar
  years, 1937-1941 / Scott H. Longert.
Description: Athens : Ohio University Press, [2019] | Includes
  bibliographical references and index.
Identifiers: LCCN 2018056334| ISBN 9780821423790 (hc : alk. paper) | ISBN
  9780821423806 (pb : alk. paper) | ISBN 9780821446799 (pdf)
Subjects: LCSH: Cleveland Indians (Baseball team)–History–20th century.
Classification: LCC GV875.C7 .L67 2019 | DDC 796.357/640977132–dc23
LC record available at https://lccn.loc.gov/2018056334

CONTENTS

ILLUSTRATIONS

Following page 78

Chapter 1

A TROUBLESOME OFF-SEASON

For Indians boss Alva Bradley, the 1937 regular season could not have arrived soon enough. The fall and winter months had been filled with controversy and debate, mostly detrimental to his ball club. Bradley, who had bought the team in late 1927, had seen more ups and downs in recent days than in his entire previous tenure. Now that opening day had just about arrived, he hoped for at least a few months of smooth sailing.

The first round of turmoil began in late September of 1936. Rumors floated around the American League that the Indians might have illegally signed pitcher Bob Feller. Still a high school student, the seventeen-year-old phenom had pitched sparingly throughout the season, but in the latter part had managed to break the American League strikeout record. Feller and his incredible fastball had brought comparisons to the great Walter Johnson and all the other speed ball kings. The Cleveland front office daydreamed of the pennants the youngster from Van Meter, Iowa, would surely bring.

The dream turned into a nightmare when, on September 23, Ed McAuley of the *Cleveland News* broke the unpleasant story. The Indians beat reporter had uncovered evidence that Feller had signed directly with Cleveland and not a minor league club. The Major League rules of 1936 stated that teams could not sign a player straight out of high school. The rule read, "Major League clubs shall sign as free agents only college players and players who

1

have previously contracted, or accepted terms, or had service, with any Minor or Major League clubs." This rule was introduced five years previously when minor league clubs were overwhelmed by the Great Depression and did not have the means to compete with the American or National League clubs for raw talent.

In his story, McAuley reported that most Major League teams flouted the rules on a regular basis. However, this case received national attention due to Feller's spectacular accomplishments while still only a schoolboy. How could he have gotten to the Majors so fast? According to McAuley, the Indians' chief scout, Cyril "Cy" Slapnicka, had allegedly signed Feller, then behind closed doors had transferred him to the Class D Fargo-Moorhead club of the Northern League.

The two organizations had a working agreement that kept Feller safely away from the other Major League teams. However, after the pitcher signed his Cleveland contract, the Des Moines, Iowa, club attempted to acquire Feller. They were puzzled by the actions of both Bob and his father William, neither of whom showed any interest in a deal. The Des Moines rep had no inkling that the Fellers had already been spoken for. When Bob set his American League strikeout record at the tail end of the baseball season, the Des Moines people knew somebody, probably Cleveland, had pulled a fast one. Lee Keyser, the Des Moines owner, wasted no time in filing a grievance with the commissioner's office. The chances of recovering Feller were nil, whereas the likelihood for a cash settlement was a good bet.

Baseball commissioner Judge Kenesaw Mountain Landis had a complicated problem to deal with. This was not a matter of some obscure minor league player that few paid attention to. No matter how the Judge ruled, his decision would be front-page news all around the country.

Landis had a strong regard for minor league players. He despised the idea of the Major League clubs having a "chain store" system that impeded the progress of young men trying to advance to the big leagues. Most clubs, particularly the Yankees and Red Sox, had extensive interests in all levels of minor league organizations. They could manipulate a player's destiny, moving him from club to club until they believed he was ready to compete at the highest level. This led to several procedures that Landis found despicable. "Covering up" meant shuttling a player back and forth to different minor league clubs to avoid scrutiny. This took place when a team in the Majors had no room for the player in question or believed he needed more time. The player wound up being "sold" to the minors, but only to a team that was part of the Major League team's chain store. This procedure could go on indefinitely, denying the player a legitimate shot at the big time.

The procedure that applied to Feller was called "recommending." A Major League team (Cleveland in this case) would sign a player (Feller), then nudge a friendly club (Fargo-Moorhead) to quietly ink him to a valid minor league contract. After a certain length of time the Major League team would advise their partner to sell the player to a higher level (the Class A New Orleans Pelicans, a long-time friend to Cleveland). From there, the Major League team would be informed what a great prospect they had, and would buy the player's contract—which is just what the Indians, acting on manager Steve O'Neill's recommendation, did. This appeared to be a legal move, with the paperwork to back it up. However, the Indians were quite careless in shifting Feller through their farm system before he had pitched a single inning for Fargo-Moorhead or New Orleans. He arrived in Cleveland during the springtime, doing some concession work at League Park and pitching sporadically for an amateur club. The Indians had beaten the system, yet Feller's great pitching late in the year completely blew up the scam.

Judge Landis had little or no sympathy for William Feller and his young son, who had stayed in step with the Cleveland front office, seemingly unaware of any wrongdoing by the Indians. The Fellers notified Landis that they were happy with Cleveland and preferred to remain even if something illegal had occurred. The judge explained free agency to them and the possibility of Bob having the once-in-a-lifetime chance to collect a gigantic payday with another Major League club. Most players would have jumped at the chance to sell their services for as much dough as possible. Here was a tremendous opportunity to make an example of the Cleveland club and score one for the little guy. But William and son were adamant about staying put, forcing Landis to ponder this one for a long while.

Another issue Judge Landis had to consider seriously was that other Major League teams had violated the same rule. Ed McAuley asserted that a highly placed team official told him that if Feller became a free agent there were about ten players on each Major League roster who could become free agents as well. If these ballplayers filed any complaints, it would turn baseball upside down. Although the Judge had no deep feelings for most of the owners, he did not relish wrecking the status quo. Landis decided to take a long fishing trip, telling curious writers a verdict probably would not be given until the first week of December.

While Bob Feller returned to high school in Van Meter, anxiety spread throughout the Cleveland front office. Alva Bradley heard reports of the Yankees and Red Sox gearing up for a bidding war should the Judge rule against the Indians. Surely the possibility of losing the greatest pitching prospect since Walter Johnson or Lefty Grove had to cause some restless nights for the Indians owner. But Bradley remained confident, at least in public, that he had nothing to worry about.

Eventually the newspapers reported that a decision would be revealed at the December 1936 winter meetings. Sure enough, on the tenth the ruling came down. The Indians were found guilty but were allowed to keep Feller. Judge Landis fined Cleveland $7,500 for their actions, payable to the Des Moines club. The Judge released a 2,500-word statement blasting the conduct of the Indians and all of baseball in general. "It turns out that in reality Fargo-Moorhead had nothing whatsoever to do with signing Feller which was done by the Cleveland club, its agent Slapnicka using for that purpose a minor league contract because he could not sign him to a major league contract," the Judge wrote. Landis then slammed the process of "recommending" and gave a step-by-step account of how the Indians had violated the baseball law. Fargo-Moorhead had received only $300 for selling Feller to New Orleans, and the Pelicans just $1,500 for moving Feller to Cleveland. The sales were noticeably below market value for a player of Feller's perceived caliber. Though the Indians were the recipient of the Judge's fury, it was Cy Slapnicka who was singled out. Going forward, the new Cleveland general manager would need to walk the line or face the consequences.

In analyzing the situation, Judge Landis did about all he could. Allowing Feller to become a free agent opened the door for any number of ballplayers to cry foul and demand their freedom. He did not have any inclination to rule on potentially hundreds of similar cases. Another factor was the Fellers' steadfast desire to remain with the Indians. The papers would have a field day with the story and hound the Judge unmercifully. It was time to move on to other things, particularly the 1937 season.

Now that the crisis had passed, the Indians considered some moves to improve the ball club. On January 18, Cleveland and the St. Louis Browns agreed on a huge six-player trade. Outfielder Julius "Moose" Solters, shortstop Lyn Lary, and pitcher Ivy Paul Andrews would come to the Indians, while the Browns would receive shortstop Bill Knickerbocker, pitcher Oral Hildebrand, and star Cleveland outfielder Joe Vosmik. The two pitchers involved were throw-ins; neither one had lived up to his potential.

The Solters-for-Vosmik part of the trade drew plenty of criticism from the Cleveland fans and several of the sportswriters. Ed Bang of the *Cleveland News* believed trading Joe was a significant error on the part of Cy Slapnicka. Vosmik made the All-Star team in 1935, leading the American League in three different categories. His .348 batting average left him one point short of the title. But he had had a mediocre season in 1936, prompting Slapnicka to reckon his left fielder was on the down side. Many fans complained to the newspapers, believing Moose Solters, a middle-of-the-road player, could not replace the Cleveland-born Vosmik.

Lyn Lary had had some good seasons with Yankees, but the Indians were now his fifth team in the American League. He could steal some bases and cover a lot of ground defensively, but his batting average had declined on a yearly basis. Bill Knickerbocker had won the Cleveland shortstop job in 1933 and held it over four seasons. His play could be termed steady yet lacking in any superior skills. The Indians front office thought some new blood on the team might spur them along. The trade inspired headlines throughout the country, yet the probability of Solters and Lary leading the team to the pennant seemed remote.

Two months later, the Indians, new players and all, gathered in New Orleans for the opening of spring training. The national reporters turned their attention to Bob Feller, filing stories on just about anything concerning him. The public ate it up, particularly Feller's politeness and "aw shucks" nature. There were many positive vibes coming out of camp, mostly courtesy of the eighteen-year-old almost-superstar.

Near the end of camp, more stories appeared revealing that once again the Indians front office was in hot water with their good friend Judge Landis. On March 29 it was disclosed that the Judge had been investigating a possible cover-up in the case of minor league outfielder Tommy Henrich. The Massillon, Ohio, product was originally signed in 1934 by Cleveland ex-player and scout Bill Bradley. Henrich reported to Zanesville, an Indians affiliate. He excelled there, triggering a rapid promotion to New Orleans. The 1936 season displayed Henrich at his best, batting a lofty .346 and compiling a gaudy total of 203 hits. Clearly he stood as one of the elite players in all of the Southern Association. In September of the same year, New Orleans questionably sold Henrich and pitcher Ralph Winegarner to the Milwaukee Brewers for $7,500. This ridiculous figure came to the attention of Billy Evans, the recent general manager of the Cleveland Indians. Evans departed Cleveland in a huff after Bradley cut his salary by 50 percent and now supervised the entire Boston Red Sox farm system. In an article in a Canton, Ohio, publication, Evans remarked that Henrich alone could easily bring a price of $15,000 to any Major League club. Stories circulated that Henrich read the article and believed a questionable deal had taken place. He did not know that Milwaukee had recently become an affiliate of the Indians. That raised the issue of who had really sent Henrich to Milwaukee, the Indians or their long-time partner, New Orleans. Over the winter months Henrich wrote a letter to Landis, politely asking for clarification of his standing. After his tremendous season at New Orleans, should he not have received an invite to Cleveland's spring training? He asked Landis who really owned his contract. The investigation began on March 29.

Rest assured that Alva Bradley did not take the ongoing probe lightly. The brunt of his anger was directed at his former associate, Billy Evans. Bradley insisted Evans had ulterior motives in writing the September article. The Indians owner told the *Cleveland Plain Dealer,* "I don't care about Henrich but I do care about learning how long Evans will be allowed to continue the tactics that have caused us trouble since he severed his connection with Cleveland." Bradley went on to insist that Evans was committing a breach of ethics in harassing his former employer.

Evans responded comically, advising reporters he did not know what "breach of ethics" meant and he would have to look it up. Bradley's angry outburst probably related to the Feller decision the winter before. Apparently Evans had flown to Des Moines, Iowa, to wait for Judge Landis to issue a ruling. In the event of Feller becoming a free agent, Evans planned to park himself on Bob's front door with a Boston contract. This irritated Bradley; throw in the Henrich situation and the messy divorce in the Cleveland front office, and it can be better understood why the owner wanted Evans cut off at the knees.

Bill Terry, the manager of the New York Giants, threw gas on the fire by saying Henrich was worth at least $20,000. To the casual observer it appeared the Indians were guilty beyond belief. Landis would conduct a thorough investigation, but given that the Feller case had occurred just three months before, it was generally thought that he would declare Henrich a free agent.

Landis cut short a Florida vacation to meet in New Orleans with Bradley and Slapnicka. Reporters, eager to file a big story, waited patiently outside the building for over three long hours. The door opened and out came the two conspirators with dire expressions on their faces. They did not comment, though any betting man would have put it all down on Henrich and the open market. Few men, including Slapnicka, escaped the ire of Judge Landis. Cy, or as reporters were now calling him, "Sly," had done it once. The chance of another victory seemed slim.

On April 15 Landis issued his decree. The decision read, "Investigation of the status of the player, instigated at his own request, discloses that he has been 'covered up' for the benefit of the Cleveland club. . . . Because of the violation of the player's rights under his contract and the major–minor league rules, he is hereby declared a free agent." Tommy Henrich was now able to negotiate with any Major League club.

Henrich took the high road in commenting to the press. He said, "I am satisfied of course with the judge's decision, although

I said before I did not appeal for my free agency. All I asked the judge to do was to decide my status—if I belonged to Milwaukee outright, to Cleveland or some other club." He immediately left the Brewers spring training site for Massillon to confer with his parents. Landis had ruled a three-day waiting period before teams could overwhelm Henrich with substantial offers. When the clock struck midnight, the New York Yankees dove in and signed Henrich to a contract. The Yanks outbid the Red Sox and Giants by offering a bonus between $25,000 and $30,000. Henrich would have a long, productive career in New York, becoming a four-time All-Star and a great complement to Joe DiMaggio.

The Indians front office committed a ghastly error in trying to hide the talented Henrich in the minor leagues. They may have decided that their 1937 outfield had no room for the up-and-coming right fielder. Earl Averill had reached his thirty-fifth birthday but still was one of the best in the American League in center field. Bruce Campbell had survived two life-threatening bouts of meningitis and looked to be as strong as ever. Moose Solters would be the starter in left field. On paper the outfield looked to be quite sturdy. Even so, a fourth outfielder had to be carried on the squad. Instead of Henrich, the Indians chose Roy Weatherly, another highly regarded young player. In his 1936 rookie season, "Stormy," as everyone called him, batted over .300. However, opposing teams soon figured out he could not handle a slow curve or off-speed pitches. In 1937 Weatherly hit an awful .201 in a limited relief role.

When the Indians decided to bring up Weatherly a year prior, New Orleans manager Larry Gilbert urged them to take Henrich instead, believing he had a much bigger upside. Cy Slapnicka did not agree. He saw the great speed of Stormy and the likelihood of his playing center field in the cow pasture of Municipal Stadium. Tommy Henrich could have filled at least the utility role on a much more productive level, and with his ability the Indians would have figured out a way to get him in the starting lineup. In any event, if the Cleveland front office had not tried to be the smartest guys in the room, a pennant or two might have been there for the taking.

The 1936–37 off-season surely caused Alva Bradley more heartburn than any other term on his record. He looked ahead to the onset of the regular season and a chance to focus on the launch of a new schedule. Nevertheless, the bad times just kept on rolling. Just prior to the start of the campaign, another depressing event occurred, though this one had no direct impact on the season. Tris Speaker, the Indian's unofficial goodwill ambassador and a fan favorite, had a severe accident. Still nimble at age forty-nine, he was attempting to build a flower box on the second floor of his suburban Cleveland home. He climbed up the porch, balanced himself, and began hammering away. Moments later the porch collapsed, tumbling the ex–Indian great sixteen feet to the ground. A lesser man would have lain there waiting for help. Not Speaker; he staggered to his feet and cautiously sat down on a lawn chair. His wife called an ambulance, which raced Tris to the hospital. The X-rays taken revealed a fractured skull, a broken arm, and a cracked bone in his right hand. Serious lacerations covered his entire face. The doctors put Tris in a hospital bed with bags of ice wrapped around his head. He could barely speak or move anything but his legs.

For a day or two the physicians feared he might not survive the injuries. To everyone's relief, Tris did beat the odds, getting back on his feet in just about a month. He missed opening day at League Park, where for the better part of twenty years he had greeted players and fans with a hearty smile and some words of encouragement. He usually stopped in the radio booth to chat with WHK announcer and ex-teammate Jack Graney. The crowd always expected to see Tris, maybe get a few words with him and an autograph for the kids at home. This year Speaker remained in his hospital bed, catching the play-by-play from old friend Graney.

After what seemed an eternity for Bradley, Slapnicka, Feller, and the rest of the Indians, it was actually time to play ball.

Chapter 2

A MAJOR SCARE

The 1937 baseball season had the word "optimism" in just about all aspects of the game. The previous year, Major League attendance rose to a noteworthy level of 7.4 million fans, a gain of 1.4 million from 1935. The large majority of teams enjoyed significant gains in attendance, with only Detroit and the St. Louis Cardinals on the negative side. The Indians reached 500,000, a sizable gain of nearly 103,000 spectators. The Great Depression still had a grip on the country, but the people who loved baseball were finding ways of scraping up a dollar or two and heading to the ballpark. Unemployment figures dropped from almost 17 percent to a touch over 14—still a troubling number, yet reason to hope that better days were ahead.

Alva Bradley shared that enthusiasm in two words: Bob Feller. Even though he had pitched just sixty-two innings in 1936, the eyes of the nation were focused squarely on the kid from Van Meter. They chose not to remark on the troublesome forty-seven walks or the eight wild pitches. Instead, fans remembered the smoking fastball that accounted for seventeen K's against the Athletics and fifteen against the Browns. With all the hype surrounding Feller, a thirty-win season plus three hundred strikeouts were universally expected.

All through spring training the crowds doubled in size when Feller took the mound. Reporters and fans followed him from the diamond to the clubhouse and back to the hotel. He signed count-less autographs and permitted lengthy interviews with anybody from the press. He had radio stations begging for live in-studio pro-grams, along with ice cream companies badgering him to eat their products during National Ice Cream Week. The Cleveland writers noted that Feller went to bed by nine o'clock each night, totally exhausted from the nonstop attention.

Manager Steve O'Neill complimented his young pitcher for displaying the knowledge and skills of a true veteran. O'Neill re-marked that Feller had remembered everything he was taught last season while handling batters as if he had been in the Majors for several years. The Cleveland skipper believed Feller's curveball had become a key weapon in addition to his blistering fastball. O'Neill made no predictions but indicated big things were ex-pected in 1937.

National columnists weighed in on Feller's impact for the com-ing season. Will Connolly, writing for a San Francisco newspaper, thought the Cleveland pitcher would be beneficial for the game. He wrote, "Interest in baseball will improve in direct ratio to in-terest in pitching feats and that's why I say Robert William Andrew Feller is a greater asset to the major leagues than our own Joseph Paul DiMaggio. It is a fact that Feller of Van Meter, Iowa and the Cleveland Indians, is doing more to accelerate interest in baseball than any rookie who has broken in during the past twenty years."

Connolly had a fair point. Though Joe DiMaggio had great ap-peal to fans in New York and his hometown of San Francisco, it would be Feller who brought more notice to baseball in virtually the entire United States. The American League owners certainly hoped Feller would live up to the extremely high anticipation and boost ticket sales at all their parks.

On Tuesday, April 20, the Indians and Tigers opened regular season play at Detroit. Veteran Cleveland pitcher Mel Harder re-ceived the start against Elden Auker. Detroit got on the board early, scoring single runs in the first and second innings, then two more in the fourth. The big blow was a long home run by outfielder Gerald "Gee" Walker. The Indians, led by Roy Hughes and Lyn Lary, managed to score three times in the early innings. After the fourth neither team was able to plate any runs, leaving the final score at 4–3 Tigers. A good-sized crowd of 38,000 fans watched the two teams' battle.

Typical early spring weather brought rain showers, canceling games until Cleveland's Friday, April 23, home opener against the St. Louis Browns. During the week the team attended a press luncheon to promote fan interest in the opener. Cy Slapnicka was the master of ceremonies, handling the brief introductions for the Indians players. Slap called up Bob Feller to say "Howdy." Feller walked to the microphone, leaned forward, and said "Howdy," then ambled back to his seat. Of course, the script was for everybody to say a few words, then be seated. The players burst out with laughter at Feller's unintentional humor. After that, when introduced, each player said "Howdy," then pretended to walk away. Feller had to be prodded to return to the speaker's podium and answer a few easy questions. Later he would understand the expectations and have a few canned sentences ready to go.

In spite of the threatening weather, the Indians front office let fans know the opener would go forward. By late morning the rain let up and a touch of sunshine broke through the overcast skies. The Cleveland fans eagerly marched into League Park, carrying topcoats in case of rain or anything else. They checked the prices at the Lexington Avenue ticket window, which showed box seats going for $1.60, reserve for $1.35, pavilion seats for 85 cents, and bleachers for 55 cents. The people with season tickets strolled behind the outfield walls, where they entered a private gate on Linwood Avenue.

The grounds crew, now run by Emil Bossard, had the field in playable shape. The infield had no large puddles, while the freshly cut outfield grass looked to be uniform in height. The bat boys were stacking the new player bats in two long rows in front of each dugout. The box seats even had new canvas covers. The only thing lacking was the ballplayers' entrance onto the field.

While ushers in bright new red jackets helped the fans track down their seats, Bob Hamilton, the long-time head of concessions, peered out from his spot under the stands, trying to gauge the exact figure of people he needed to feed. Ready for the vendors were a half-ton of juicy hot dogs, another half-ton of freshly roasted peanuts, 400 cases of beer, 750 cases of soda pop, and, for good measure, 100 large boxes of assorted candy. Modern equipment allowed Hamilton to keep the hot dogs sizzling, the peanuts toasty, and the beer and soda pop ice cold.

A recent study in *Baseball Magazine* had revealed that peanuts were the number one seller at Major League ballparks, followed closely by Coca-Cola and soft drinks of assorted flavors. It seemed the fans in the sun-drenched bleachers swigged the greatest amount of cold soda and spent the most money of any portion of seats. The folks under cover did not have to deal with the bright sun and tended to load up on peanuts and popcorn. Hearty concession sales were vital for teams struggling to make a small profit. The magazine noted that concession sales kept several teams afloat during the early years of the Great Depression.

Before long the Indians jogged out to the field, splendid in their home whites with scarlet trim and the Indian chief on the left sleeve. They wore black caps with a red C and black socks with three thin white stripes. The uniforms were manufactured by Blepp-Coombs Sporting Goods Stores, a Cleveland retail giant located at 55th and Superior.

The fans cheered loudly for their favorite veterans, including Earl Averill, Hal Trosky, Bruce Campbell, Sammy "Bad News" Hale, and catcher Frankie Pytlak. They hollered for starting pitcher Johnny Allen while he tossed his warmup throws. As expected, a huge roar went up from the stands when Bob Feller left the dugout to play catch. Though he would not pitch until Saturday, all eyes were on him. He finished his throws, then had to run the gauntlet of reporters and at least one radio host with a live microphone.

The pregame revelries began with Mayor Harold Burton throwing out the first pitch. It took him four tries before he sailed one across home plate. The large crowd rose to its feet when a group of dazzling chorus girls from Playhouse Square lined up smartly at home plate. The Indians nearly knocked each other down scrambling out of the home dugout and dashing to a spot in front of the eye-catching ladies. Roy Weatherly proved he was the fastest ballplayer on the club, outrunning everybody to get a choice location for the photos.

With this appealing highlight, the pregame ceremonies ended. Allen tossed his warmup pitches and the game got underway.

Through much of the 1936 season he had displayed a violent personality, ready to fight umpires, opposing players, managers, and anybody who seemingly wronged him. The Cleveland fans wondered if he would continue the outrageous behavior in the new season.

To the relief of the 20,752 patrons, the Browns went out easily in the top of the first inning. Allen faced three batters without screaming at anyone. The Indians' new shortstop, Lyn Lary, came to the plate to face St. Louis starter Elon Hogsett. The veteran pitcher, formerly of the Detroit Tigers, eventually sported a high lifetime earned run average of over five runs per game. Lary swung at the first pitch, lining a double down the right-field line. Roy Hughes walked and Earl Averill laid down a sacrifice bunt to move the runners to second and third. That brought up slugging first baseman Hal Trosky. He did not disappoint, lining a shot to deep right field, where Beau Bell made a nice running grab. Lary, who had tagged up at third, scored the game's first run without difficulty.

Cleveland broke the game open in the fourth inning with a barrage of singles and doubles, scoring five runs. An error by Browns third baseman Harlond Clift scored Hale, then Lyn Lary belted his second double to right field for another run. Roy Hughes followed with another two-base hit to score Johnny Allen and Lary. Trosky singled to cap the scoring and put the game out of reach. Hogsett took a seat on the bench to watch a parade of four Browns relief pitchers finish the game.

Johnny Allen gave up seven hits in the fifth through seventh innings, but managed to dance out of trouble, allowing only two runs in his nine-inning stint. One of the runs came via a booming triple by former Indian Joe Vosmik. The temperamental Allen pitched well, in spite of throwing just eleven innings in spring training. He kept himself under control, only tossing the rosin bag a couple of times when he disagreed with the home plate umpire.

The 9–2 victory pleased the crowd, who were also entertained by a wild brawl in the right-field seats. It took a handful of police to break up the fight between several obviously drunken fans. Later some of the colorful bunting hanging from the upper level caught fire due to a careless fan lighting his cigar. Quick-thinking young men attempted to douse the flames with beer and soda until water was located to put out the blaze. All of the rousing activity, plus a total of twenty-two hits between the two teams, made the game last an unusually long two hours and forty-five minutes.

The Indians to a man were jubilant in the clubhouse. There were plenty of smiles, including Johnny Allen yelling from the showers, "I only need nineteen more wins!" They had played hard and hustled, completely deserving the one-sided win. Manager Steve O'Neill talked happily with reporters, pleased that his boys had put on a good show. Now all attention turned to Saturday's game and the season debut of still–high schooler Bob Feller.

Throughout spring training, every pitch Feller threw, every warmup toss he made, was carefully scrutinized by reporters and fans. Now, on April 24, the baseball realm would see how he fared. At game time there were 12,000 fans in the seats, a fine crowd for the day after the home opener. Among the ticket holders were an unusual number of young boys, already members of the growing Feller fan club. They anticipated a big win, with at least eighteen or twenty strikeouts.

For St. Louis, leadoff hitter and former Indian Bill Knickerbocker walked to home plate. Feller started with a few curveballs when suddenly a severe pain raced through his elbow. He panicked for a moment, not sure what to do. Feller desperately wanted to make a good showing, especially in his first start of the year. His elbow throbbing, he made the decision to keep the pain to himself. He shook off the signs from Frankie Pytlak until he saw the one for a fastball. Feller blazed away, though the aching in his arm was almost unbearable. He stuck with the fastball, trying not to make eye contact with his puzzled catcher.

Knickerbocker looked over several pitches, then trotted to first with a walk. After a fly ball for out number one, Joe Vosmik stepped up to the plate. He picked out a fastball for a sharp base hit. Feller kept throwing the hard one, but could not find the plate, walking outfielder Beau Bell and player-manager Rogers Hornsby. That brought in the first run of the ball game, still leaving the bases loaded. The free-swinging Harlond Clift chased three fastballs for the second out. After another walk forced in run number two, Catcher Rollie Hemsley lined a base hit to make the score 4–0.

Feller got the third out and walked back to the dugout without talking to Steve O'Neill or Pytlak.

In the second inning Feller loaded the bases again, this time with none out. After he retired Beau Bell, Rogers Hornsby came to the plate with a choice opportunity to crack the game wide open. In spite of the mounting pain in his elbow, Feller gamely struck out the Browns' big hitter. Harlond Clift swung away, lofting a fly ball to Bruce Campbell. The fans stood and applauded their hero for escaping the inning unscathed.

The Indians batters came to life in the bottom of the second inning. Sammy Hale smacked a double to left field and Campbell walked. St. Louis pitcher Jim Walkup checked the runners and delivered to Frankie Pytlak, who hammered the ball to the fence. Both runners scored while Pytlak raced to third with a triple. Feller came to bat with a chance to cut into the lead. Once again the fans stood as Feller singled, scoring Pytlak from third. Now the Indians trailed by only a run.

Feller struggled through another four innings until he gathered his courage and confessed to O'Neill that he had hurt his arm. Trainer Lefty Weisman took Feller to the clubhouse and carefully examined the arm. It did not appear to be anything serious, allowing Feller to advise reporters he would throw again in a few days. Though the Indians lost the game, 4–3, the big story in the papers was the scary arm injury and the possible ramifications.

On the positive side, Feller had struck out eleven batters in his six innings. After giving up the four runs, he blanked St. Louis over the next five innings. He did walk six Browns. Walks were a major concern of the front office, but out-of-town writers would reference them as evidence that Feller was just wild enough to be effective.

Several days later the elbow had shown little improvement. Cy Slapnicka called team doctor Edward Castle to examine his ailing pitcher. A complete assessment revealed several torn fibers just below the elbow. Dr. Castle instructed Feller to rest the arm for two weeks before doing any kind of throwing. The diagnosis calmed Slapnicka and Alva Bradley, but they maintained a small amount of worry. The two men had made a large investment in the hard-throwing right-hander. They could stand another couple of weeks, but anything more might be viewed as a serious predicament.

Trainer Lefty Weisman believed a bone in the right arm might have been dislocated from the elbow. Weisman had no formal medical training, but had spent over fifteen years treating damaged ballplayers. He recommended a visit to a bonesetter practicing several blocks from League Park. Cy Slapnicka quickly discounted the suggestion, preferring to take the advice of experienced doctors. His lack of faith in Weisman proved to be a major error in judgment.

On Monday, May 10, Feller left Cleveland on a chartered airplane bound for Des Moines, Iowa. He was returning home to Van Meter to rest his arm and attend his high school graduation. He was taken aback by all the local folks waiting to greet him and asking pointed questions about his pitching arm. Feller thought he could go home and escape all the attention; however, any plans to rest quietly and study for finals were quickly foiled. He spent any time he could find cramming for final exams, which took place Thursday. The subjects tested were physics, literature, American history, and psychology. Feller passed with ease, scoring two seventy-nines, a seventy-four, and a seventy. Not bad at all when you consider he had left school over two months ago, yet still retained a good portion of what he had learned over the winter.

The much-anticipated graduation took place on Friday evening. The high school auditorium had just four hundred seats available, usually more than enough for any occasion. It proved to be totally insufficient, as approximately eight hundred curious people jammed inside the tiny hall. Among the crowd was an army of newspaper reporters and radio men with microphones. WMAL radio, all the way from Washington, DC, set up their equipment for a live broadcast to be aired nationally. The parents and relatives of the twenty graduates were shocked by the ruckus around them. This kind of attention was usually reserved for the president of the United States.

Feller arrived at the auditorium wearing a new dark gray suit with a red rose pinned to his lapel. He could not help but note the large contingent of reporters and radio announcers just below the stage. As class president, he addressed the audience in a low voice, speaking rapidly. He said, "When I was playing baseball in high school, little did I realize that I would be playing big league baseball today." He reached for his diploma, nearly dropped it, then scrambled back to his seat. The other graduates, clearly nervous in front of all the reporters and microphones, stumbled through their orations and songs. With the motto "The higher we rise, the better the view," Bob Feller's high school days were officially over.

A few days later Feller left Van Meter to meet up with the Indians on their eastern road trip. Besides his much-publicized injury, there was a list of mounting issues facing the ball club. On May 1, Johnny Allen complained of severe pain in his abdomen. The Indians rushed him to a St. Louis hospital, where doctors diagnosed Allen with a flare-up of appendicitis, but were certain he could avoid any immediate surgery. Manager O'Neill had begun the season with Allen as his ace and Feller a likely candidate for number two. In just a few weeks the only healthy pitchers were veterans Mel Harder and Earl Whitehill. Denny Galehouse, still learning the ropes, would be pressed into immediate service.

Three days after Allen went down, the Indians faced the Washington Senators. Mel Harder pitched a decent game, going six and two-third innings while allowing five runs, three earned. His teammates played little defense, committing four errors, including one by each of the infielders. Roy Weatherly added to the sloppy play, heaving a throw from center field to the wrong base, which allowed runners to advance into scoring position. A frustrated Steve O'Neill severely chewed out Weatherly when he came back to the dugout.

Reliever Joe Heving replaced Harder and held the Senators in check for the next three and a third innings, leaving with the score deadlocked at 5–5. Newly acquired Carl Fischer took the mound for the top of the eleventh, promptly walking Ben Chapman. Buddy Lewis singled, then Joe Kuhel sacrificed the runners to second and third. After a strikeout of Jon Stone, Steve O'Neill had now seen enough of Fischer, and motioned for Whitlow Wyatt to enter the game. The situation worsened as Wyatt gave up a base on balls to Al Simmons. The fans at League Park squirmed in their seats when Ben Chapman inched down the third-base line. Wyatt began his delivery as if there was nobody on base. All three runners took off, with Chapman sliding effortlessly home ahead of the pitch. Incredibly, a rare triple steal had just been executed against the hapless Indians. Three straight base hits followed, forcing O'Neill to go to the bullpen once more. Long-time veteran Willis Hudlin entered the game, serving up a single and a double before finally retiring the Senators.

Seven big runs had just crossed the plate against three miserable Indian relievers. The frustrated crowd let go with a steady chorus of jeers while the home team, heads bowed low, trotted off the field. The Senators won by a lopsided score of 12–5. Tomorrow's newspapers were sure to be filled with some extra-colorful reporting.

Those fans who picked up a copy of the *Cleveland News* were aghast to read Ed McAuley's headline feature. It was an open letter addressed to Manager Steve O'Neill, titled "Get Mad Steve and Stay Mad!" McAuley had gone over the edge in a massive critique of the Indians manager. The sports editor accused O'Neill of being easy on his players, allowing them too much freedom on and off the field. He warned that if this type of lax authority continued, a change in managers just might occur. McAuley wrote, "I don't want the public or anyone else to fire you Steve, and that's why I'm taking the liberty of speaking frankly."

The revealing open letter cited numerous examples of Indians ballplayers making foolish mistakes on the base paths. Later in the piece McAuley briefly tried to tone down his ire by adding, "I am not trying to second-guess. You've made some mistakes Steve. You haven't played the percentages like you did last season." McAuley gave further space to the lax attitude the players seemed to be carrying with them. He noted a recent road trip where, after some tough losses, the Indians were enjoying themselves on the train home, wolfing down steaks and playing poker without a care. Apparently McAuley believed O'Neill should have stepped in and ripped the players for having a good time.

McAuley heaped more criticism on the manager, dredging up the 12–5 loss to Washington and all the gaffes perpetrated by the bungling infielders and pitcher Wyatt. Though in some ways the sports editor was trying to be a cheerleader, the open letter, taken as a whole, was a hatchet job of epic proportions.

Fans were quick to respond. Letters poured into the *Cleveland News* offices defending O'Neill. One fan wrote, "I was astounded and shocked to read in the big type in the *News* last night Mr.

McAuley's gratuitous and hypocritical advice to manager Steve O'Neill. If the Indians could have a one month moratorium on Mr. McAuley and the other press box experts, then the ball team might have a reasonable chance to show what it has."

Another fan explained the season had barely started. It was not the time to be calling for the manager's head. The letter asked how O'Neill could be responsible for the Yankees having much better players. Or how he could stop his pitchers from falling asleep on the mound? The fan ended by adapting Alva Bradley's now-famous line, "The owner hires the manager, but the fans fire him." The letter concluded, "The fans fire the manager, maybe the fans can fire you too."

Steve O'Neill had just begun his second full year of managing the Cleveland Indians, after assuming the job in August of 1935 when Walter Johnson was fired. He had spent seventeen years in the American League as a top-flight catcher, playing the great majority of his career with Cleveland. In the 1920 championship season, he caught an incredible 149 games while batting over .300. In his long stint in the Majors, O'Neill gained a reputation as one of the toughest catchers in all of baseball. He blocked home plate with a ferocity rarely seen. Opposing managers screamed at the umpires when he shifted his body into the baseline even before he had the baseball. Runners dashed home and collided with the broad-shouldered catcher, who rarely dropped a throw. Ed McAuley had really gone out on a limb in questioning the toughness of Steve O'Neill.

Just a few days after the article and fans' response, the Indians entertained the Yankees at League Park. The arrival of Gehrig and company and the initial Ladies Day of the season boosted the Friday crowd to over 15,000. The women marched to the ballpark two hours early with boxed lunches and decks of playing cards to keep busy until game time. More often than not, juicy red apples, ripe bananas, and large pieces of cake were delivered by the ladies to Jack Graney in the WHK radio booth. If he was in a generous mood, some of the bounty would find its way into the Indian clubhouse, where the players devoured the prize.

Denny Galehouse opened the game for Cleveland. A Yankee base hit brought cleanup hitter Lou Gehrig to the plate. In the off-season Gehrig had gone Hollywood, auditioning to replace actor Johnny Weissmuller in the popular Tarzan features. Although Lou did not pass the screen test, photos of him in the famous loincloth appeared in newspapers throughout the country. When Gehrig stepped into the batter's box, a large group of ladies stood up and gave the Tarzan yell. Laughter rocked the stands while Gehrig stood at home plate, staring at the crowd.

In the bottom of the first, the Indians added to the good-humored mood at the park by hammering New York pitcher Bump Hadley for five runs. Earl Averill belted a home run in the fourth inning to make the score 6–0. Galehouse blanked the Yankees for seven innings until he ran out of gas in the eighth. After one run had scored, George Selkirk clouted a three-run homer to cut the lead to 6–4. Manager O'Neill called for reliever Carl Fischer. The thirty-one-year-old pitcher had bounced around the American League, doing time with Washington, St. Louis, and Detroit. He looked fairly good in Cleveland's spring training and subsequently made the club as a late-inning option. He entered the game with Tony Lazzeri at first and Roy Johnson batting. The Indians fans were no longer smiling from ear to ear. They cringed as Johnson lined a base hit, moving Lazzeri to second.

Fischer stood rigid on the mound, waiting for the sign from catcher Frankie Pytlak. He continued to stare at home plate, oblivious to the runners. Lazzeri, now an aging veteran with heavy legs, took off for third, stealing the base with ease. Steve O'Neill flew out of the dugout and raged at his relief pitcher. Whether he was taking Ed McAuley's advice to get mad or simply asserting himself, he screamed at Fischer to go to the clubhouse and pack his bags. Fischer's days with Cleveland were abruptly over.

In the bottom half of the inning, Pytlak doubled and came home on a single by Roy Weatherly. That made the score 7–4, with the Yankees coming to bat in the ninth. Pitcher Earl Whitehill came in to close out the game. With one out and a runner on first, Joe DiMaggio grounded to third, where Sammy Hale fielded the ball and fired to second to start a game-ending double play. But short-stop Lyn Lary inexplicably dropped the throw. To further compli-cate matters, Whitehill walked Lou Gehrig to load the bases. Bill Dickey stepped to the plate with a chance to do some real harm.

Instead, he hit a soft bouncer right back to the mound. Whitehill had only to whip the ball home for the force play and give Pytlak a chance to throw to first to end the game. For some odd reason, he chose to whirl around and throw to second. Lary barely fielded the throw, touched second, then fired in the dirt to first baseman Hal Trosky. The ball got under Trosky's glove and rolled into foul territory. Two runs crossed the plate while Gehrig raced to third and Dickey to second. The crowd had gone full circle from leisurely watching a blowout to standing up and screaming at the Indians players. Luckily, Whitehill got the last out before a major riot ensued. Cleveland, in spite of playing like amateurs, had won 7–6, yet the fans were boiling and muttering to themselves about the poor exhibition they had just seen.

Although the season had a long way to go, the Indians had stumbled out of the gate. Silly errors all over the field, Feller's arm injury, and Johnny Allen's appendicitis caused sportswriters and fans to ponder if the 1937 campaign was already headed for disaster.

Chapter 3

BROADWAY AND A MOOSE

E ven though the Indians were struggling, there were a few bright spots to ease some of the fans' anxiety. Lyn Lary got off to a hot start, batting near .400, though, as already noted, the veteran shortstop had some difficulty fielding his position. Lary also stole a few bases, reminding fans he still had the good speed and baserunning ability that most of his teammates lacked. To date, the Indians front office had to be pleased with at least part of the big trade with the St. Louis Browns.

Lynford Lary was born in Armona, California, on January 28, 1906. He played all three big sports in high school in Visalia, earning a reputation as one of the premier athletes in the state. After graduation he decided to attend college at the University of California. Just before he officially enrolled, he got an offer to play semipro ball. Lary had little money to pay for a college education, making it an easy decision to forget higher learning and go for the cash instead. Soon the Oakland Oaks ball club in the Pacific Coast League offered a contract for the 1925 season. Lary jumped at the chance to make some decent money and began to concentrate all his efforts on becoming a professional ballplayer.

After several seasons at Oakland, Lary became one of the most sought-after prospects in the league. In 1928 he batted .314, getting the rapt attention of the New York Yankees. The Major League club wanted Lary and second baseman Jimmie Reese as a package deal. The two represented the slickest fielding combination in the entire PCL. Both players eagerly signed deals, then traveled cross-country to report for 1929 spring training. The Yankees turned heads by paying Oakland an outrageous sum of $125,000 to acquire the great double-play combination. Years later, the Yankee front office ranked this deal as one of the poorest transactions they had ever made in the history of the organization.

Lary impressed his new teammates from the start, eventually beating out Leo Durocher and grabbing a spot in the starting lineup, which included the marquee names of Ruth, Gehrig, and Bill Dickey. Jimmie Reese, on the other hand, would flame out quickly, setting up Lary as the lone survivor of the six-figure transaction. In his first season, the shortstop played in eighty games and batted a reasonably good .309. The following year Durocher was gone, traded to the Cincinnati Reds. In 1930 Lary hit for a lower average but played in 117 games and scored 93 runs. He really hit his stride in 1931, belting 10 home runs and knocking in 107 along with 100 runs scored. The Yankees now had at least something to show for the $125,000 spent.

While living in New York City, Lary gravitated toward the high-society nightlife. He saw every new movie and attended all sorts of trendy Broadway plays. He began to dress like a movie mogul, often being seen wearing the latest fashion of flannel trousers, brightly colored silk shirts, and navy blazers with coordinated handkerchiefs in the breast pocket. In addition, he smoked a pipe, looking every part the Hollywood director. One day Babe Ruth walked into the Yankees locker room and noticed Lyn wearing one of his classic outfits. The Babe smiled and said, "Hi, Broadway!" The nickname stuck immediately and followed Lary the rest of his playing career.

Though Lary had a great season in 1931, another milestone was just around the corner. While watching a new feature film, he indirectly met his wife-to-be, the beautiful Mary Lawlor. The two did not have a conversation because Mary was on the screen, the lead actress of the popular comedy being shown. Lary viewed the movie several times, convinced he had found his one true love. Via a great stroke of luck, Miss Lawlor would soon leave Hollywood for an extended run on the Broadway stage. Lary wrangled tickets to the play and, through a mutual friend, David Marks, got a quick introduction. The encounter did not go well, as Mary paid little attention to the smitten Lary. Undeterred, he thought he could impress her by dropping off complimentary box seat tickets to the next Yankee game. The day came and Lary kept peering into the stands, hoping to catch a glimpse of the classy star. Much to his disappointment, the actress never arrived. He discovered later that Mary knew nothing about baseball and had no interest in seeing a game.

Broadway Lyn did not give up the quest, persuading his Marks to set him up with Mary for an evening of dinner and dancing. This time the two celebrities really hit it off, dancing to the popular song "Lucky in Love," and soon were an item. After a brief courtship they were married on July 14 in New York City, with Babe Ruth serving as the best man. With no time for a honeymoon, the young couple cruised around town in a huge eight-cylinder automobile with Lary's name plate on the side door.

Ballplayers around the American League took notice that Lary had landed a genuine Hollywood star. Though many of the guys dated beautiful women, Broadway Lyn had outdone them all. He would lead the Major Leagues until Joe DiMaggio wed the spectacular Marilyn Monroe more than twenty years later.

Certainly 1931 was a great year for Lary, yet an incident on the ballfield would mark him for the rest of his time in New York. In late April the Yankees were in Washington to play the Senators. In the top of the first inning, Lary reached base with a clean single. There were two out when first baseman Lou Gehrig smashed a tremendous drive to deep center field, heading straight for the bleachers. Lary sped past second while the ball cleared the center-field wall, hit the concrete, then bounced back onto the field. He raced to third and rounded the bag, looking back to see the Washington outfielder holding the ball in his glove. Despite the Senators standing at their positions without moving, Lary wrongly assumed the ball had been caught and headed for the Yankees bench without touching home plate. The Yankee dugout, watching the flight of Gehrig's monstrous home run, failed to notice Lary had stopped before crossing home. The Iron Horse rounded third and touched home, only to be called out by the umpire for passing Lary on the baseline. The ruling gave Lou a triple, but no runs were credited to New York thanks to Lary's remarkable lapse. Of course the Senators won the game by two runs.

Dan Daniel, the fine New York sportswriter, later mused that Lary had some issues in his head. He wrote, "Lary had a blind spot in his mentality. Sometimes under pressure he'd hold the ball too long and suddenly haul off with a wild heave."

The Yankee shortstop could not offer a valid reason for pulling up halfway down the baseline and jogging to the dugout. Later he did say he thought the ball had been caught, but it was still difficult to understand his not touching home plate just to be sure. If he had turned around, he might have noticed Gehrig still running about thirty feet behind him. The most amazing thing about the incident came to light at season's end. Gehrig and Ruth tied for the lead in round trippers with forty-six. If Lyn had continued home that day in Washington, Gehrig would have won the crown outright with forty-seven.

In 1934 the Yankees were no longer thrilled with their short-stop, and sent Lary to the Boston Red Sox. Over the next few years he had stops in Washington and St. Louis before arriving in Cleveland for the 1937 season. Manager O'Neill soon learned that his new ballplayer still had a strong hankering for the nightlife. Lary did not drink excessively or get into trouble, but saw no reason not to stay out late at the clubs and socialize until the dawn. This behavior lasted all through his time with the Indians. In spite of the late hours, Lary continued to lead Cleveland in hitting for a good portion of the season. He seemed to be undergoing a rejuvenation with the Indians.

As the season entered June, Cleveland had a record of 19–14, actually not a bad total when your number one and number two pitchers are out of the lineup. Johnny Allen made a slow recovery from the appendicitis attack, pitching only two innings of relief on May 11. He waited nine more days before starting against Chicago. He had tremendous support from his teammates, who bashed twenty-one hits and scored sixteen runs, but Allen retired in the third inning, too fatigued to go any further.

At the end of May Allen regained his old form, pitching a complete-game victory at home against Chicago. Also in his old form was a classic temper tantrum directed at home plate umpire Johnny Quinn. Throughout the game Allen was haphazardly tossing the rosin bag all around the pitching mound. Quinn spoke to him about it, then walked to the mound for a confrontation. Allen waited a moment, stared at the ump, and fired the ball right into Quinn's chest protector. The baseball caromed all the way to the first base dugout. Maybe Quinn was too startled, but, to the shock of everyone at League Park, he did not toss the demented pitcher from the game.

Once again Allen enjoyed outstanding support in the 15–3 win over the White Sox. Hal Trosky homered, Earl Averill hit a three-run shot, and newcomer Moose Solters slammed a bases-loaded home run far over the right-center-field wall. The game was a coming-out party for Solters, who had four hits in five trips and five RBIs to lead the offense. The Cleveland front office let out a sigh of relief over Solters's huge performance. Alva Bradley and Cy Slapnicka had taken some intense heat from the fans for swapping hometown hero Joe Vosmik for Solters. They expected some big hitting from Moose to justify trading their All-Star left fielder. It would take more than one big day at the plate to silence the critics, but the grand slam gave them a boost in the right direction.

Moose Solters was born in Pittsburgh on March 22, 1908. His family came from Hungary and settled in Pennsylvania, where his father found work in the coal mines. As a young boy, Moose spent a great deal of time shagging batting practice fly balls for the Pittsburgh Pirates. When old enough, he joined his father and two brothers laboring in the dangerous mines. Education was not in the picture, though Solters did attend Fifth Avenue High School for a year, where he was able to play football as a hard-running halfback.

Out of school while still of high school age, he played Sunday baseball for the Colonial Mine #4 club in the Frick River League. Moose was a big boy now, nearly six feet tall and weighing over two hundred pounds. He had black hair and brown eyes to go with a big grin whenever he spotted a friendly face. Not the stereotypical "Moose," he was able to run quite well while showing lots of agility in the outfield. He was once timed at 3.6 seconds running from home plate to first.

In a short while, Moose became one of the top players in the Frick League, swatting tremendous home runs wherever he played. In the spring of 1927, a telegram arrived at the Solters home, addressed to J. Solters of the Colonial Mine team, offering a tryout with Fairmont, West Virginia, of the Mid-Atlantic League. Moose thought about it, then urged his older brother Frank, a fair ball-player himself, to report instead. As a loyal brother and dedicated to his family, Solters wanted Frank to get a shot at the minor leagues. Moose believed his own time would come soon, so why not let his brother get an opportunity first?

Frank reported to Fairmont and homered his first time up. He then fanned three straight times, and the manager became suspicious. This did not look like the scourge of the Frick River League, and Frank reluctantly admitted the same. He soon packed his bags and went home to Pittsburgh, thanking his younger brother for the chance. Moose, satisfied his brother had gotten the tryout, quickly traveled to Fairmont for his professional debut. The early results were far from overwhelming. Solters had an awkward batting stance, sometimes swinging while he was off-balance. His first season he hit only .271, not quite terrorizing the pitchers of the Mid-Atlantic. He remained at Fairmont for the next two seasons, slowly raising his average to a respectable .294. In the fall and winter months Moose did some hard labor, driving and unloading a delivery truck and working odd jobs in a grocery store and bakery.

For the next three seasons he became a baseball nomad, playing for Shreveport in the Texas League, then Albany and Binghamton in the New York–Pennsylvania League, and finally the Baltimore Orioles of the International League. Moose played there for a meager salary of $150 a month. The team had low expectations of their new outfielder, starting him off as an occasional bench player. An injury got him into the regular lineup and Moose went on a tear, boosting his average to a splendid .363. He also managed to score 123 runs, catching the interest of the Boston Red Sox.

Moose eagerly signed a contract to play for Boston in the 1934 season. After a good showing in spring training, he appeared in the opening day lineup, playing right field and batting sixth. He remained a starter, delivering timely base hits and driving in his share of runs. On May 23, the Red Sox faced the Indians, with Mel

BAD BOYS, BAD TIMES

Harder doing the pitching. The Cleveland ace threw one of his sharp-breaking curveballs, which bore in on Moose and struck him in the hand. Umpire Charley Donnelly claimed the ball hit the bat, not allowing Solters a free trip to first. Within moments the hand began to swell, forcing Moose out of the game. Later he went for an X-ray, which revealed the hand was indeed broken. The injury sidelined him for almost a month.

With the hand not healing well, Moose had difficulty swinging the bat for the remainder of the season. Still, he batted .299 for the year, an acceptable total for a first-year player. He had shown more than enough ability to receive a contract for the 1935 season. Moose got off to a slow start in his second campaign, batting less than .250. After only twenty-four games, the Red Sox shipped him to St. Louis for second baseman Oscar Melillo. The change in scenery proved to be a great move for Solters. He finished the year with 18 home runs and 112 RBIs. In a game against the Detroit Tigers, Moose showed awesome power, crushing three straight home runs off Elden Auker. In his next trip up he lined a pitch deep toward the right-field wall. Pete Fox raced back and made a leaping catch to keep Solters from at least extra bases. Even with Fox's circus catch, Moose still had a tremendous day, gaining notoriety as one of the American League's better power hitters.

Living in St. Louis, Moose had the opportunity to pal around with Joe Medwick, his counterpart with the Cardinals. Solters would proudly tell anybody listening that the two of them were the only Hungarian American ballplayers in Major League Baseball. Whenever they met, one would yell, "Hey Polack!" The other would yell back "How ya' doin Hunkie?" Then both would sit down, have some laughs, and catch up on the latest gossip.

In 1936 Solters played to an even higher level, knocking in 134 runs, good for fifth in the American League. Manager Rogers Hornsby worked with Moose to get him to set his feet in the back of the batter's box. The new stance allowed him to see the ball just a fraction longer. The results were positive, allowing Solters to make better contact and become a real threat. Cleveland took notice, starting talks with the Browns front office to acquire Moose. It would take a six-player deal, but Cleveland got their man for the 1937 season.

With Johnny Allen seemingly healthy again and Moose Solters asserting himself, the only Cleveland player still unable to contribute was Bob Feller. He had seen an army of doctors, yet his elbow still badly ached whenever he tried to throw. The first week of June, Cy Slapnicka announced Feller was leaving town to visit friends in Milwaukee and get some additional rest. Stuart Bell, the sportswriter for the *Cleveland Press,* did not buy any part of the story. Bell had been around the block more than a few times and knew when something other than the truth was being peddled. Investigating the flimsy tale, he discovered that Feller had an appointment with a specialist in arm injuries. The physician had invented a machine that could take one's arm and massage it for an extended period. Though the treatment was experimental, Slapnicka had run out of ideas on how to fix the most valuable arm on the Indians pitching staff.

Cleveland reporters were constantly badgering the general manager on why Feller's arm issues were taking so long. Frustrated, he tried to arrange the Milwaukee trip without arousing suspicion. But after Stuart Bell foiled his secret plans, all the Cleveland papers had stories about exactly what the Indians were up to and why Feller had to leave the city.

On first glimpse, the Milwaukee trip seemed to be a success. Feller had several mechanical treatments that significantly reduced his constant elbow pain. Back in town, the moment came to test his throwing arm under game conditions. Feller returned to League Park and started throwing off the pitching mound. Within minutes the same discomfort returned. Slapnicka had few choices remaining before declaring Feller on the shelf for the rest of the year. The only possible solution was to see the bonesetting doctor Lefty Weisman had earlier recommended. Ironically, his office was just a home run's distance from League Park. Feller took the short walk and had Dr. A. L. Austin do a thorough examination. After some manipulation, the physician believed the ulna bone, connecting to the elbow, had been dislocated. He firmly grabbed Feller's wrist with one hand, then popped the elbow hard with the other. Feller felt a tremendous pain, then nothing. The arm appeared to be fine.

The doctor reassured Feller he could start throwing whenever he felt ready. By today's standards he would have rested for weeks;

however, the Indians' fortunes were reaching a critical point. The front office, worried about dwindling gate receipts, wanted Feller starting as soon as possible. A day later he resumed throwing, this time curveballs and all. Two days went by and the arm had miraculously responded. Feller announced to the papers he had the green light to pitch full-time.

The euphoria over Feller's return was only momentary, as bad news came from Boston. On June 20 Johnny Allen complained of severe stomach pains. A local doctor examined him and determined his appendix was moments away from bursting. Allen was taken to Palmer Memorial Hospital, holding ice bags on his tender stomach. A hospital surgeon performed the surgery, and Allen came through without any complications, yet he would likely be on the shelf for a month if not more. The starting rotation would not be at full strength until August.

Steve O'Neill chose to start Feller on July 4 at Municipal Stadium. Alva Bradley had committed to play a series of games at the new facility, the most since he had taken the team back to League Park after the 1933 season. Bradley had incurred the wrath of the city of Cleveland by exercising an out clause in his lease. He claimed the ball club had lost money playing at the 80,000-seat stadium and thus elected to move out of downtown and relocate to ancient but comfortable League Park. Now, four years later, Bradley had a notion that a playing a select number of games at the lakefront might attract some bigger crowds.

The Yankees were always a terrific draw, and holiday games usually brought exceptional numbers. In addition, Cleveland was bringing back the highly popular Great Lakes Exposition for a second summer. This large venue had state-of-the-art attractions, restaurants, and exhibits and happened to be located next to Municipal Stadium, along the edge of Lake Erie. Alva Bradley expected a large group of out-of-town visitors to stop by the Expo, then take in a ball game.

The return of Bob Feller drew a total of 35,000 eager fans to the stadium—an excellent crowd, yet nowhere close to a record. Jo-Jo White led off for the Tigers by drawing a walk. Feller then ignited the crowd by striking out Bill Rogell, Charlie Gehringer, and the always dangerous Hank Greenberg. During the flurry of strikes, White stole second and third, but could not advance any further. The Indians scored in the bottom half of the inning when Roy Hughes singled, went to third on Earl Averill's base hit, then scored on Hal Trosky's sacrifice fly.

Feller cruised along until the top of the fourth. He had been throwing mostly fastballs with a few curves mixed in to keep the Tigers off balance. Greenberg led off the top of the inning with a walk. Goose Goslin hit a grounder to Lyn Lary, who kicked the ball around for an error. Rudy York then laid down a perfect bunt, just inside the third-base line. Feller picked up the ball and heard catcher Frankie Pytlak yell, "First base!" At the same time, Detroit third-base coach Del Baker yelled even louder, "Third, third!" Feller turned and threw a strike to third base. Unfortunately, no Indian stood near the bag, and the ball rolled all the way into the left-field corner. By the time Moose Solters recovered the baseball, Greenberg had scored while Gehringer reached third and York second.

Probably somewhat rattled, Feller grooved a fastball to right fielder Pete Fox, who lined a base hit for two more runs. The Indians now trailed 3–1. At this point the young pitcher bore down, retiring the side without any further destruction. Manager O'Neill, despite hearing a chorus of boos, told Feller he was finished for the day. It had been only four innings, still Feller showed the form of the kid who had dazzled the American League at the end of the 1936 season. He had allowed only one hit while striking out four. The three runs were unearned, though Feller himself was responsible for the throwing error that allowed Greenberg to score. Considering he had not started a game in over two months, the results were more than positive. Nevertheless, Cleveland lost 3–2.

After the game O'Neill told reporters, "I thought the kid had done enough work for a beginning and I didn't want him to press too hard to make up for what happened in that fourth inning." Feller announced his arm had come through just fine. He now believed he could take his regular turn in the rotation. Good news all around.

The next day Cleveland traveled to St. Louis for a doubleheader. As usual, the lowly Browns were completely out of the running, already twenty games below the break-even mark. Either buoyed by Feller's return or frustrated by their own .500 record, the Indians pummeled St. Louis, 14–4 in the first game and even worse in the nightcap, 15–4. Slugger Hal Trosky was the hero of game one, detonating three home runs along with seven RBIs. The lineup produced a total of seventeen hits, manhandling former teammate Oral Hildebrand for eleven tallies before he left the game. After a brief rest, the Indians recorded twenty-one hits in game two, including home runs by Moose Solters and Roy Weatherly. Even though they were far behind the Yankees in the pennant chase, Cleveland had a potent crew of hitters who could explode at any time. Averill, Trosky, Bruce Campbell, Lyn Lary, and Solters were capable of destroying American League pitchers, yet they were prone to episodes of poor play, exasperating the front office.

On July 18 the high-flying Yankees were in Cleveland for a Sunday game at Municipal Stadium. Once again, Alva Bradley proved he was a shrewd operator, betting the matchup of Bob Feller versus Joe DiMaggio and Lou Gehrig would draw a monstrous crowd. When the game began, there were 59,884 raring-to-go fans eager to see what a healthy Feller could do.

The 1937 season had thus far yielded a 10 percent increase in attendance over the previous year. Few people were willing to say the Great Depression had already peaked, but Major League owners were starting to note a positive trend. Bradley had the best of both worlds, scheduling his potential big dates at the mammoth Cleveland Municipal Stadium while drawing fair-to-middling numbers weekdays at League Park.

The New York Yankees were quite a drawing card at home or on the road. At any city they visited, an exceptional number of people would come out to watch the best team in either league. Cleveland fans had been packing League Park to see the Yankees for years. Babe Ruth had launched colossal home runs over the high right-field wall, and later Lou Gehrig joined Ruth in an awesome show of power not seen before. Ruth was gone, but Gehrig was still around, and Joe DiMaggio had created new interest in the Yankees with his superior all-around play. At age twenty-two, Joe D. had already begun to demonstrate his claim to be the next Yankee superstar.

On this day, eighteen-year-old Bob Feller took the mound to challenge the pennant-bound club from New York. Despite his young age, he already had impressive credentials in his brief career, including shattering the American League single-game strikeout record. The Cleveland sportswriters went all out in their game stories. Ed McAuley stated, "The dimple-chinned Bob Feller from the furrows of a farm in Iowa against the swarthy Joe DiMaggio from the humble home of a fisherman on the coast of San Francisco. Make or break hero or goat, the two outstanding youngsters of modern times."

The atmosphere at the stadium was reminiscent of an opening day. A U.S. Army squadron went through a number of drills, followed by a Scottish fife-and-drum corps marching smartly about the field. A group of fans from Buffalo presented gifts to two former minor-league Bisons, Yankee manager Joe McCarthy and Cleveland's Frankie Pytlak. A similar group arrived from Pittsburgh to honor their favorite son, Moose Solters. The Fellers made the long-distance trek from Iowa, their first opportunity of the year to see Bob on the mound. With all the pregame ceremonies, the game started nearly twenty minutes late.

Feller and Yankee starter Red Ruffing were impressive from the onset. Neither team scored until the visitor half of the third inning, when shortstop Frank Crosetti led off with a walk and moved to second on an infield ground out. Up to the plate came "Joltin'" Joe DiMaggio. Crosetti edged off second base, and on the pitch raced for third. DiMaggio sent a scorching ground ball at third baseman Sammy Hale. "Bad News" knocked the ball down, but before he could pick it up Crosetti came sliding hard into the third-base bag. His foot kicked the ball into foul territory, out of Hale's reach and far enough for Crosetti to scramble to his feet and score the game's first run.

The Indians tied the game in the seventh inning on singles by Trosky, Hale, and Pytlak. In the ninth the score remained 1–1. Feller had thrown well over a hundred pitches, yet still had plenty of steam on his fastballs. Leading off the ninth was Red Ruffing, already a two-time strikeout victim. A good-hitting pitcher, Ruffing caught up with a fastball and lined a base hit. Crosetti dropped a sacrifice bunt near the mound. Feller picked up the ball and threw wild to first, leaving runners on first and second with nobody out. He then walked third baseman Red Rolfe on four straight pitches.

As if somebody had written a clever script, Joe DiMaggio slowly walked to home plate. Bases loaded, nobody out, and the score tied. There were the two rising young stars at a do-or-die moment. The huge crowd roared when Feller eyed the plate, then threw two sizzling fastballs by Joe D. The next pitch was an off-speed curveball that got too much of the plate. Di Maggio swung and hammered the ball way back in left field. Moose Solters raced to the wall but watched helplessly as the drive landed well into the seats for a grand slam home run! Di Maggio had won the battle in spectacular style. Steve O'Neill trotted to the mound to ask his pitcher if he wanted out. Feller refused to leave the rubber, intent on finishing the game. The final score stayed at Yankees 5, Indians 1.

Feller's last delivery to retire the side gave him an out-of-this-world pitch count of 171. He recorded seven strikeouts, eight walks (yes, that's right), and one hit batter. Feller held the powerful Yankees in check for eight full innings, something that most pitchers in the American League could not do. Although his record for the season slipped to a surprising 0–4, Feller had served notice that the best was yet to come.

At the beginning of August the Indians were still a few games under .500. Steve O'Neill tried to tighten things up by banning poker games and posting an earlier curfew. The restrictions did not turn the club around, though one player in particular began to heat up. After resting for three weeks, Johnny Allen, fully recovered from his dangerous surgery, received the okay to pitch again. On August 14 he went seven innings in a 4–3 win over Chicago. The win boosted his record to five wins and no losses.

Five days later Allen won again, easily beating St. Louis 9–1. Six wins without a defeat was a nice record, but Allen was setting in motion a remarkable winning streak. No doubt making up for lost time, Allen refused be beaten, lifting his record to 8–0 at the end of the month. He began September by defeating the hopeless Browns, 15–3. Bruce Campbell and Moose Solters each drove in three runs to help Allen to win number nine without a blemish.

The streak rolled on through the month, with Allen topping the Red Sox, Senators, Tigers, and White Sox. His outstanding pitching woke up the ball club, lifting them above .500 and into the first division. On September 21, Allen beat the Senators in a complete-game victory, 6–3. Hal Trosky slammed a bases-loaded home run to seal the win. With two weeks left in the season, Allen was now a lofty 13–0.

The Indians were playing their best ball of the season. Bob Feller had hit his stride, while Mel Harder collected a number of wins. They had no chance to catch the Yankees, but the team proved they could play at a more than competitive level.

On September 26 Cleveland took a doubleheader from Detroit. Allen won his fourteenth without a loss, while Feller struck out ten in a trouble-free second-game victory. On the last day of the month, the two aces pitched the Indians to another doubleheader victory, this time over the White Sox. Allen faltered a bit, giving up an uncharacteristic four runs. Earlier in the season the team would have folded, but three RBIs each from Trosky and Solters led to a 6–4 win. Johnny Allen now had an unbelievable record of 15–0. He would likely get one more start in October against Detroit.

Feller had a terrific outing himself, holding Chicago to one run over nine innings. He had the fastball hopping, striking out eleven batters in the 4–1 victory. Fans all over Cleveland shook their heads and took a deep sigh at what might have been. Cleveland now had the two finest pitchers in the American League. It is not inconceivable to project that barring the injuries, Feller and Allen might have won quite a few more games between them. That conjecture puts the team squarely in the pennant race, just behind the Yankees. The outlook was bright for the 1938 season.

Allen had one more chance to get his sixteenth straight victory and tie the American League single season record held by greats "Smoky" Joe Wood, Walter Johnson, and the still-pitching Lefty Grove. Although the season was closing up for Detroit and Cleveland, 22,000 interested Tiger fans paid to see the game. Allen was paired up against Jake Wade, an erratic pitcher who could be really good or equally bad. In the bottom of the first inning, Pete Fox doubled with one out. Allen got the next hitter, bringing Hank Greenberg to bat. Entering the game, the big first baseman already had a spectacular year with an incredible 182 RBIs. Allen delivered and Greenberg hit a ground ball toward Sammy Hale. It appeared to be a routine play, but somehow Hale could not get his glove down, and the ball slowly rolled into left field. Fox scored with what proved to be the only run of the entire ball game. The up-and-down Wade stopped the Indians on one hit, depriving Johnny Allen of win number sixteen and an undefeated season.

Allen would lead all Major League starting pitchers with an unreal winning percentage of .938. In 173 innings of work, he allowed only four home runs and posted a career-best ERA of 2.55, good for third place in the American League. In two years of pitching for Cleveland, Allen had an impressive record of thirty-five wins and only eleven losses. One can only wonder what might have happened if he had not suffered the two attacks of appendicitis.

Throughout the victory streak, Allen kept his outbursts and combative personality under control. But after losing his final appearance of the season and a chance to tie the American League record, Allen reportedly let it all go. Franklin "Whitey" Lewis, at that time a writer for the *Cleveland Press,* later claimed that Allen went after Sammy Hale at least twice. Round one occurred in the visitors' locker room, where the two had words and the fight was on. Several players and Manager O'Neill had to step in and separate the two. In the dining car on the train back to Cleveland, Allen supposedly had more choice words for Hale, initiating round two. Once again O'Neill had to get between the angry ballplayers and stay there until the train reached Cleveland. None of the other Cleveland reporters mentioned the incidents. Either it was a case of what happens in the locker room stays there, or the confrontation may have been exaggerated. In any event, it was an attention-grabbing story and something that fit right into Johnny Allen's mode of behavior.

The Indians finished the year fourth in the standings, with eighty-three wins versus seventy-one losses. Their inspired play in September, featuring twenty-three wins and thirteen losses, enabled them to remain in the first division. The Yankees swept everybody away, winning 102 games while losing only 52. They would cruise through the World Series, needing only five games to put away their cross-town rival the New York Giants.

Alva Bradley and his group of shareholders had now completed ten seasons running the ball club. In all these years they were never a serious threat to win a pennant. Bradley had gone through three different managers in that time period, each with similar results.

With the 1937 season concluded. he had to mull over the status of current manager Steve O'Neill.

In early October the Cleveland newspapers floated rumors that Bill McKechnie might be willing to manage the Indians. The veteran was highly regarded by most Major League owners and front office people. A former player, McKechnie had seventeen years of National League managing experience with Pittsburgh, St. Louis, and recently Boston. While Alva Bradley did not comment on the speculation, the will-he-or won't-he grew until days later, when McKechnie signed on to pilot the Cincinnati Reds. Bradley then issued a statement saying that O'Neill was staying unless someone decidedly better came along.

On October 20, apparently Bradley did find someone he deemed worthier. He announced that O'Neill had been fired and Oscar Vitt, currently the manager of the Newark Bears, had accepted the job. O'Neill was generously offered a job in the Indians organization as a scout, but the deposed manager rightly asked for and received permission to look for other jobs. Bradley told the papers, "Changing managers is the most unpleasant feature of my job. It's just one of those things that have to be done. The show must go on."

The decision to replace O'Neill was a debatable one. It speaks of impatience by Bradley in his efforts to field a top-flight ball club. He seemed to overlook the fact that his two best pitchers had missed large portions of the season. That in itself ruined the Indians' chances of finishing any higher in the standings. Certainly O'Neill had made some mistakes during the season. He gave his players a lot of leeway and expected them to respond accordingly. He kept an even temperament when the team struggled and Bradley wanted specific answers. Perhaps had he shouted a few more times or shown some frustration to Bradley, he might have kept his job.

Be that as it may, O'Neill had no control of Johnny Allen's appendix issues or Bob Feller's sore elbow. The two pitchers, counted on to lead the rotation, won only twenty-four games between them. The remaining staff of the All-Star Harder, Hudlin, Galehouse, and Whitehill went 44–45. Had some of those guys, particularly the last three, stepped up, a change in managers might not have taken place. Bradley did not follow his usual motto that "The owner hires the manager, the fans fire him." In this instance he listened to nobody, informing the press the show must go on. Indeed it would, with Oscar Vitt running that show—or circus, depending on how one looked at it.

Chapter 4

ROLLICKING ROLLIE

In what was hopefully not an omen of things to come, Indians general manager Cy Slapnicka suffered a heart attack just before the start of the annual Major League meetings in early December. While attending a banquet in Milwaukee, he became uncomfortably ill but attributed the chest pains to a simple case of indigestion. At 3 a.m. he realized the pain had gone far beyond indigestion. He reached for the phone and called the room of Indians scout Bill Bradley to tell him to get a cab and rush him to the hospital. The doctors confirmed that Slapnicka had experienced a heart attack and restricted him to a cumbersome oxygen tent. He would be out of action for an extended period of time. Alva Bradley's right-hand man usually had an active role in talking trades and ideas with the other team representatives. Now Bradley only had Oscar Vitt with him, who was not expected to have much of an impact due to his unfamiliarity with the club.

The team did formally announce that they had completed a deal with Milwaukee of the American Association, sending three players to the club for highly touted third baseman Ken Keltner. The Indians had actually bought Keltner's contract at the end of August; however, the transaction was not complete until the three players were sent. Keltner had emerged as a star player for the Brewers, batting over .300 and handling third base at a Major League level. He would report to spring training and be given a legitimate shot to win a starting job.

The most unexpected proposal of the meetings came from none other than Alva Bradley. He announced a revolutionary plan to bring night baseball to Cleveland. Bradley cited the recent success of the Cincinnati Reds, who had held seven games at night, which drew a total of 130,000 fans. The Cleveland owner firmly believed the time had come to play ball games under the stars, and he was stepping forward to lead the charge. He had done a thorough study and was preparing to invest $75,000 at Municipal Stadium to install the proper lighting.

The standing rule on night baseball stated, "Any club desiring to play night baseball must apply to the other seven teams for permission which if granted at all would be granted for one year only." Bradley would have quite a chore on his hands in convincing a majority of American League owners to support his innovative plan.

The owners reserved the right to decline a request if the club had been operating at a reasonable profit by daylight. Only for a club in financial straits might the owners consider endorsing an emergency measure. Bradley's did not fit that description.

The owners politely listened to Bradley's arguments, then adjourned to discuss the proposal. In a short time they returned a one-sided vote of five against the lights and just two, Chicago and St. Louis, in favor. The other owners still believed baseball should be played in the daytime, and did not consider that fans might embrace the idea of playing ball after sundown. The Cleveland boss told reporters, "Naturally I'm disappointed. Night baseball in Cleveland would have meant a lot to the club and new fans." Bradley took some solace in the ball club netting a profit of $190,000, the highest amount during his tenure.

The other business was more mundane. The season would open on April 19 and close on October 2. The All-Star Game was awarded to the Cincinnati Reds. Some disagreement occurred over the type of ball to be used: the American League owners favored the livelier ball used in their league for more hitting, while their counterparts in the National League preferred their league's dead ball to highlight pitching. The meetings ended with no other significant business or any blockbuster trades.

In the middle of January 1938, Bradley made known to Cleveland fans that he wanted to schedule twenty-five games at Municipal Stadium. He proposed that all Sunday games and holiday dates be played at the seldom-used facility. He acknowledged that Bob Feller and Johnny Allen were big draws, and as many fans as possible should have the chance to see them in action. He added that the Cleveland Baseball Company would put in a strong bid for the concessions at all games played at the stadium.

Bradley's plans were a mixed blessing to Cleveland City Council. They would be able to negotiate with the ball club for a percentage of the gate while keeping all parking revenues. On the flip side, council knew few other concession companies qualified to handle the food and drinks required for a crowd of 50,000 or 60,000. Once again they had little choice but to yield to Mr. Bradley, who had taken away $50,000 in city rent when he vacated the stadium after the 1933 season. There had been several different administrations of city managers and mayors, yet none had been able to keep Alva Bradley from imposing his will on the city of Cleveland.

A month later, activities in the League Park office began to gather speed. Player contracts were being negotiated at a rapid pace, while plans for spring training were just about finalized. Bob Feller was rumored to have been offered a substantial deal of $17,500 plus a bonus for attendance at the games he pitched. Feller's strong performance in September convinced a now-healthy Cy Slapnicka that his pitching prodigy was just about on par with the best pitchers in baseball. Johnny Allen got a tremendous contract calling for a team-high salary of $40,000 for two years. It seemed most of the players were able to get raises without much of a tussle from the front office.

Baseball Magazine published an old classic anecdote about salary negotiations between players and owners. The tale concerned Colonel Jacob Ruppert, the proprietor of the New York Yankees. Ruppert's grandfather and father had founded a large brewery in the New York area years ago, where they produced the popular Knickerbocker Beer. Colonel Ruppert was already an enormously wealthy man when he purchased the Yankees in 1916. With some wise player acquisitions named Ruth and Gehrig, the Yankees became the top-drawing team in all of baseball. Knowing the franchise had cash to burn; the players started to get aggressive in their contract demands. Waite Hoyt, one of Yankees' best pitchers, met with Ruppert about his salary for the next season. A frustrated Ruppert, said, "Hoyt where's this going to end? Ruth wants more money, Gehrig wants more money, Pennock, Meusel and all the others want more money. What do you fellows think I am anyway, a millionaire?" Hoyt's reply went unrecorded.

Alva Bradley and his front office remained quite energetic throughout February. An announcement soon came that the Indians had acquired St. Louis Browns catcher Rollie Hemsley for third baseman Roy Hughes and backup catcher Billy Sullivan Jr. Cy Slapnicka had had his eye on Hemsley for some time. The initial motivation came from Bob Feller, who been barnstorming with Hemsley and loved the way he caught a game. He mentioned this to his general manager, who started efforts to get the veteran in a Cleveland uniform. The Browns hesitated at a Frankie Pytlak–Rollie Hemsley straight-up deal. Slapnicka countered with a starting third baseman and an alternate catcher. This time the Browns said okay.

Rollie Hemsley came to Cleveland with some outstanding credentials. An All-Star in 1935 and 1936, Hemsley had excellent defensive skills along with an above-average bat. He knew how to handle his pitchers as well as call a good game. He did not shy away from collisions at home plate, nor did nagging injuries force him out of the lineup. Bruised shins and swollen hands were just part of the everyday routine for Rollie. There did exist one small detail that made Cleveland his fifth stop in the Major Leagues. Hemsley had a severe problem with alcohol, and it was becoming worse each season.

Ralston "Rollie" Hemsley was born on June 24, 1907, in Syracuse, Ohio, located in the southeast portion of the state. The small Meigs County mining town sat across the Ohio River from West Virginia. Local folklore claimed when the river reached a certain low point, anybody could wade across and visit the neighboring state.

Rollie's father, Joe, had a keen interest in baseball. When not laboring in the coal mines, he played or watched games at the nearby King Field. Rollie and his brothers, Doug and Joe Jr., followed the head of the family to the mines, collecting six dollars a day for backbreaking work. Rollie would later remark, "Baseball's a soft job compared to blasting your way through those hunks of coal."

When Rollie reached his twelfth birthday, he began training to be a big-time catcher. Joe took him into the backyard and threw him curveballs by the hour. Before long Rollie played at King Field, catching for Joe's semipro team. The ballpark had a grandstand, a dirt field, and a deep center field, complete with a wide area of cornstalks. Teams from the Ohio Valley League scheduled games at the ground, and occasionally a Major League club stopped by for an exhibition game.

Rollie, now known as "Dutch" by his teammates, proved fearless behind home plate. He would reach a height of five feet, ten inches and never weigh more than 170 pounds. He had unusually big hands that helped him stop pitches in the dirt and whistle throws to second base. He played like a polished veteran, soon drawing attention from several minor league clubs. At age seventeen he got an opportunity to join the 1925 Frederick, Maryland, club in the Blue Ridge League. Rollie showed steady progress in his three seasons in Frederick, batting .311 in 1927 with nine triples and twelve home runs. In one of the games Rollie went five for five with two home runs, two doubles, and a single. In another contest he took part in a rarely seen double play. With a runner on first base, the batter lifted a short fly into right field. The Frederick first baseman dashed to the outfield and made a fine over-the-shoulder catch. Hemsley, alertly noticing that the base runner had strayed too far from first, whipped off his mask and sprinted down the first-base line. He yelled for the ball and got the return throw before the startled runner could slide back to the bag. These top-rate performances earned him a promotion to Wichita of the Western League, though he never actually played a game there. The Pittsburgh Pirates tracked Rollie down and bought his contract outright. Hemsley would report in 1928 to spring training and compete for a spot on the roster.

The Pirates were not aware that Rollie had begun drinking in the 1927 season. To complicate things, the Pirates' star outfielder, the great Paul Waner, besides being a tremendous hitter and all-around player, had a serious problem with alcohol. Before long the two players became drinking buddies, starting Rollie on an eleven-year binge. He often arrived at the ballpark with abrasions on his face and sometimes a grotesque black eye. Regardless, he managed to play through the hangovers, well enough to remain the backup catcher.

In one particular game he got livid with umpire Bill Klem regarding his judgment of balls and strikes. Rollie called Klem a "blind bat." Klem replied, "Young man, you've been drinking!" Hemsley fired back, "And from the way you're umpiring, you could have too!" The veteran umpire then told the fuming catcher to go take a seat on the bench and sober up for the remainder of the game.

In spite of this terrible behavior, Rollie somehow improved his game, working his way up to be the Pirates number one catcher. In 1931, just after the regular season got underway, manager Jewel Ens agreed to let Hemsley stop home in Syracuse for a day before embarking with the team on their first road trip. Rollie took off and was not heard of or seen again for a full week. He did not try to contact the Pirates front office during the entire time he went AWOL. He eventually reported with a flimsy explanation he was sick. Ens, completely fed up, suspended him for two weeks, then traded him to the Chicago Cubs.

Rollie moved on to a new environment in Chicago that featured two of the most notorious drinkers in all of baseball, outfielder Hack Wilson and pitcher Pat Malone. In no time at all, Rollie became completely unhinged. The reporters soon noticed his bloodshot eyes and disheveled appearance. Manager Rogers Hornsby, hardly a friend to the ballplayers, somehow tolerated the mischief of his new catcher. Gabby Hartnett caught most of the games, leaving Rollie to play once or twice a week. Still, he was effective, batting .309 in sixty-six games.

It took Hornsby another year to tire of Rollie's bad conduct. Before the start of the 1933 season, Hemsley went to the Cincinnati Reds in a five-player trade. Chicago received slugger Babe Herman in exchange for four players from the Cubs. Rollie floundered in his new environment, batting a feeble .190 in forty-nine games. He only made it to August before the Reds released him, putting his career in jeopardy.

In an exceptionally strange set of circumstances, the St. Louis Browns claimed Rollie. Certainly they needed help anywhere they could find it; however, their new manager happened to be none other than Rogers Hornsby. Why the former Cubs boss believed Hemsley could be of any help is puzzling. He had seen the outrageous behavior, the black eyes, the cuts and bruises, yet still wanted Rollie to catch for him.

Before packing his things and reporting to St. Louis, Hemsley got into a scary automobile accident. He walked away from the crash, and when he caught up with the Browns, Hornsby penciled him into the lineup. But while dressing, his new teammates noticed the gruesome cuts and bruises covering his body. Several told Rollie to talk with Hornsby and sit out the game. He advised them all to shut up and mind their own business. He likely feared that if the manager found out, his days with the Browns might be over before they started. Rollie caught the game and finished the year with the club.

In the first half of 1934 Hemsley found a way to slow down the drinking and played great ball. The newspapers raved about his batting, his work behind the plate, and his clever handling of the pitching staff. The new Rollie lasted until midseason when the Browns finished a series in Chicago. Before leaving for Detroit, manager Hornsby notified the players they could take in the World's Fair and catch a late train east. The players dressed quickly and ambled off to the fair. Rollie left the clubhouse with pal Frank Grube and headed in a completely different direction. The two partied until late in the evening. In due course they reached the train station several hours after their ride had left. The boys drank some more, then caught an early morning train bound for Detroit. Riding with them were renowned bandleader Ted Lewis and his entire orchestra. The musicians matched the ballplayers bottle for bottle. Upon arriving at the station, Hemsley and Grube dove into a cab. At this point they had been celebrating for well over twelve hours.

They rushed to the hotel, hoping to sober up a little then report to the ballpark. Both reached the revolving doors at the same time and pushed in the opposite directions. Neither man would yield, causing the mechanism supporting the doors to snap. Maintenance people were summoned to repair the whole thing while guests of the hotel stood by and had to wait to get in or out.

Hemsley and Grube raced to the park, arriving in time for practice. Manager Hornsby eyed both of them and called for the team to line up. He then asked each and every player if they enjoyed the World's Fair. One by one the guys said yes, they had a great time. When Hornsby reached Grube he asked him the same question. Grube said he had fun there. Hornsby smiled and said, "You are fined $150." Several players later he stood directly in front of Rollie. Asked the same query, Hemsley said he had a great time. This time Hornsby smiled and said, "You are fined $300." The catcher frowned and blurted out, "Why is my fine $300?" Hornsby calmly replied, "Because you are more valuable to the club!"

All seemed well until late August, when Rollie got into a much-publicized bar fight. On a day off he rented a car and wound up in a tavern legendary for drawing rowdy sailors just off the boat. According to Hemsley, he was relaxing at the bar when one of the drunken sailors bumped into him. The two had words and within minutes were brawling inside, then on the streets outside of the bar. Several other sailors joined the fight; prompting a call to the local police, who arrived within minutes. As they were struggling to pull apart the severely drunken warriors, Rollie, according to the police, belted one of the cops square in the face, then tried to take his badge. The police subdued Hemsley and carted him off to jail. He was charged with drunk and disorderly conduct and driving without a license. The Browns gave him an immediate fine and suspension.

Rollie later claimed the charges were unjustified. He explained to reporters, "I was in a tavern when a sailor bumped up against me and I told him to watch his step. A row followed and I knocked the sailor cold. I did not resist the officer and he did not strike me, nor did I try to hit him." Nobody bought Hemsley's version of the incident, and the charges remained along with the fine and suspension.

The national newspapers began calling him "Rollicking Rollie" or "Jolly Rollie," pegging him as a fun-loving guy who sometimes went too far. They, like much of the population, did not understand that Rollicking Rollie could not help himself. One drink would lead to two, then to seven or eight. He had a disease that no large fines or man-to-man talks would help. At times he went completely sober for several weeks, then something would set him off and the drinking would start all over again. His alcoholism did not allow him to have a beer or two and be on his way like most of his teammates. Rollie had a dangerous problem that went unabated for quite a long time.

Even during the off-season, Hemsley could not ease off on the alcohol. He bought a farm in Missouri, where he relocated his wife, Mildred, and young daughter, Joan. Rollie had some hunting dogs that he took deep into the wooded area on the farm. While searching for rabbits or squirrels, he always had a pint or two with him. He might go missing for several days until Mildred had to navigate the dense woods and bring him home.

Family members still relate a story about Rollie. Back in Syracuse, he liked to join his buddies for a jaunt down Route 124, where a string of popular taverns did business. One evening Rollie informed Mildred he would be borrowing the brand-new car he had just bought for her. Blanching at the thought of her husband careening down Route 124 and wrecking her car, she ran to the kitchen, grabbed a large knife, hustled to the car, and slashed the tires. A set of new tires was needed, but the car was saved from destruction.

With the bad events piling up, it would seem that Rollie's career had reached a critical point. But in spite of all the riotous times and the all-night partying, Rollie somehow had an impressive season in 1934. Catching 123 games, he batted .309 with 133 hits and 7 triples. He did even better in 1935, earning a place on the All-Star team. He caught 141 games, a career high, while batting .290. He led the American League catchers in assists, while allowing only three passed balls the entire year. He accomplished this with many a black eye and impaired vision from the swelling. On one occasion he shuffled hungover into the ballpark with one eye completely closed and the other about half as bad. Manager Hornsby told Rollie that as punishment he would catch both ends of the doubleheader. Someway he managed to do the job without completely falling apart.

Although putting together several impressive seasons, Rollicking Rollie continued with his outrageous conduct. Regardless of this, he repeated as a 1936 All-Star. His on-field talent got the attention of several American League teams in addition to Cy Slapnicka. Talks were held with the Browns at the winter meetings, but nothing solid came to pass. In the meantime, Hemsley continued to solidify his reputation as the wildest man in baseball. According to Dan Daniels, a drunken Rollie boarded a Browns train to Washington with a basket of live frogs. He then entered the sleeping car and threw a frog into each player's berth. On another occasion he patiently waited for his teammates to turn in for the night, then stole everyone's shoes and hid them in another compartment.

In spring training of 1937, Rollie added to his long string of outlandish behavior. The Browns were traveling to Laredo, Texas, for an exhibition contest. After the game, the players had a train waiting to take them to San Antonio, where the team was staying. Few were surprised when Rollie vanished, missing the train ride back to camp. He had crossed the border into old Mexico to sample some of the famous local tequila.

Late that same evening he found his way back to San Antonio with a girl on each arm and two bottles of liquor stuffed in his back pockets. He stumbled into the lobby of the Browns' hotel, where idling near the entrance were, of all people, new St. Louis owner Don Barnes, new general manager Bill Dewitt, and manager Rogers Hornsby. The men stared at Rollie for several minutes, then left for their rooms. Hemsley knew he could not talk his way out of this one.

The next morning Hemsley received a message to see his bosses immediately. The end result of the less-than-friendly meeting was a substantial fine and suspension. Rollie estimated he racked up a whopping total of $20,000 in fines, almost certainly the most of any ballplayer of his era. The deductions in pay never had any effect. He simply moved on to the next episode.

Over the course of the 1937 season, Hornsby grew weary of trying to curb Rollie's behavior. He let the other American League clubs know his catcher was on the trading block. Near the end of the season, the Tigers showed interest in completing a trade for Hemsley. The Browns happened to be in Detroit for a late September series. After one of the games, Rollie, totally drunk stumbled into the team hotel. He raised a ruckus in the lobby, bad enough for the Detroit front office to hear about it. That incident killed any chance of a trade happening.

Even with all of this history, Slapnicka remained intent on acquiring the biggest headache in all of baseball. Perhaps he thought new manager Oscar Vitt had the right stuff to tame Rollie and convert him into a model citizen. Possibly the general manager believed he could show the catcher a better way. The Indians still had Frankie Pytlak, a good backstop the front office would keep around for insurance. Be that as it may, the Cleveland Indians hadn't the vaguest idea of what they were truly in for.

Chapter 5

VITT TAKES OVER

On February 19, 1938, Bob Feller arrived in Cleveland to sign his generous contract for the upcoming season. A gala event was planned, including a live radio broadcast from the remarkable new studios of WTAM. A huge investment from NBC Radio enabled construction of a modern building on Superior Avenue downtown to house the state-of-art-facilities. The radio executives from New York were on hand as the public got its first view of the broadcast area and related studios. Approximately 650 guests attended for an evening of cocktails, a swank dinner, and dancing. At 9:00 p.m. a live broadcast of music from New York swept through the new sound system. At the half hour the entertainment switched to a local dance band and several comics who were performing at the nearby Palace Theatre.

Then came the main event of the evening. Out to the podium walked WTAM sports reporter Tom Manning, decked out in a fancy tailcoat. Behind him were Alva Bradley and national celebrity Bob Feller. The invited guests toned down their conversations to watch the two men put their signatures on a contract for $17,500, a considerable deal for a player yet to win more than nine games in a season. Feller assured the crowd his arm was fine, he had actually grown a half inch, and was primed for a big season. The extraordinary program ended moments later with a live hookup to the BBC in London, bringing the unmistakable chimes of Big Ben direct from Westminster Palace. It was a truly a modern evening for all who attended, a chance to see and hear the best of Cleveland and the world.

Within days the Cleveland players would gather from all around the country and head south for New Orleans. This spring had some real significance in bringing in new ballplayers and a first-time Major League manager in Oscar Vitt. Much of the hype around Vitt's hiring was positive, citing him as a man who could whip the Indians into shape and mold them into a pennant contender. Alva Bradley spoke highly of his new field boss, telling reporters, "I was deeply impressed by his personality. I believe he has the dynamic qualities a baseball leader needs."

Baseball Magazine had similar plaudits for Vitt. The article read in part, "Oscar is well-equipped to handle any disorder or dissension that may crop out on his club. He was matured in the Detroit clubhouse during the seething days of Ty Cobb when the place was frequently a fiery furnace of discord." The Cleveland players did not exactly conjure up visions of a fiery furnace, though in players like Johnny Allen and the freewheeling Rollie Hemsley loomed the potential for big trouble. Vitt had spent his entire managing career in the minor leagues. He had many years of dealing with willing young ballplayers struggling to make it the Majors. Now he had to prove his worth with a team of veterans in their late twenties or early thirties who had yet to win. Quite a challenging scenario to walk into.

Oscar Vitt was a native of San Francisco, California, where he was born on January 4, 1890. While just a youngster he developed great foot speed, enabling him to outrun the bigger boys intent on giving him a whipping. At times Oscar stood his ground, threw several punches, then raced away to safety. He played a lot of handball, not doing much on the baseball diamond until high school. He attended a technical school, where he studied architecture.

On April 18, 1906, when Vitt was sixteen years old, he and his family were sleeping at home when the one of the most powerful earthquakes ever recorded leveled much of the San Francisco area. An estimated 3,000 persons died. The Vitts were fortunate to experience only minor damage, as many of the nearby homes and those around the city were destroyed or needed major repair. The study of architecture turned out to be a huge financial windfall for young Vitt. He had recently taken several courses in bricklaying, roofs, and chimney repair.

Within hours he formed Vitt and Company, offering chimney repairs at eight dollars a job. He and a friend moved around the broken city, finding work in just about every neighborhood. In only one month Vitt and Company grossed a weighty $650. A promising career in home repair awaited, yet Oscar felt the strong pull of organized baseball. After several years of semipro ball, he landed a contract with the San Francisco Seals of the Pacific Coast League. Vitt failed to hit .300, but his fielding was above average and the foot speed helped him leg out infield hits and take the extra base.

In 1912 the Detroit Tigers acquired Vitt, giving him considerable time at third base. Manager Hughie Jennings loved Vitt's style of play. Whether diving for ground balls, running out every ball in play, bunting, or stealing bases, he was a throwback to the nineteenth-century player who fought for every square inch. They called him scrappy, peppery, a happy warrior. Jennings, in his days as a National League Baltimore Oriole, had used that type of hustle and bench jockeying to great advantage. Vitt, even though a first-year player, fearlessly shouted at both his teammates and opponents throughout each game. Although standing no more than five foot eight and weighing about 150 pounds, he had no fear of any player in the American League. Even Ty Cobb caught some of Oscar's venom.

At certain times Cobb could be overaggressive on the bases and get himself thrown out while streaking for an extra base. After one of those incidents, Vitt yelled to him, "For Christ's sake why don't you carry an anchor with you!" Everyone on the Tigers bench and in the grandstand knew Cobb would not let that remark go by. A moment later the "Georgia Peach" walked over to Vitt and sharply told him, "Hey listen busher, keep your trap shut if you know what's good for you!" Before Vitt could answer, catcher Oscar Stanage stepped in between the two and stopped Cobb from doing any harm.

Eventually Cobb and Vitt reached an understanding, enough so that the Tigers outfielder looked out for the scrawny third baseman. The Tigers were playing the Yankees when Vitt attempted to score from second on a base hit. The throw from the outfield arrived in plenty of time for catcher Les Nunamaker to block the plate. Lesser men might have tried to slide and avoid contact with the six-foot-two, 190-pound catcher. Vitt never hesitated, lowering his head and crashing into Nunamaker at full speed. Fans shuddered as Vitt careened backwards and landed hard on his back. He was out in every sense of the word. It took a moment or two to gather himself, but when Vitt reached the Tiger bench, Cobb stopped by and said, "Kid, I'll take care of that."

Later in the series, Cobb was leading off second base when a Tiger base hit gave him the chance for revenge. He rounded third, picking up speed as he flew down the baseline. Once again Nunamaker got the throw in time, wheeling toward Cobb to block him off the plate. The collision at home literally shook the earth. The Yankees catcher flew backwards on impact, his cap and one of his shinguards soaring through the air. Cobb scored the run, but more important was standing up for a teammate—something that Vitt greatly appreciated. When the two players met at the Detroit bench, Cobb said, "I guess he'll be a little more careful about the right of way next time!"

Vitt hustled his way through seven full seasons for Detroit. His finest year was 1915, when he had career highs in just about every hitting category. On the defensive side, he led all American League third basemen in putouts and assists. All was not a bed of roses playing for Detroit, though. He had the unwelcome distinction of taking a Walter Johnson fastball squarely between the eyes. Vitt crumpled to the ground and lay unconscious for several minutes. He slowly opened his eyes, glad to be back among the living. Teammate Donie Bush stood above him, kicking Vitt in the legs and yelling at him to get up and quit his stalling. Sympathy was not a quality common among rough-and-tumble ballplayers in the early part of the twentieth century.

After ten years in the American League, the last three with Boston, Vitt signed on with Salt Lake City. He played two more years before putting away his glove and starting on his long managerial career. From 1926 through 1934 he ran the Hollywood Stars, winning a minor league pennant in 1930. He managed Oakland in 1935, then moved all the way across the country to pilot the Newark

Bears of the International League. He had tremendous success there, winning the 1937 pennant by a staggering twenty-seven and a half games. The Bears topped off the regular season by winning the Little World Series against the Columbus Redbirds. Vitt got the attention of Major League owners, particularly Alva Bradley. He liked everything about Vitt, especially his managerial motto, "Win everything in sight and never stop winning."

One area that Bradley may have overlooked was the incredible talent on the Newark Bears, a Yankee Farm team. With up-and-coming stars like Joe Gordon, Charlie Keller, Spud Chandler, and George McQuinn, it did not take a fabulous manager to guide them into first place. Possibly Bradley thought any manager who could win a league by such a dominating margin should be able to help the troublesome Indians. With that in mind, the reins were handed to the forty-seven-year-old Oscar Vitt.

The 1938 edition of the Cleveland Indians featured a lineup of proven veterans along with several talented young players on the verge of breaking out. The only experienced addition was Rollie Hemsley, anticipated to battle Frankie Pytlak for the starting catcher's job. The outfield seemed already set, with five-time All-Star Earl Averill in center field, Bruce Campbell still holding down the right-field job, and last year's acquisition Moose Solters in left. All three were capable of hitting over .300 and driving in a large share of the runs.

Big Hal Trosky had a lock on the first baseman's job, usually leading the team in home runs and RBIs every season since 1933. Trosky had the misfortune to play in the American League at the same time as superstars Lou Gehrig, Jimmie Foxx, and Hank Greenberg, who left Trosky somewhere in the shadows. Sammy Hale had been with the Indians for six seasons, alternating between second and third base. Hale had arm issues that hampered his throwing, although his skill at the plate had not been affected. Lyn Lary entered his second year as the Indians shortstop with little competition. The front office expected him to play steady ball and be a leader out on the field.

The pitching staff had proven winners in Johnny Allen and Mel Harder. Bob Feller had shown a world of potential in his first two campaigns, and now was expected to be among the best pitchers in the game. Willis Hudlin and Earl Whitehill were the only other candidates for the starting rotation. Both pitchers were well past their primes, with Whitehall at thirty-nine years old and Hudlin thirty-two. Between them they had spent twenty-seven years in the American League. If either one had just had ten or twelve wins left in his arm, that would be enough to complement the other three starters.

Oscar Vitt's ball club worked out in New Orleans to get in shape for the upcoming season. Normally spring training came and went without any front-page news or shocking revelations. The players sweated through workouts, talked about how great they felt, and let reporters know big things were up ahead for the new season. The sportswriters sent home optimistic stories, exhibition game summaries, and the comings and goings of the players on the fringe. There was always time for everybody to go out in the evenings and check out the swinging night life in downtown New Orleans.

For the most part the players had their fun but knew enough to get back to the Roosevelt Hotel at a reasonable hour. At the end of March, Rollie Hemsley, unable to restrain himself with all the enticing nightclubs and hot spots just a few blocks away, went out for a late-night adventure. He partied hard, waking up in his hotel room in the late morning hours too sick to take part in batting practice. He notified Vitt and the coaches, then went to his room to try and sleep it off. A photographer had followed Rollie back to the hotel. He tried to get a picture as he entered his room, but Rollie slammed the door in the photographer's face. About a half-hour later someone knocked loudly at his door. Exhausted and hungover, he opened it to find the same man still trying to get a photo. They struggled for a moment, then Rollie pulled out a dresser drawer and smashed it over the photographer's head. The camera fell to the floor, broken into pieces.

Soon the residents and staff at the high-class Roosevelt heard about the incident. Oscar Vitt suspended Rollie, tacking on a significant fine. The regular season had not yet begun, and Hemsley had already started to rack up discipline penalties. Fans began to wonder if the hard-living Rollie would be on the club on opening day. Gordon Cobbledick wrote in the *Plain Dealer,* "[Hemsley's] leadership along the primrose path might take some other Indians astray, and there probably aren't any other who can stand the pace he sets." The question remaining was whether the nervous front office could stand the pace either.

With Hemsley's status in the air, the Indians left New Orleans to make the long trek back to Cleveland. On the way were exhibition stops in many of the southern cities. For the fifth year in a row, the New York Giants traveled with the Indians, providing the opposition at many of the locations. There were games in Alexandria, Louisiana; Birmingham, Alabama; Meridian, Mississippi; and several other cities and towns. Crowds averaged between three and five thousand per stop. The clubs got a large share of the gate from local promoters eager to host a Major League ball game and make something of a profit. It was win-win for all concerned, particularly the fans who traveled from all around the southern states to see a Carl Hubbell or a Bob Feller pitch three innings. In the days before television, the exhibition games were a once-a-year delight for the populations that lived great distances from the Major League cities.

The extended barnstorming trip had its finale in Charleston, West Virginia. From there the Indians rode home to Cleveland to prepare themselves for the opener. The starting lineup had one significant change in it. Oscar Vitt penciled in a new third baseman with just two years of minor league experience. He had shown immense promise in spring training, enough to win the job outright. His name was Ken Keltner.

Kenneth Frederick Keltner was born on the south side of Milwaukee on October 31, 1916. He attended high school there, playing just about every sport available, including ice hockey. While a member of the football team, a nagging ankle injury prompted him to concentrate on baseball alone. Keltner played amateur ball for several different teams, including one backed by a mortuary. When the season ended, he switched to fast-pitch softball, garnering all kinds of attention for his exceptional talent.

In 1936 a local umpire noted Keltner's skills and accompanied him on a visit to Allen Sothoron, the manager of the Milwaukee Brewers. A brief tryout convinced Sothoron, a one-time Major League pitcher, to offer a contract. Keltner signed and was sent to Class D Fieldale, Virginia, a member of the Bi-State League. Though a long distance from home, Keltner quickly developed into an outstanding ballplayer. In one season at Fieldale, he batted an impressive .360 while powering 12 triples and bashing 33 home runs. The Brewers were satisfied enough to bring Keltner back to Milwaukee for the 1937 season. He made the transition flawlessly, knocking out 27 home runs and hitting .310. At this point the Indians became interested, securing Keltner's contract for the large amount of $40,000 and three players.

Keltner reported to the Indians spring training in something less than top-flight condition. The *Cleveland News* observed that "Keltner is a chunky German of the type that put on weight rapidly." The reporter did mention that the new third baseman had great hands, a strong arm, and excellent reflexes.

The Indians sorely needed a dependable third baseman who could handle his position without the glaring errors of his predecessors. Sammy Hale's bum arm led to a move to second base, allowing Keltner to show off his well-above-average fielding skills. He helped nail down a roster spot in the course of the exhibition tour with the New York Giants. In the first two games, Keltner walloped three home runs, convincing Slapnicka and Vitt they had indeed found their man.

With the addition of Ken Keltner, the Indians were primed and ready to open the season at Municipal Stadium. Fans had to get used to the idea of driving their cars or hopping on a bus to find their way downtown toward the lakefront. Alva Bradley predicted record attendance, as well he should, with an 80,000-seat facility. The weather cooperated with blue skies and an unusually warm April day. Though a strong wind came blowing off Lake Erie, the temperature steadily climbed to a pleasant seventy-seven degrees. Men discarded their winter overcoats to arrive at the stadium in shirtsleeves.

At nine o'clock in the morning the concession staff was already hard at work. The mouthwatering roast beef and corned beef had to be cooked and simmered for at least six hours. Bags of popcorn were being produced at a rate of fifty bags every two minutes. Bread trucks lined the streets with several thousand loaves of warm fresh bread and hot dog buns.

At least ten tons of ice were needed to cool the thousands of soda and beer bottles. An opening-day crowd had the capacity to devour up to 34,000 tasty sandwiches. including hot dogs, cool off with 3,000 or so bricks of ice cream, and wash it all down with refreshing lemonade, soda pop, and beer. Several hundred vendors, from small boys to grown men, handled the concession sales for 10 percent of the gross. Selling beer had the potential to earn more than a few bucks, while hot dogs had the greater volume. Vendors were always looking to hawk the higher-priced items, leaving the popcorn and candy bars for the youngest boys. The ten- and eleven-year-olds stood in a line, their oversized vendor coats falling far below their waists.

There was money to earn even after the game finished, in the "blow-off sales," where vendors lowered their prices and sold items to fans needing food for the drive home. Men on their way back to the office might want a hot dog and a cold beer to get them through the overtime hours. There were many ways to make a buck.

The crowd assembled on April 19 added up to 31,600. It was a new record for the Cleveland Indians, yet still left almost two-thirds of the stadium seats empty. Major League attendance for opening day, including Cleveland–St. Louis, reached 250,000, a robust start for the new season. Owners looked ahead to a money-making summer. They had scrimped and saved for quite some time, and prospects were now bright for a continued stretch of profitability. The red lines in the company books were beginning to give way to black ones, much to the relief of the clubs that had struggled mightily throughout the Depression of the 1930s. The team owners could now sit back in their private boxes, shaking hands and counting the dollars about to be added to their savings accounts. Even Judge Landis might be seen cracking a small grin. Though probably not.

The opening-day ceremonies at Municipal Stadium were nothing out of the ordinary. Manager Vitt received an authentic Native American headdress from a rodeo troupe that was performing at the midtown Cleveland Arena. The Indians and Browns marched to center field for the raising of the flag. And that was all the pregame pomp. The Indians took the field with a few of the players wearing their new windbreakers under their jerseys. Owner Bradley had paid the pricy amount of $16.50 each for the cold-weather protection. If nothing else, his boys were the best-dressed players on the field.

Jack Graney sat behind the WHK microphone for his seventh year as the Indians' play-by-play announcer. The veteran now had a partner, Pinky Hunter, to handle the between-innings conversation. This addition allowed Graney a short break while the teams exchanged positions on the field. Soon broadcasts would ease into the two-man format that allowed fans to acquire the maximum amount of information each and every game. Hunter contributed scores from around the American League, did updates, handled some of the live commercials, and provided a somewhat comic foil for Graney's observations.

At the Cuyahoga County Jail, 450 prisoners enjoyed Graney and Hunter's broadcast of the opening game, thanks to the county sheriff and his deputies, who hooked together fifteen loudspeakers to relay the play-by-play. It is safe to say there were no prison breaks or mass riots from the time Johnny Allen threw his first pitch.

In spite of the warm weather and a new manager running things, the Indians played badly, losing to St. Louis 6–2. The Browns broke the game open in the fifth inning with four big runs. George Mc-Quinn, one of Oscar Vitt's young players from the 1937 Newark Bears, led off the inning with a double. Don Heffner walked and Buck Newsom, the Browns' starting pitcher, bunted a popup that fell behind the pitcher's mound. That loaded the bases and brought up the leadoff hitter, rookie Mel Mazzera. Johnny Allen let go with a fastball, plunking the first-year player in the side. Ex-Indian Billy Sullivan grounded to Hal Trosky, who let the ball get past him into right field for two more runs. Sam West, the Browns center fielder, lofted a sacrifice fly to Earl Averill for the final run. Cleveland, save for a solo home run by Trosky, never threatened, and the home opener was lost.

The next afternoon the two clubs relocated to League Park. Here Bob Feller would make his highly anticipated 1938 debut. One year ago under the same surroundings, Feller had injured his elbow, a costly blow for the team. Now he had to deal with the lofty expectations still following him since his first start in 1936. Feller had yet to pitch a full season for Cleveland, and undoubtedly he wanted nothing more than to show everybody he had the liveliest arm in the Major Leagues. He took the mound in great health and superb conditioning and with a new catcher in Rollie

Hemsley, a proven game manager. All signs pointed to a successful afternoon.

Only 4,500 fans turned out to see Feller's initial appearance. Probably ten times as many regretted staying at the office or their business when they heard the final score. Feller had total command from the first inning, spotting his fastball and curve where the St. Louis hitters could barely make contact. There were many weak ground balls to the infield and only six fly balls to the outfield, all of them of the routine variety. Feller pitched like a true veteran, moving the ball around rather than winding up and throwing blazing fastballs right down the middle of the plate. The Browns were surprised with Feller's maturity, being constantly fooled by the pitch location. Through five innings they failed to get anything resembling a base hit.

Billy Sullivan came to bat in the top of the sixth inning with one out. He bunted the ball halfway between the mound and home plate. Feller came charging down and grabbed the ball, but had to turn toward first to make his throw. The ball and runner arrived at the same time, resulting in a call of safe from umpire Eddie Rommel. Nobody argued, and the Browns got their first and only hit of the game.

After a brief slumber, the Indians' offense woke up. They scored three in the second, the highlight being Lyn Lary stealing home against pitcher Jim Weaver. The play before, Bruce Campbell had easily stolen second without a throw. Manager Vitt, coaching third, noticed how little attention Weaver was paying to the base runners. He gave Lary a quick nod and the shortstop dashed for home and scored. That was all the help Feller needed, but the Indians came up with six more tallies, including a double and triple from Trosky. The final score was 9–0.

After the game, reporters crowded around Feller to ask him about the bunt single and close play at first. In typical Feller style, he told the *Plain Dealer*, "I threw it with everything I had and if he beat it out it couldn't be helped." Another writer asked why Feller did not just throw the ball away for an error and preserve the no-hitter. Rather than show any contempt for the silly question, he smartly replied, "I don't think that fast!"

At nineteen years old, Bob Feller had nearly thrown his first no-hitter. He struck out only six and walked the same number, but he had shown the poise of a ten-year veteran. Surely Rollie Hemsley had helped by calling a good game, but almost all the credit went to the young man from Van Meter, Iowa. All the fans who witnessed the game agreed Feller had arrived as a first-rate pitcher.

The Indians moved on to Detroit, where they kept their winning ways going. They took three in a row from the Tigers, using some big hitting from Hal Trosky and Earl Averill. The win streak was apparently a little too much for catcher Rollie Hemsley. After the final-game victory, the team had a midnight train ride to Chicago. With a more than enough hours to kill, Rollicking Rollie visited at least several bars, then moseyed his way back to the team hotel. In the lobby stood Oscar Vitt, relaxing before the cab ride to the rail station. He noticed Rollie staggering around by the front doors, obviously full-blown drunk. Vitt approached the wayward player, loudly voicing his disapproval. He ordered Rollie to get the first train back to Cleveland, where he could meet with Cy Slapnicka and discus his new suspension. Hemsley tried to argue he was not drunk, he only had a couple of drinks. Vitt just shook his head in frustration.

The Cleveland reporters soon surrounded Vitt, looking for an interesting quote or two. Vitt had a few words to say. "The only rule about drinking on this ball club is stop when you have had enough. If a fellow wants to take a couple of glasses of beer or even a couple of high balls after a game, why I am for it. But I insist they know when they've had enough."

Vitt's rules were adequate for the casual drinker who knew when to stop. Like all the other managers before him, he had no idea what do about Rollie's problem. The season was only six games old and Vitt had already suspended Hemsley twice, the first time during spring training. Now it would be Cy Slapnicka's predicament to deal with. At first glance it seemed the Indians general manager had no plan on the table. When Rollie arrived in Cleveland, he told reporters he certainly had not had too much to drink and the suspension was clearly not justified. Slapnicka did not agree, telling the *Plain Dealer,* "Oh sure, listen to him you'd think he was a saint and that we were all wrong. I saw myself that he was drinking Sunday night." Alva Bradley had a straightforward comment. "He plays ball for six months only. He should be able to behave himself or if he can't he should get a job as an ice man."

Meanwhile Johnny Allen took some of the glaring spotlight away from Hemsley. In his recent win against the Tigers, Allen had had several arguments with the umpires, nearly getting sent to the clubhouse. Vitt had to sprint onto the diamond to stop Johnny from going too far. On April 28 at St. Louis, Allen completely lost his temper, charging home plate while kicking dirt in every direction. It was the bottom of the fourth inning, and the Indians were pounding the Browns all over the lot. There did not seem to be any plausible reason for blowing up. However, Allen was in the midst of giving up four runs to St. Louis, likely bringing his volatile temperature to a boiling point. Home plate umpire Bill McGowan had a long history with Allen, setting the stage for an unforgettable confrontation.

A pitch came in that looked to be a strike, but McGowan loudly indicated a ball. The call enraged Allen, who sprinted off the mound, ready to send the umpire halfway to the moon. For several minutes some choice words, unprintable in the newspapers, were hotly exchanged between Allen and McGowan. Frankie Pytlak joined the frenzied argument, as did Lyn Lary and eventually manager Vitt. Curious reporters studied Allen's face, later describing him as "white with rage."

McGowan decided he had had enough of the angry one. He raised his right arm, signaling the Cleveland pitcher out of the game. Within seconds the banished Allen turned with both fists clenched and came within inches of McGowan. Vitt had no choice but to bear-hug his pitcher and twist him away to avoid certain bloodshed. In a moment Allen partially regained his composure, reluctantly walking toward the clubhouse while spot starter Denny Galehouse hurriedly threw his warmup pitches.

Fortunately for everyone concerned, especially Allen, Cleveland won the game, 11–6. Ken Keltner hit his first home run as an Indian, along with a triple and three RBIs. Galehouse finished the game with five and one-third innings of excellent relief, allowing only one more tally. The Cleveland sportswriters, particularly Ed McAuley, upbraided Allen for his childish behavior. He had let the team down on numerous occasions and showed no signs of changing his ways. Manager Vitt had directed hundreds of players in his minor league days, but had not seen the likes of Johnny Allen and Rollie Hemsley. He had to figure out a way to get both players to toe the line and do their jobs like the remainder of the squad. Soon the Indians would earn a national reputation as one of the most difficult teams in baseball.

Chapter 6

JEFF AND JOHNNY

A t the end of April the Indians sported a fine record of 8–3. Sure, the season had just begun, but the team appeared to be following up on the strong finish of 1937. The hitting was good, the pitching better than average, and the defense, though spotty at times, had improved. While most of the players were rapping the baseball, Moose Solters struggled mightily in left field. For one reason or another, the hard-hitting Moose could not get himself started at the plate. He had been hitting fourth in the order, the prime spot ahead of proven batters Earl Averill and Hal Trosky. Much had been expected, but Solters failed to produce as he had the previous year. His disappointing start left the door wide open for an eager Jeff Heath to get a shot to play left field.

John Geoffrey Heath was born in Fort William, Ontario, Canada, on April 1, 1915 The small town on the shores of Lake Superior had been connected to the fur-trading business since the seventeenth century. Both French and British merchants prospered in Fort William, eventually battling it out for control of the money-making territory. The British were the victors, controlling all the trading until the industry gradually faded out. In 1970 several towns, including Fort William, consolidated to form the present-day city of Thunder Bay.

Heath's parents came from jolly old England, where his father, Harold, was a soccer player of some renown. When Jeff reached his first birthday, the family relocated to the northwest United States, settling in Seattle, Washington. Harold either owned or managed a local hardware store.

As a young boy, Jeff played a form of baseball with his neighborhood pals. The boys, not yet ready for grade school, apparently made up the rules as they went along. A neighbor recalled seeing a game between the four- and five-year-olds where Jeff made contact, dropped the bat, and ran to third base, then all the way around to home. To all who took part, it was a legal play.

Jeff attended Garfield High School, where he played varsity football and baseball immediately. Already near six feet tall and weighing 200 pounds, he developed into a bone-crushing fullback, running wild against all the other high schools. In the December 1933 city championship game, the Garfield Bulldogs faced off against Lincoln High in front of over 25,000 fans at the University of Washington football stadium. Jeff, still a junior, had a tremendous day, catching two touchdown passes in Garfield's 19–7 win. In the second quarter, Lincoln had the ball deep in their own territory. Their running back slashed through the Garfield line, broke a tackle, and was off to the races. Jeff sprinted down the field after him. Using all of his speed, he made a touchdown-saving tackle at the three-yard-line. Several plays later, Lincoln fumbled, ending the drive without any points. Jeff's play turned the momentum around, putting the Bulldogs in control for the rest of the game. He led his conference in scoring with forty points and was named to the 1933 All-City team.

Jeff also had tremendous success at baseball. Typical box scores showed him getting three hits in four at bats, usually a home run and double and at least several RBIs. He graduated in the spring of 1934 as one of the top athletes ever to play at Garfield High School.

Before long Jeff attracted the interest of the University of Washington, which offered him a football scholarship. Colleges such as Alabama, California, Oregon, and Fordham were on the short list as well. They called him a "muscle man," with a big upper body capable of knocking tacklers several yards backwards. A good-looking guy with wavy brown hair, brown eyes, and confidence in everything he did, Jeff had it all.

While mulling over the football offers, Jeff spent the summer playing semipro baseball with the Yakima Indians. The team was managed by former Cleveland Indian George Burns, a key member of the 1920 World Champion ball club and the 1926 American League MVP. Heath dominated at the plate, batting well over .400 for the season.

In late August, Heath was selected for an amateur all-star baseball team to board a steamship and sail all the way to Japan for an exhibition tour. The group was coached by two former Major League players, Max Carey, the base-stealing whiz of the Pittsburgh Pirates, and outfielder Leslie Mann, a member of the 1914 Miracle Braves. The squad, considered to be the elite amateur players from all around the United States, ranged in age from nineteen to twenty-three.

The tour left San Francisco near the end of September, bound for Honolulu, Hawaii. From there it was straight to Japan for a series of seventeen games in the country's largest cities. Jeff played well on the trip, bashing a home run during a game in Tokyo. Wire photos sent from Japan showed the young team eagerly sitting down for dinner with a large number of beautiful geisha girls at their service.

On the voyage home the boys were notified that the entire team was to represent the United States in the 1936 Olympics hosted by Germany. They would play a series of exhibition games to demonstrate the American dominance of the sport. The twenty-year-old Jeff Heath, already an experienced tourist to an Asian country, would now have the opportunity to see much of Eastern Europe. As enticing as the offer must have been, professional baseball interrupted the world traveler.

George Burns had not forgotten the stellar play of his former Yakima outfielder. Keeping things in the family, Burns got in touch with Indians scout Willie Kamm, another ex-member of the Tribe. Kamm rode the rails to Seattle, Washington, to meet with Heath and offer him a minor league contract to start the 1936 season with Zanesville, Ohio, of the Mid-Atlantic League. Heath already had several offers from clubs in Washington, including his hometown of Seattle. Where many young ballplayers would have jumped at the first contract shoved under their nose, Jeff waited for the best deal to come along. He took his time, sifting through the proposals to get as much up-front money as possible. He viewed the negotiations as a business, and tried to obtain the most money he could to get his young life started on the right path. Ultimately he signed with Kamm, obtaining $3,500 immediately and another $1,500 for the remainder of the year.

Over the winter, Jeff attended several classes at the University of Washington. He made a practice of running at the college indoor track, often chalking up a mile or better. Playing a lot of competitive handball kept him in top shape before the beginning of spring training. In the classroom he became quite enamored of books on all subjects, often in later years taking a load with him on the road. With his education and self-assurance, he had little problem asserting himself on the field and in the clubhouse.

In 1936 Heath left Washington to make the cross-country trip to Zanesville, Ohio. The Greys had an excellent ball club, featuring players such as future Cleveland Indian Oscar Grimes. They would win the league championship that year. On May 3 Zanesville hosted the world-class Pittsburgh Crawfords for an exhibition doubleheader. The Negro League club had a fearsome roster, with the battery of the great Satchel Paige and peerless catcher Josh Gibson. Speedster "Cool Papa" Bell played center field, while Judy Johnson was at third base. This packed lineup had enough stars to compete with a Major League club, let alone a Class C one. The Crawfords easily swept the doubleheader, with Paige throwing an impressive 7–0 shutout in game two. Heath batted fourth and played left field in both games, doing nothing of note in either contest.

Competing against the teams of the Mid-Atlantic, Heath had little trouble in piling up some amazing statistics. He batted an outstanding .383 for the season, with 28 home runs and a remarkable 187 RBIs. The Indians front office promoted him to Milwaukee in 1937, where he shone once again, hitting .367 in one hundred games. Jeff received a late-season call to join the Indians, where he got into twenty games and batted only .230. Even with the low batting average, he received an invite to report to New Orleans in 1938 for spring training with the big boys.

At New Orleans the Cleveland reporters labeled Heath smiling and carefree. Easygoing as he was, they noted that when something went wrong he got a strange look in his eyes, like a stern warning sign to back off. Mostly he was self-assured, though; he told Ed McAuley of the *News*, "I'm a candidate for any job in the Indians outfield. And when I say any job I mean Averill's as well as either of the others." As a young man Heath greatly admired Earl Averill, another resident of the state of Washington. The high regard ceased when the confident first-year player reported to camp believing he could unseat the ten-year vet and perennial All-Star. On opening day Averill stood in center field, warding off the challenge. Heath sat on the bench waiting for manager Vitt to give him a chance anywhere in the outfield. It would come soon enough.

The Indians kept winning ball games all through May. At the end of the month they had a superb record of 24–12, three and one-half games ahead of the Yankees. Of course, a lot of baseball remained to be played, but Cleveland gave their fans plenty of excitement in the early going.

On Sunday, May 22, the Indians and Yankees met for a showdown at Municipal Stadium. The late spring weather cooperated, with sunny skies and temperatures in the mid-sixties. The recent play of the home team really got the city excited. At five a.m. several dozen people mustered in front of the stadium ticket office. A few hours later the number grew into the hundreds. Trains arrived downtown carrying people from as far away as Buffalo and New Castle, Pennsylvania. By game time the crowd had swelled to 62,244, a tremendous number for early in the season. Bob Feller had some issues with his back, but warmed up anyway and started the game. He had to leave after three innings, but held the Yankees scoreless.

In the bottom of the fourth, with the Indians already up 3–0, Earl Averill came up with the bases loaded and two out. Yankees pitcher Monte Pearson, the ex-Indian, had few friends remaining in Cleveland. When he was traded to the Yankees in 1936, he called out several of the Indians players, including Averill. Nobody, especially the Cleveland center fielder, forgot what Pearson had done. With the fans urging him on, Averill punched a base hit to left field, scoring two runs. An inning later runners were on second and third when once more Averill came to the plate. He lined another base hit, scoring two more runs. The Indians now led 6–0.

In the New York half of the sixth, Lou Gehrig smacked a long drive between the outfielders. With the ball rolling deep into the outfield, Lou had a sure triple. As he rounded first he slowed up, appearing to be in some kind of pain. He stopped at second, motioning for the trainer to come out. After talking it over with the trainer and manager Joe McCarthy, Gehrig stayed in the game. He would score on a base hit, but when the Yankees took the field for the bottom of the sixth, Babe Dahlgren trotted out to first. Gehrig's consecutive game streak was intact at 1,992, but fans wondered what had happened to the best player in the game.

The Indians won the ball game by a decisive score of 8–3. First-year pitcher Johnny Humphries, in relief of Feller, got the win, and Mel Harder entered the game in the seventh to finish things out. Except for Feller, everyone who started the game had at least one hit; even the rookie Humphries had a single and drove in a run. The giant crowd snarled traffic for over two full hours, yet few people grumbled after the one-sided victory.

When the game concluded, the sportswriters marched into both locker rooms. Although they wanted to hear from the victors, most of them rushed to the visitor's side to talk to Lou Gehrig. With his record-setting consecutive-game streak on the line, they were looking to determine how badly Lou was injured. Fans from all around the United States were monitoring the streak, eager to find out any new details. If he couldn't go the next game , it would be a major scoop.

The reporters nearly tripped over one another to reach Gehrig's locker. There was Lou, smiling and ready to talk. He said, "Sure I'm all right. It was just another attack of that cutting pain across my back. I'm pretty bad for five or six hours but after the hot towels do their work, I'm as fit as ever." That was enough of an explanation for all concerned. Fans reading the papers on Monday read the articles and nodded their heads, believing Gehrig had some kind of sore back. After all, he was the "Iron Horse" of baseball. He never got an injury severe enough to force him to miss a game. Just about everybody that followed the national pastime believed the injury would fade in a short time, permitting Gehrig to play on for the long term. Nevertheless, the back pain was probably an undetected symptom of the frightful disease that would claim Gehrig's life in just three years.

On Memorial Day, May 30, the Indians returned to Municipal Stadium for a holiday doubleheader with Chicago. The White Sox themselves were not a great draw, but with Feller and Allen scheduled to pitch, a total of 38,615 fans turned out, eager to see Cleveland's best pitchers for the price of a single game. Feller proved he had recovered from his aching back, leading Cleveland to a 5–2 win. He had difficulty finding the plate, walking eight batters, but allowed only five hits in breezing to the victory. Earl Averill knocked in two runs on two of the Indians' twelve hits.

Johnny Allen did even better in the nightcap, holding the White Sox to just four hits and a single run. He was a one-man wrecking crew with two big singles and three runs driven in. Frankie Pytlak had three hits, including a triple, as the battery mates completely stole the show. Since the beginning of the 1937 season Allen had now won an eye-popping twenty-one out of twenty-three decisions. No pitchers in either league could come anywhere near to Allen's numbers. If he continued along those lines and with help from Feller, the Indians had a legitimate opportunity to roll to a pennant.

Alva Bradley had chosen wisely for the select games at Municipal Stadium. In only three scheduled dates, the home opener, a Sunday game with the Yankees, and the holiday doubleheader topped out at 132,468 fans or an average of over 40,000 per date. Bradley had a keen knack for gauging fan interest, and so far in 1938 he had it down remarkably well.

The next morning the *Plain Dealer* had two front-page articles on the doubleheader. One had the usual summary of the games, while the other had a much different take. It read in part, "It's Baseball in 1938, not War! Take off your coat and start in on the peanuts and thank your stars you are watching baseball instead of mobilization. Baseball players leaning over the edge. Nobody with a grenade. Planes in the air advertising a horse race not a bomber anywhere."

The implications of the article were clear. Though the threat of war in Europe had much of the world consumed with anxiety, the United States had little to worry about. The German War machine stood poised, ready to march over Europe at any time. Surely many folks in the United States had genuine worries about relatives overseas, but few were concerned about safety here at home. We had a strong ally in England ready, and the idea of a foreign invasion over the Atlantic Ocean seemed quite remote. Therefore, on Memorial Day, Americans could flock to the ballparks and eat their hot dogs and peanuts, thinking of nothing but baseball. They did, to the tune of 330,448 people attending the eight games in the American and National League. The Yankees, at home against the Red Sox, drew 82,980. Baseball was thriving with seemingly nothing to fear from a potential German onslaught overseas.

Other than Rollie Hemsley's suspension in late April and Johnny Allen getting thrown out in Detroit, things were amicable in the Indians clubhouse. New manager Oscar Vitt had the team playing well, with few or no complaints. Fans waiting for the usual team collapse were silent as the season progressed into June. Cleveland went on an eastern road trip and on June 7 was playing the Red Sox at Fenway Park. Johnny Allen started the game by giving up a two-run homer to slugger Jimmie Foxx. Nothing unusual here, as Foxx would go on to hit four home runs in the series.

Even with a lead, the Red Sox batters and Manager Joe Cronin whined to umpire Bill McGowan about Allen's sweatshirt. They claimed the ratty old shirt had several frays along the elbow that made it difficult to see the baseball. In addition, Allen had cut slits in the shirt for ventilation, and the Boston hitters argued that all this interfered with their line of sight. McGowan, who had tossed Allen from the Detroit game, had no sympathy for the Cleveland pitcher. Before Allen could start the second inning, McGowan stopped the game, advising Allen to go to the clubhouse and get a new sweatshirt. Allen became infuriated (what a surprise) and refused to change. He argued he had used the same sweatshirt since opening day and none of the other umpires had a word to say about it.

McGowan refused to budge, again ordering "Jawin' John" to go get a new undershirt. While the Boston fans howled, Allen stalked toward the Indians dugout and vanished into the clubhouse. McGowan waited five minutes, then ten minutes, and still no Allen. Manager Vitt, after arguing with the home plate umpire, went to the clubhouse to find his riled-up pitcher. Lyn Lary ran from his shortstop position to the clubhouse to see what was going on.

Allen sat in a chair by his locker, refusing to change his shirt. He would not listen to reason, venting his anger at McGowan and the Red Sox batters. Vitt could wait no longer, relaying to the bullpen to get reliever Bill Zuber warmed up and in the game. Allen not only hurt himself by his actions, he let down the team by once again allowing his emotions to get the best of him. Zuber, rushed into the game, gave up three runs on four hits. Vitt had to summon the bullpen once more, calling on Johnny Humphries to relieve Zuber. Humphries pitched an outstanding game, going six and a third innings without a run while the Indians clawed their way back to a wrenching 7–5 win. Before the players took off their uniforms and showered, Vitt stormed into the clubhouse and served up a hefty $250 fine to Johnny Allen.

When the reporters stopped by the locker room, some of the Cleveland players defended Allen, claiming McGowan had a grudge against him and that's why the skirmish occurred. They believed the sweatshirt issue was ridiculous and McGowan had gone too far in ordering Allen to get a new shirt. Some of the guys even insisted McGowan had said some nasty things about the Indians in general and was completely out of line. In fairness to McGowan, regulation 25 of the American League rulebook read, "American League pitchers will not be permitted to work with ragged or slit sleeves which have the effect of confusing the batter."

Be that as it may, the incident was picked up in every major newspaper across the country. Reporters and columnists weighed in on who was wrong or right. A Texas newspaper believed umpires who were hostile to a particular team should not be assigned to work any of their games. They advocated that umpire schedules be done in private and on a week-to-week basis, allowing changes for player-umpire issues. The paper had an interesting point; however, Allen had a beef with most of the American League umpires. It really didn't matter who was on the bases or behind the plate.

All three Cleveland papers had in-depth stories about the now-famous sweatshirt. Allen, after regaining his composure, spoke freely with reporters. "I wore that shirt all last season without anyone complaining," he said. "There's not so much as a loose thread waving in the wind. Those slits can't possibly have the slightest effect on the batter. Anyway I was ready to go back in the game. I even was going to change the shirt and I sent word to that effect but he [Vitt] replied it was too late."

Stuart Bell of the *Cleveland Press,* the most outspoken of the Indians sportswriters, wrote, "There was absolutely no excuse yesterday for him walking off the field whether his shirt sleeves were illegal or not. If the umpire asked him to change his shirt he should have done it." Bell was right on point with his comments. Allen ought to have considered the game and his team before anything else. He could have obeyed McGowan and sometime later filed a protest with the league office. Allen, unfortunately, was too self-centered to do this. There have been many bizarre incidents throughout baseball history—a batter running to third on a ground ball, for instance, or Germany Schaefer racing from second base to first in an attempt to draw a throw. Allen's display in Boston has to rank right up there.

The *Cleveland News* could not resist publishing a silly poem about the ill-advised behavior of Allen.

> The umps, they're doing Allen dirt,
> They're even picking on his shirt.
> All of which makes Johnny mad,
> And leaves him $250 in the rad!

The story of Allen's troubles did not let up for quite some time. Alva Bradley wanted to make some kind of gesture in hopes that Allen might put aside the debacle and move forward. He announced that the Higbee Company, a popular downtown Cleveland department store, would offer $500 to display the Allen sweatshirt. By mere coincidence, Higbee's director was Chuck Bradley, Alva's brother and part owner of the Indians. Somehow the two got together and hatched the scheme. Curious people came from all around northeast Ohio to see the infamous sweatshirt that had cost Allen $250. At a later date Bradley approached his pitcher and gave him the check for $500. That act seemed to quiet down Allen considerably. Fortunately for all concerned, Allen did not have any more serious outbursts for the rest of the season.

Whether the Allen problem had an effect on the team is not known, but they lost the last two games in Boston. With the lead down to three and a half games, the team now faced a huge weekend series with the defending champion Yankees.

Due to all the attention, the *Press* borrowed the huge mechanical scoreboard owned by the May Company, another of the thriving department stores downtown. It was normally saved for World Series time. The *Press* set it up in Public Square, brought in a teletype line from Western Union, and prepared to have the sports staff shout out the play-by-play of the weekend games. Eager fans, not wanting to wait for the recreated game broadcast by WHK, filled every inch of the square to get the game results in real time.

As it turned out, the Yankees clobbered the Indians 8–2. Bill Dickey hit two home runs while Lou Gehrig added another. Saturday's game was rained out, probably a good thing for the Indians. On Sunday, Cleveland led 6–5 when Bob Feller came on in relief of the beleaguered Johnny Allen. With a runner on, Feller served up a 400-foot game-winner to rookie Joe Gordon, leaving the Indians a scant one and a half games ahead in the standings.

Ten days later, New York came to Cleveland for a well-anticipated rematch with the margin still a game and a half. They had four games to play: a single date on Tuesday, a doubleheader on Wednesday, and another single game on Thursday. Though it was only the latter part of June, Indians fans treated the series as if the American League pennant was on the line. At the start of Tuesday's game, some 20,000 fans stacked themselves into League Park. Bob Feller pitched against Red Ruffing in what turned out to be a crowd-pleasing slugfest. The Indians won the battle 10–5, with Jeff Heath belting a key two-run home run and contributing four RBIs. Rollie Hemsley, just recovered from a broken finger, had three hits and batted in three more. Feller got the victory despite a shaky appearance, giving up five runs and walking an improbable nine Yankees.

The home team had drawn first blood. The next day, starting early in the morning, the trains rolled in on the hour, bringing several thousand fans from Erie, Pennsylvania, and all parts of western Ohio, headed for Municipal Stadium. Along with the baseball nuts came out-of-town reporters, enough to saturate the entire press box. Cars started to fill the stadium parking lots with license plates from Indiana, Pennsylvania, and Michigan. Since a huge day was expected at the municipal lots, the city parking fee was temporarily raised to a steep seventy-five cents per car. Extra salespeople manned the ticket windows at eleven a.m., eyeing the lines of customers stretching over a hundred feet long. Since summer had officially arrived, the men dusted off the shiny white straw hats, while the ladies were seen wearing loud multicolored bandanas.

Cleveland City Hall and the courthouse on Lakeside Avenue were practically deserted as an unofficial half-day holiday allowed employees to dash for the stadium. Among those taking the short walk down Lakeside was Safety Director Eliot Ness and his wife. The nationally famous lawman was putting down the mug shots and incident reports long enough to see the Indians' and Yankees' confrontation. A veteran policeman on duty at the stadium remarked that he had not seen such a spirited crowd since the 1920 World Series at League Park. Truly the Cleveland fans had a raging case of premature pennant fever.

When Mel Harder let go with his first pitch, a magnificent crowd of 67,459 fans was in attendance. Several thousand had to stand due to the Great Lakes Exposition of 1937 borrowing seats from the upper left- and right-field stands. The Indians front office had dallied in reinstalling the seats, not anticipating a need for them anytime soon.

A number of spectators brought their own cameras to take action shots of the players. This was a new phenomenon happening around Major League parks. Portable cameras had become more affordable and lightweight, so in addition to bringing home a score card and team pennant, one could take snapshots and have them developed at a number of camera outlets. Fans added photos to their scrapbooks along with the game summaries and articles from the newspapers. A new cottage industry was born.

In the top of the first inning, the Yankees went down without incident. In the Cleveland half Lyn Lary came to the plate and coaxed a walk from starter Lefty Gomez. The vast crowd roared when Bruce Campbell punched a single, putting runners on second and first. Sammy Hale laid down a well-placed bunt just to the right of the pitcher's mound. Gomez fielded the ball, then heaved it over third baseman Red Rolfe's head toward the left-field corner. Lary scored easily, while Campbell sprinted all the way around the bases to plate the second run. Earl Averill, always dependable in the clutch, laced a single to center field, scoring Hale from second for the third run of the inning before Gomez could halt the carnage.

Mel Harder pitched his best game of the season, limiting the Yankees to one run over seven and one-third innings. Johnny Humphries relieved Harder in the eighth and recorded his second save. Final score: Cleveland 3, New York 1. The second game of the doubleheader still had to be played, but fans had already had plenty to cheer about. They celebrated at the concession stands, seeking respite from the heat, now peaking at eighty-six degrees. Usually the fans were able to count on a nice cool breeze coming off the lake. But on this day the flag stood limp on the pole: no wind, just oppressive heat and humidity everywhere. To contend with it, spectators bought a record 30,000 ice cream bars and 20,000 beers. Hot dogs were flying off the grill: 40,000 for the day. The new Cleveland Concession Company, in its short tenure, could not keep pace with the demand.

Game two had Johnny Allen facing off against Monte Pearson. Neither side did anything until the bottom of the third, when Bruce Campbell walloped a three-run homer into the right-field stands. The Indians collected a total of fourteen hits, including a double and triple from Hal Trosky and three singles from Jeff Heath. Allen allowed only four hits in cruising to a 7–1 victory and a sweep of the critical doubleheader. The Indians starter now had nine straight wins for the year after his loss on opening day. Cleveland's lead over the Yankees climbed to four games, while Boston trailed by three and a half. There was still one more game to play, but the Indians could do no worse than take three out of four.

On Thursday at League Park, New York salvaged the final game by a score of 8–6. Bill Dickey and Lou Gehrig had home runs to pace the New York attack. Denny Galehouse could not hold back the Yankee offense, yielding four important runs in the first two innings. Even so, the Indians had shown the skeptical hometown fans some excellent baseball. They remained alone in first place, staying on course to challenge for their first pennant in a long eighteen years.

At the end of June, hanging on to a four-game lead over the Yankees, the Indians faced the Tigers in a wild showdown at League Park. Bob Feller had a one-sided lead of 9–3 going into the top of seventh, but Detroit pushed across two runs in their turn at bat to narrow the gap. Feller started the eighth with two walks, which caused his removal in favor of Johnny Allen. With nobody out, the Tigers were far from done, touching Allen for a triple and a double to close within one, 9–8. Two consecutive fly balls scored the tying run before Allen got Hank Greenberg on another fly ball to retire the side. In the bottom of the ninth, two Indians were out when Frankie Pytlak slashed a triple to deep left center. When Allen stepped up to the plate, the fans shifted uncomfortably in their seats, certain the game was about to go to extra innings. The pitcher took a mighty swing and lined a base hit for the game-winner. Not only did Allen have the deciding hit, he boosted his record to a stellar 11–1, and the team's record to an excellent 40–22. The Indians could do no wrong, or so it seemed.

Alva Bradley plots strategy with American League president Will Harridge and National League president Ford Frick, December 1936. *Author's collection.*

High school senior Bob Feller crams for final exams, April 1937.
Feller graduated from Van Meter High in May. *Cleveland Press Collection—*
Michael Schwartz Library, Cleveland State University.

Feller walks to the Cleveland dugout after pitching against St. Louis, April 1937. He had already injured his right elbow but said nothing until the sixth inning. *Author's collection.*

Women fill the grandstand at League Park for Ladies Day, 1937.
The female fans were just as boisterous as their male counterparts.
Cleveland Press Collection—Michael Schwartz Library, Cleveland State University.

Ken Keltner at bat, ca. 1938. Keltner joined the Indians in 1938 and became a fixture at third base. One of the best-fielding infielders in the American League, Keltner was largely responsible for stopping Joe DiMaggio's hitting streak at fifty-six games. *Bruce Milla collection.*

Lyn Lary takes a drink, ca. 1938. Lary was a disappointment at shortstop but married to Hollywood actress Mary Lawlor. *Bruce Milla collection.*

The infamous Johnny Allen sweatshirt on display at Higbee's Department Store, June 1938. Notice the holes in the right sleeve. *Cleveland Press Collection—Michael Schwartz Library, Cleveland State University.*

Part of the record-breaking crowd at Municipal Stadium watching the Indians sweep the Yankees, June 22, 1938. More than 67,000 fans attended, the highest total ever for an afternoon doubleheader. *Author's collection.*

Indians Frankie Pytlak and Hank Helf pose for photos on August 20, 1938, after catching baseballs dropped 708 feet from the Terminal Tower. The stunt was set up by the Come-to-Cleveland Committee and drew thousands of spectators. *Author's collection.*

Indians players relaxing at the Café du Monde in New Orleans after practice, March 1939. *From left:* Jimmy "Skeeter" Webb, Al Milnar, Jeff Heath, Bill Zuber, Ray Mack. *Author's collection.*

Judy Garland gets ready to perform the national anthem, opening day at Municipal Stadium, April 18, 1939. Alva Bradley stands to the left, Mayor Harold Burton to the right. A smiling Oscar Vitt is standing against the grandstand. *Cleveland Press Collection—Michael Schwartz Library, Cleveland State University.*

A stone-faced Cy Slapnicka ponders Rollie Hemsley's future with the Cleveland Indians, April 1939. Hemsley would shortly enter Alcoholics Anonymous and become sober. *Author's collection.*

Rollie Hemsley clear of black eyes and bruises, April 1941. With the help of AA, Rollie turned his life around, becoming an All-Star in the 1939 and 1940 seasons. *Author's collection.*

The Fellers quietly celebrate on the morning of April 17, 1940, the day
after Bob's opening day no-hitter against the Chicago White Sox.
Feller would have a tremendous season, nearly pitching the Indians
to the pennant. *Author's collection.*

Lou Boudreau (*left*) and Ray Mack (*right*), ca. 1940. The two arrived in August 1939 to form one of the top double-play combinations in the American League. Boudreau would become player-manager of the Indians in 1942. *Ray Mack family.*

Cleveland manager Oscar Vitt ponders his future with the ball club,
June 1940. The Indians' player revolt shocked Vitt and the nation.
Author's collection.

Happy fans line up at the League Park ticket window, August 1940.
Even with the players' revolt, the Indians battled for the pennant until
the end of September. *Cleveland Press Collection—Michael Schwartz Library,
Cleveland State University.*

THE MUCH ABUSED CLEVELAND INDIANS OF 1940

Front row (left to right): Ben Chapman, Sammy Hale, Frankie Pytlak, Oscar Melillo, Johnny Bassler, Oscar Vitt (Manager), Roy Weatherly, Ray Mack, Johnny Allen.

Center row (left to right): Louis Boudreau, Luke Sewell, Bob Feller, Al Milnar, Roy Bell, Trainer Lefty Weisman, Al Smith, Joe Dobson, Harry Eisenstat and Nate Andrews.

Back row (left to right): Bill Zuber, Oscar Grimes, Russ Peters, Cal Dorsett, Mel Harder, Hal Trosky, Ken Keltner, Jeff Heath, Johnny Humphries, Rollie Hemsley and Clarence Campbell.

Indians team photo: the "Crybabies" of 1940. They would push for the removal of manager Oscar Vitt and get roasted in the national papers. Despite the trouble, they came within a game of winning the pennant.
National Baseball Hall of Fame Library, Cooperstown, NY.

The Dodgers' Leo Durocher and Cleveland's Roger Peckinpaugh look over the new batting helmet worn by Joe Medwick, March 1941. It would be many years before batters used the protection on a regular basis. *Author's collection.*

Bob Feller accepts congratulations from teammates and club stockholders after pitching the only opening day no-hitter in Major League baseball history, April 16, 1940. *Bruce Milla collection.*

Chapter 7

MUNICIPAL STADIUM

As the season neared the halfway point, Oscar Vitt showed early signs of disintegrating under the pressure of a hard-fought pennant race. The Indians still led the American League, but Ol' Os, as he liked to call himself, had his first meltdown as a Major League manager. Vitt became furious when his team lost a tough 9–8 decision on the road to the Washington Senators. He told Gordon Cobbledick of the *Plain Dealer*, "I've been in baseball for nearly 30 years and I've never seen as bad a defensive team as this one—either in the major's or minor's. Of the 26 games we lost we've beaten ourselves out of 13." Vitt had nearly lost his composure in the Senators' half of the ninth inning. With the game knotted at eight runs apiece and a Washington runner at third, Jeff Heath caught a short fly ball in left field. The runner tagged up and sprinted for home in what should have been a close play. For whatever reason, Heath lost his grip on the ball and sent a wobbly throw that barely reached home plate and allowed the runner to score easily.

Vitt also had choice words for Roy Weatherly in right field. Replacing an injured Bruce Campbell, Weatherly failed to hustle on several occasions, a practice Vitt would not tolerate. Ol' Os was the king of hustle throughout his playing days, and expected no less from each of his players. He always coached third base in Hughie Jennings style, yelling encouragement and jumping up and down, much to the amusement of the fans. From time to time Vitt would vent his frustration for all to see, shaking his head or outstretching his arms when one of his players committed an error or took a called third strike. The guys slowly started to notice the antics but said nothing. In time that would surely change.

On Sunday, July 3, a classic old-timers game came to League Park. It was a great afternoon for nostalgic Cleveland fans, as the World Champion 1920 Indians matched up against the 1908 Cleveland Naps. It was the thirtieth anniversary of that near-pennant-winning team. The Naps fought to the wire, losing to the Detroit Tigers by just a half-game. The rules at the time did not require Detroit to play a rained-out game from earlier in the season. Thus, the Naps were denied a chance for a playoff, and that group of talented ballplayers never got to a World Series.

The younger 1920 team had most of their roster on hand for the contest. Tris Speaker, Stan Coveleski, Larry Gardner, Bill Wamby, Elmer Smith, Joe Wood, and others were on the field for the champs. The 1908 squad, most of them in their mid- to late fifties, had Bill Bradley, George Stovall, Joe Birmingham, Earl Moore, and ringers in former Chicago White Sox ace Ed Walsh and Boston's Cy Young. Napoleon Lajoie, everyone's favorite, had fallen ill several days earlier and had to stay away from the park.

Cy Young, at an energetic seventy-one years old, started the game for the 1908 squad. The fans stood and cheered for their old hero as Cy pitched to four batters, then left the field. Moments later the crowd erupted when Elmer Smith cracked a long home run high over the right-field wall. Memories flooded back to game five of the 1920 series, when Smith, in the opening frame, belted the first-ever grand slam in the postseason. Later Joe Wood thrilled the fans by driving a pitch all the way to the scoreboard in deep center field. He jogged into third base with a triple, then scored on Elmer Smith's double. Youth won out in end, as the 1920 edition smoked the older players 8–0.

Three days later the sixth Major League All-Star game was held at Crosley Field in Cincinnati. Earl Averill, named to the team for the sixth straight year, appeared along with American League stalwarts Jimmie Foxx, Charlie Gehringer, Lou Gehrig, Bill Dickey, Lefty Gomez, and catcher Rick Ferrell. Johnny Allen and Bob Feller were on the pitching staff, the initial time for both players. Allen pitched the middle three innings, allowing one run on a triple by Mel Ott and a single by Ernie Lombardi. The National League won the game 4–1. In six years of All-Star play, the American League still enjoyed a four-games-to-two lead.

After the break, the Indians went on the road, eventually winding up in New York City. With the two clubs still fighting for the pennant, some less than good-natured words went back and forth during the pregame workouts. Lefty Gomez started things by singling out old teammate Johnny Allen. Gomez said, "I hear you're working tomorrow, so am I. Well tough luck. You can't win them all." Allen stared for a few seconds then shot back, "You ought to know!"

Yankee coach Johnny Schulte yelled to Hal Trosky, "You gotta get votes to make the All-Star team. Your own manager wouldn't even give you a vote." This remark stemmed from earlier comments by first baseman Trosky that he deserved to be on the American League roster. He had some credibility, since he was hitting well over .300 and driving in his share of runs. Lou Gehrig was not having a strong first half, which encouraged Trosky to speak out. Of course Jimmie Foxx had to be the starter, and Hank Greenberg was right behind in the voting, but Trosky had a legitimate argument that he should be one of the substitutes. Gehrig was the sentimental choice, leaving the Indians star out of the picture. Though Oscar Vitt quickly denied that he failed to vote for Trosky, some of the players may have had their doubts. If there was any honeymoon for Vitt, one had to believe it was about to cease.

The Indians, despite the taunting, beat the Yankees 5–3. Earl Averill hit his tenth home run, while Trosky singled in two more. Mel Harder pitched extremely well, evening his record at 7–7 and showing again that he could limit the New York hitters as few pitchers could. Cleveland maintained the inspired play through the month of July, peaking on the thirtieth with a mark of 53–30. New York was still a game and a half ahead, with three more wins and the same number of losses as the Indians, and the Yankees were poised to go on one of their classic hot streaks, leaving the rest of the American League in their wake. Once again the pennant chase was about to trend in a different direction, one that did not favor Oscar Vitt and his ball club.

It probably would not have made a difference, but Johnny Allen injured his pitching arm sometime in July. He managed to win his thirteenth decision against two losses, yet over the rest of the season he would win only one more game. He continued to pitch his regular turn, but rarely lasted more than a few innings, due to painful arm that hindered his effectiveness. The injury left Bob Feller and Mel Harder as the only reliable starters on the club.

With the Yankees destroying the rest of the American League, Alva Bradley canceled plans to play all the September home games at Municipal Stadium. He had envisioned making a box-office killing as the Indians chased the pennant through the last month of the season. Though his dreams were ruined, he had still seen attendance rise significantly from April through most of July. The team would make a robust profit regardless of how attendance fared for the balance of the season. At least it was something positive from a season that had so much promise from the outset.

On Wednesday, August 3, the Indians and Red Sox met for a doubleheader at Municipal Stadium. A vocal crowd of 36,397 was on hand to celebrate Earl Averill Day. After ten productive years, friends of Averill decided it was time to organize a tribute to one of Cleveland's finest ballplayers. Al Maharas, the owner of the popular State Café Chop House, led the effort. Maharas and ten other well-connected gentlemen created a souvenir program, which sold for twenty-five cents. Numerous restaurants, beer distributors, gas stations, and retail shops took out ads of different sizes. The Cleveland Baseball Company bought a full-page ad, while smaller space was purchased by Tris Speaker, Billy Evans, the broadcast team of Jack Graney and Pinky Hunter, and team trainer Lefty Weisman. Averill had a home in the eastern suburb of Cleveland Heights, making that area a prime target for advertising. It seemed that most of the merchants on Cedar and Lee Roads bought spots, covering several pages. The payoff for all that advertising took the form of a dazzling new Cadillac sedan.

First up was a huge display of flowers, enough to fill Averill's greenhouse back in Snohomish, Washington. Earl had been in the flower business back home for several years. Then each team presented him with a number of autographed scorecards to commemorate the event. Ed Bang of the *Cleveland News* spoke about all the contributions Averill had made as a long-time Cleveland Indian, including 222 home runs and 115 triples plus a lifetime batting average of .324. Jack Graney brought out his portable microphone and presented the beautiful new car. Averill sat on the fender and was slowly driven around the stadium for a victory lap while fans stood and cheered.

Averill, now in his mid-thirties, had filled a tremendous void left when Tris Speaker retired. Many fans believed nobody would be able to replace the Grey Eagle at the plate or especially in the outfield, where Speaker routinely outran line drives hit far over his head. Averill came along and won over the Speaker fans by smashing a home run in his first at bat as an Indian. He did not cover as much ground as Speaker could, yet he made a number of spectacular plays in center field, more than enough satisfy the skeptics.

As well as being an All-Star player, Averill had a soft spot for the boys and men who clamored for his autograph or a simple handshake. Just two months earlier, a man from Dover, Ohio, had traveled to an Indians game in hopes of getting Averill's signature on his scorecard. The gentleman was crippled by a severe mining accident that had left him in a wheelchair. Friends in Dover got an ambulance to transport him for the long ride to League Park. After the game the man was taken to the outside entrance of the Indians locker room. While he waited, the players had to shower and dress quickly to catch their train for the upcoming road trip. The police came by to chase away all the children hanging around to talk with their favorite Indians. Hal Trosky walked out and stopped long enough to sign the man's scorecard. A few moments later, out came Averill, hurrying to catch a waiting cab for the train station. Other players might have ignored the fan and kept on running, but Averill stopped for a moment, quickly signed the scorecard, and shook hands. The man asked if there was any way to get a signed baseball as well. Averill smiled, ran back into the clubhouse, and snatched a new baseball. He put his name on the ball, said goodbye, then hurried for the cab. If anyone deserved a special day at League Park, it was surely Earl Averill.

Other than the day for Averill, the Indians' fortunes in August began a steep decline. In a doubleheader at St. Louis, Moose Solters got a rare start in the outfield. Jeff Heath had won the starting job back in July, demoting Moose to occasional pinch-hitting duties. In game one Solters reached first base on a fielder's choice. Seeing the steal sign flashed, he edged off first, only to get quickly picked off. In his next at bat, in the eighth inning, Moose singled to center field. He made a big turn going around first, raced halfway to second, then changed his mind and scampered back toward first. The relay throw was right on the mark, arriving an instant before Moose slid into the bag. The umpire called him out, ending a horrendous day for Solters. When the Indians took the field in the bottom of the inning, Solters was on the bench, replaced by Roy Weatherly. Oscar Vitt went nuts after the game, calling out Moose and several other players. Vitt said Solters was as good as gone from the team. He told Gordon Cobbledick, "I feel sorry for the guy but he'll never get a chance to repeat those boners while I'm running this club."

Alva Bradley stood firmly behind his manager, declaring a housecleaning would be in order and that Vitt would wield the broom. Lyn Lary ranked at the top of the list with Sammy Hale, Solters, and, surprisingly, Earl Averill. Lary had fallen out of favor through some troubling erratic play. He had a tendency to throw to the inside of the first-base bag, forcing Hal Trosky to reach across his body just in front of the batter hustling down the baseline. Sooner or later Trosky risked a collision that could easily end up with a broken bone or two.

Vitt aired further complaints about just about everybody on the team. Even Bob Feller did not escape harsh words from the manager. Ol' Os believed Feller's high leg kick prevented him from throwing strikes. He wanted Feller to adopt the same leg extension that most other American League pitchers used. Now in his third season with the Indians, Feller was being asked to change his delivery while keeping the same speed. True enough, the bases on balls were still a problem; nevertheless, that was a lot to ask of your best pitcher, only nineteen years old. Feller did the wise thing and did not respond in the papers.

The vast majority of Major League managers kept their barbed criticisms behind closed doors. Occasionally they would spout off to reporters, but those instances were few and far between. Manager Vitt did not seem to have any reservations about saying derogatory things concerning his players to anyone who would listen. His players either heard or read about the denigrating talk and became resentful. It would take some time for them to react, but the seeds were planted in 1938.

The Indians were no longer earning headlines on the playing field, so the Come-to-Cleveland Committee fostered an idea that would revive interest throughout the United States. The committee, with the approval of the Indians management, advertised a scheme planned for the morning of August 20. Their idea was to break the world record for catching a baseball dropped from the greatest height. The current record was established in 1908, when Senators catcher Gabby Street caught a ball dropped 555 feet from the Washington Monument, and had faced few challenges since then. The Cleveland committee had faith the record could be beaten, and hoped to lure thousands of interested spectators downtown. An Indians player would stand on the fifty-second floor of the landmark Terminal Tower and drop twelve baseballs to the ground. Attempting to snag at least one of the throws would be catchers Rollie Hemsley, Frankie Pytlak, and the seldom-used Hank Helf, as well as two former catchers, Indians coaches Wally Schang and Johnny Bassler.

The publicity stunt gained serious momentum until Oscar Vitt announced on the seventeenth that Hemsley and Pytlak were barred from the attempt due to safety concerns. He allowed both coaches and Hank Helf to try for the record. It must have seemed a good idea to keep your two best catchers away from a speeding baseball hurtling 708 feet straight down.

On the morning of the twentieth, an animated crowd estimated at 10,000 people gathered at the base of the Terminal Tower. Ropes were put up to keep the spectators at a safe distance, although who could be sure what a safe distance was? Newsreel camera crews and radio announcers from several Cleveland stations set up their equipment to capture the event for posterity. A moment later the Indians representatives arrived on Public Square. Apparently Vitt had changed his mind, since Hemsley and Pytlak joined Helf at the bottom of the tower. Ken Keltner was designated to be the man on the fifty-second floor, dropping the baseballs at one every two minutes.

Some of the Indian players and coaches wore construction helmets for protection, though few people seemed to worry if a blow to the head might cause severe injury. After everything appeared to be in order, Keltner waved from above and dropped the first baseball. Several mathematicians on hand estimated the ball's speed at an absurd 138 miles per hour. The first baseball landed on the concrete and rocketed back up over 100 feet in the air. That probably should have convinced all those participating to give it up, but this was 1938, and ballplayers still had little interest in wearing batting helmets or any kind of protection. They were fearless.

In spite of the chance of disaster, the show continued. On the fourth throw, Hank Helf zigged and zagged across the concrete sidewalk and made a successful grab. The crowd went wild, as the old record was now shattered courtesy of the Indians' third-string catcher. People shouted from the windows of the Hotel Cleveland, including several Chicago White Sox, biding their time before the afternoon game. More spectators were sensibly viewing the show from inside the Higbee Company and behind the walls of the Terminal Tower itself.

Even though the record was broken, the high-flying baseballs kept coming. A slight wind blew in north from the lake, causing the next throw to veer dangerously close to the throng behind the ropes. Luckily, nobody got hit, and Keltner dropped another missile. Frankie Pytlak, all of five feet, seven inches, changed course several times, planted his feet, and caught the speeding ball, making it two for the day. Pictures of the two successful players were seen the next day in newspapers all across the country.

The Come-to-Cleveland Committee had pulled off a tour de force that local folks would remember for many years to come. The event brought a massive number of people downtown, many of whom stopped by the lunch counters and restaurants or did some shopping at the department stores. With the help of the Indians, particularly the courage of Helf and Pytlak, the show produced a morning of fun and excitement that lessened the anger at yet another pennant lost to the powerful Yankees.

The disappointing Cleveland season ended on October 2 with a doubleheader at Municipal Stadium. The Detroit Tigers were in town for what would normally represent two meaningless ball games. But this time 27,000 fans bought tickets, eager to see if Hank Greenberg, who already had fifty-eight homers in the book, would break Babe Ruth's single-season home run record. Two more would tie Ruth at sixty; three more would set a new mark. Bob Feller had the start in game one, making the challenge even tougher for the hard-hitting Greenberg.

Benny McCoy, the Detroit second baseman, led off the game. Feller had his fastball crackling, striking out McCoy on three straight pitches. After the Indians went out in the bottom of the first, Greenberg led off in the top of the second. With fans making plenty of noise, Feller whiffed the Tigers first baseman, then struck out two more to fan the side. He did the same in the next two innings, racking up a remarkable ten strikeouts in four innings.

The crowd began to home in on the strikeouts, paying much less attention to Greenberg and his chase of the Babe's record. Feller resembled the kid who just two years ago had nearly tied the American League record with fifteen K's, and a month later equaled Dizzy Dean's Major League record of seventeen. This outing Feller had his sharp-breaking curve working along with his unparalleled fastball.

The fans paid little notice when Detroit scored two runs in the sixth inning and two more in the eighth. They bellowed their approval when outfielder Chet Laabs fanned in the eighth inning, bringing the count to sixteen.

Pete Fox led off for the Tigers in the top of the ninth. Feller, his fastball still blazing, sent Fox to the dugout, victim number seventeen. Roy Cullenbine singled, bringing Hank Greenberg to bat for the last time in game one. He made contact but lifted a harmless fly to center field, where Roy Weatherly made the catch. In four attempts Greenberg failed to homer, hitting one double, striking out twice, and flying out. In all fairness, he had to contend with a pitcher who had overwhelming stuff.

Catcher Birdie Tebbetts, one of two Tiger players who had not struck out, drew Feller's seventh walk of the game. Even though he had grown tremendously as a pitcher, the bouts of wildness were a semiregular occurrence. Chet Laabs, already a four-time strikeout victim, stepped warily into the batter's box. Feller, ignoring the two runners, went to a full windup to get every inch of power behind his throws. Laabs looked mesmerized, failing to move his bat off his shoulders. Feller threw a strike, then a ball. By this time just about everybody in the stadium was standing. Another strike zipped by Laabs, then another, and the deed was done. Bob Feller had smashed the Major League strikeout record with eighteen!

The bewildered Laabs had fanned an incredible five times, pitcher Harry Eisenstat and shortstop Mark Christman three times, and McCoy, Fox, and Greenberg twice. Few Cleveland fans were concerned that the Indians lost the game 4–1. They had seen Bob Feller establish a modern-era pitching record, one that would stand for another thirty-one years.

Feller also led Major League pitchers with 240 strikeouts in 277 2/3 innings. He had started the day with 222, four behind Buck Newsom. For the season he won seventeen games, lost eleven, and struck out 7.8 per nine innings. He also led the American League in walks with a whopping 208. Feller had opened the season with a near no-hitter against St. Louis, then in his final start set a new standard for strikeouts in either league. Though he fell short of the twenty wins that the Cleveland front office expected, he had had an exceptional year. He was on the brink, it seemed, of becoming the number one pitcher in all of baseball.

Other Indians had excellent seasons in 1938. In his first full season, Jeff Heath proved to be one of the best-hitting outfielders in the American League. A terrific second half put him at .343, just six points behind Jimmie Foxx in the race for the batting title. He led the league with 18 triples and had 21 home runs and 112 RBIs. Earl Averill batted his usual .330 while finishing second to Heath with fifteen triples. Ken Keltner played outstanding throughout the year, finishing with 26 homers and 113 RBIs. The high point came on a September 11 doubleheader against the St. Louis Browns, when he hammered out seven straight hits, including two long home runs and a double. The Indians were pleased with their rookie third baseman and not at all disturbed by the high price they had paid for his minor league contract.

Rollie Hemsley visited with Cy Slapnicka right as the season came to an end. Rollie picked up a nice bonus of $1,000 and a large diamond ring for his wife or daughter. The money and the ring were not part of his contract; they resulted from a verbal agreement at a late April meeting. At that time, Rollie came to Slapnicka's office, pleading for reinstatement after the recent suspension in Detroit. After much thought, the general manager dangled the bonus offer if Rollie could stay out of trouble for the entire season. Somehow he did, which in itself was a tremendous feat. He may have snuck a drink or two when nobody was around; nevertheless, his name appeared in the papers only as part of the box scores. Rollie would later reveal that the moment he cleaned out his locker, he streaked for the nearest tavern and got plastered. One might say he was getting a jump on the 1939 season.

Chapter 8

LET THERE BE LIGHT

Throughout the off-season, Alva Bradley had one single purpose in mind. He would use any means available to get league approval for the installation of lights at Municipal Stadium. To make this a reality, Bradley had to secure the votes of at least four American League owners. In 1937 he had had approval from only two, Chicago and St. Louis. He recognized that the owners from New York, Boston, and Detroit were vehemently opposed to any form of night baseball. That left Connie Mack of Philadelphia and Clark Griffith of Washington as the only potential allies Bradley needed to lock up.

In August 1938 Bradley got a key endorsement from Philadelphia's Earle Mack, Connie's son. The younger Mack revealed to a local paper that he had no disagreement with night baseball in any of the American League cities. Though the winter meetings were four months away in December, Bradley figured he had the third vote and only needed one more to get the nod for installing lights. Of course, Connie had a say in the matter, but the prospects were bright.

At some point in the fall, Clark Griffith let the owners know he intended to ask for waivers on first baseman Zeke Bonura. Griffith had a verbal agreement with the New York Giants to purchase the power hitter for the tidy sum of $25,000. For this to happen, all the American League owners had to let Bonura pass. Alva Bradley thought the matter over and realized he had some strong cards to play. The minor league meetings were to be held in the first week of December. He instructed Cy Slapnicka to make the rounds at the get-together and let it slip that the Indians were thinking of claiming Bonura for the A.L. waiver price of only $7,500. This was a polite warning to Griffith that it would be in his interest to vote yes on Bradley's night-game proposal and then collect the extra $18,000 from the Giants. If the long-time Washington owner voted against Bradley, the deal with New York was all but dead. The Indians had Hal Trosky well established at first base, but Bradley was willing to throw away $7,500 to show his contempt if Griffith voted no.

The meetings convened in New York on December 12, and, after some talk back and forth, the owners voted 4–3 in Cleveland's favor. The fourth and deciding vote came grudgingly from Clark Griffith. One could call the proceedings a bit of horse trading, but Bradley showed extraordinary resolve in pulling off the vote. The previous year he had politely asked for approval; this time he utilized the power of the almighty dollar to get what he wanted. The rest of the formidable owners surely got the message.

The remainder of the annual winter meetings had a few interesting proposals tossed about. The Yankees wanted to start paying their ballplayers salaries on the first day of spring training. The normal routine was to begin payouts on the opening day of the regular season, then the first and fifteenth of the month the rest of the way. The Yankees' reasoning was that players who were thinking of holding out could not resist the idea of a late February or early March paycheck. If the proposal was enacted, the Yankees were confident all the clubs could save money because the number of holdouts would sharply diminish, leading to less negotiating and thus to cost savings. Though New York presented a good case, the other owners, not willing to dole out salaries early, voted the proposal down.

Another interesting proposal came forward for the owners to consider: raising the waiver price to $10,000. This idea apparently came forth to discourage owners from claiming a player for no reason other than gamesmanship. A recent example had been when Alva Bradley threatened to claim Zeke Bonura to coerce Clark Griffith into supporting him on night baseball. Another scenario was that an owner with a lot of cash in his pocket might claim a player to prevent his fellow owner from getting a better deal in an interleague transfer. Not all of the moguls were best friends, so raising the waiver price might prevent this form of mischief.

While the bosses negotiated, reporters filed stories about some potential trades about to take place. The hot rumor concerned the Indians acquiring veteran outfielder Ben Chapman from Boston for Earl Averill and Sammy Hale. Bradley and Slapnicka denied the stories, but the smart money was on Chapman to be in the Cleveland outfield come 1939. The team was certain another big bat in the lineup would improve their chances of unseating the Yankees. Chapman was an experienced ballplayer capable of batting over .300, stealing bases, and contributing better-than-average defense. On December 14, the Indians traded pitcher Denny Galehouse and minor league shortstop Tommy Irwin to Boston for Ben Chapman. The Red Sox had no second thoughts about dealing a pretty fair outfielder. They had confidence in a promising new guy named Ted Williams to fill the void.

Ben Chapman was born in Nashville, Tennessee, on Christmas Day, 1908. He had no choice but to be a ballplayer, as father Harry spent thirteen seasons in the minor leagues, and uncles Jim and John toiled in the minors for many years as well. While he was still a young man, the Chapman family moved to Birmingham, Alabama, where Ben attended classes at Phillips High School. He excelled at all sports, including football, basketball, and baseball, and even found a few minutes to run track. What separated Chapman from other athletes was speed. He could outrun just about everyone on the football field and circle the bases quicker than anybody on the diamond.

When he reached his senior season, Purdue University extended a scholarship offer. Ben readily agreed to head north to Indiana, until the New York Yankees approached with a bona fide contract to play ball. Soon he forgot about Purdue, as he made his 1928 debut with Asheville, North Carolina, of the South Atlantic League. Chapman hit a solid .336 for the year, earning a promotion to St. Paul, Minnesota, in the American Association. Once again he batted .336, though this time with a noteworthy 31 home runs and 222 base hits.

The Yankees had seen enough. They added Ben to the 1930 roster. Playing most of his games at second and third base, he had a fair to middling rookie season, then really blossomed in 1931, when he stole a league-high 61 bases to go with 17 home runs and 122 RBIs. Now playing the outfield, he seemed to be the perfect complement to Babe Ruth and Lou Gehrig, able to get on base and score runs courtesy of the big guns.

While Chapman thrilled Colonel Ruppert and manager Joe McCarthy with his outstanding play, he started to alienate his teammates with his contemptible behavior. On one fine day Chapman provoked Ruth by angrily telling him, "If you were paid as much as you're worth you'd be making less than I am." This may have been retaliation for an earlier remark from the Babe after Chapman unsuccessfully tried to steal third with two out. The Yankee great told Ben he must have rocks in his head.

Even though Chapman continued to play exceptional baseball (he was an All-Star from 1933–36), the unfortunate incidents started to pile up. He had difficulty handling the endless taunts from fans in the outfield bleachers. On one occasion he sprinted to the stands, vaulted over the railing, and chased a fan completely out of the ballpark. While playing in Philadelphia, Chapman attempted to steal second. Enraged when umpire John Quinn called him out, he grabbed the baseball and tried to pound umpire Quinn in the head. A swift ejection from the game followed, but the infuriated Yankee again charged the umpire. Several teammates had to hold him back and escort him to the locker room. The next day he received notice of a fine and three-game suspension from the league office.

By 1934, Chapman had already become an outsider to his ball club and many of the loyal New York fans. He complained repeatedly that the aging Ruth could no longer handle playing right field and was hurting the team's chances of reaching another World Series. Chapman grumbled that due to Babe's decreasing mobility, he himself had to cover parts of right field from his center-field position. He told the papers anonymously that "if Ruth had plenty of money put away it was time for him to quit, but if Babe wasn't well fixed financially he should keep on playing."

The next day, a furious Ruth stalked into the Yankee clubhouse demanding to know who said it was time to retire. Chapman had enough guts to stand up and admit it, yet somehow no punches were thrown between the two antagonists. The newspapers did not let go of the story, resulting in fans roundly booing Chapman at most of the American League parks. Few could question the hard truth that Ruth had slowed down noticeably and could not cover right field in an acceptable manner. Yet the Babe had revolutionized the game, bringing excitement and popularity to baseball like none before him. He was the Sultan of Swat, the man who crushed sixty home runs in a single season. Chapman's caustic remarks were completely out of bounds.

The unkind words to Babe Ruth were only the beginning of the storm. In a home game at Yankee Stadium, some vocal fans in the outfield bleachers began to ride Chapman. It did not take long for a response from the heated outfielder. Assuming the men heckling him were Jewish, he unloaded on them with some choice racial slurs. The men were offended, as was every Jewish fan in hearing range. The situation deteriorated to the degree that friends of Chapman organized a banquet and invited anyone who had a grievance against the outfielder to attend and talk it out. Whether or not the Yankees front office ordered him to, Chapman or a ghostwriter issued a statement to the papers. It read, "Please express my deepest appreciation to all my Jewish friends who attended the banquet. And I only hope that everyone believes me when I say I respect and honor their race and religion and meant no malice toward them. I am extremely sorry for the entire affair at the park."

Before the start of the 1935 season, Chapman put up $50, wagering he would not kick over any water buckets, throw any bats, or fight with any fans. New York scribe Dan Daniel wrote in his column, "He is a fine young man, he should be an approximation of Cobb. He has the body, the speed, the aggressiveness at times. But he has certain complexes."

Chapman had a difficult time enduring days on the field when he failed to hit safely or committed an error. He brooded about his lack of success rather than looking at the complete picture. The Yankees were a tremendous team, always in the hunt for the pennant and World Series. Chapman did not seem to be able to enjoy the team's accomplishments when things went badly for him individually. In June of 1934 his wife divorced him, which made sensational news all around the country. Chapman was one of those people who cannot get out of their own way.

In the winter of 1936 Ben declared himself a holdout, wanting a better deal from team owner Colonel Ruppert. Being as stubborn as possible, Chapman did not sign his contract until April 4. It was the longest holdout in Yankee history. He missed all of spring training, joining the team in the latter stages of exhibition play. While he bided his time in Alabama, a group of Jewish Yankee fans delivered a petition to New York headquarters demanding Chapman be traded away. The petition had an incredible total of 10,000 signatures covering its many pages. Despite his conciliatory statement two years ago, there were still thousands of paying customers who despised him.

Once again a statement attributed to Chapman was released to the New York papers. It said, "The first thing I want to do is to make my peace with the Jewish fans at the stadium. I understand that some of them have signed a petition asking that I be traded. I had a little trouble with a couple of Jewish spectators in 1934 but last year I took a lot of riding without ever making a return. In Birmingham I have a lot of Jewish friends I play baseball and basketball at the Young Men's Hebrew Association. I am going to do my part in creating a better feeling."

It is not clear if the fans gave him any a chance at redemption. There was really no time, as the Yankees had resolved to move Chapman to another club before the June 15 trading deadline. With one day left to swap players, they sent him to Washington for outfielder Jake Powell.

This move appeared to be a calculated risk for Clark Griffith and the Senators. Three years earlier their new outfielder had gotten into an ugly fight with Washington second baseman Buddy Myer. The two traded punches after Chapman, spikes flying, slid hard into Myer, who was trying to apply the tag. After several minutes of fighting, the combatants headed to the Senators dugout, where the corridor leading to the visitors' clubhouse was. As Chapman reached the steps, Washington pitcher Earl Whitehill greeted him with several loud obscenities. That started another battle, with a Chapman right hand knocking Whitehill on his back. It took a group of players to restore order and get Chapman out of the

Senators dugout and on his way to the Yankee clubhouse. For his wild antics the American League handed out a fine and a three-game suspension. It remained to be seen if Chapman could mend fences with his new teammates and help them in the outfield.

His tenure in Washington lasted less than a year. On June 11, 1937, the Senators traded pitcher Buck Newsom and Chapman to Boston for brothers Rick and Wes Ferrell and part-time outfielder Mel Almada. The Red Sox wanted a veteran outfielder, while the Senators coveted an All-Star catcher like Ferrell. In the 1938 season, Chapman batted a career high of .340 and played a fairly decent outfield. He did not know it, but he was on a temporary assignment until Ted Williams had enough minor league experience to join the Sox.

Another reason occurred on May 5, when Chapman got into a tussle with Detroit catcher Birdie Tebbetts at home plate. A called third strike infuriated him, and when Tebbetts chimed in with a few offhand comments, Ben starting throwing haymakers at the backstop. The two men battled for a round or two until teammates pulled them apart. The usual fines and suspensions followed.

A day later the Tigers traveled to New York City to start a series with the Yankees. In his superb autobiography, *Birdie: Confessions of a Baseball Nomad,* Tebbetts shares a pregame meeting with Lou Gehrig. The Yankee star wanted to know if Birdie was still fuming at Chapman and whether he would fight him again. The answer was yes and yes, causing the usually even-tempered Gehrig to offer a brand-new suit if Tebbetts battled Chapman a second time and landed at least two good shots. The conversation took place two years after Ben had left the Yankees, verifying that some bad feelings still lingered on in New York.

With all the baggage Chapman had, it is a wonder the Indians wanted him anywhere on the roster. They already had the angry Johnny Allen, the hard-drinking Rollie Hemsley, and the night owl Lyn Lary. Perhaps Bradley and Slapnicka had so much faith in Oscar Vitt they thought he could turn anybody around. That was yet to be seen.

With the Chapman trade finalized, the Cleveland front office turned to other matters. Alva Bradley acknowledged that the team had earned over $30,000 profit by scheduling games just at

Municipal Stadium. City officials quickly let him know they were unhappy with their share of the receipts and demanded to renegotiate. Bradley had to consider bumping up the city's share, while soliciting bids for the installation of lights. The price for light towers seemed to be in the neighborhood of $60,000 to $70,000. A great amount of steel was required for the towers, and light sockets had to be installed on the stadium roof. The extensive work would take at least several months. As the rules stated, only seven games were allowed, and a new clause mandated games had to be completed no later than 11:15 p.m.

Bradley had numerous reasons to be confident of big crowds at the night games. He intended to start either Feller or Johnny Allen for most if not all of the scheduled contests. The two great pitchers were capable of drawing thousands of extra fans each time they worked. Included in his estimates were the people who worked a 9–5 day and, other than weekends, rarely saw the Indians compete.

Another factor in the optimism was a new U.S. Census Bureau study revealing in the last few years, the average worker's pay rate had significantly improved, from $9,665 in 1935 to $11,393 in 1938. Simply put, families now had more disposable income to spend.

Earlier in December, Colonel Leonard P. Ayres, vice president of Cleveland Trust Bank, issued his annual business forecast. His speech, held at the downtown Hotel Carter, had 1,000 optimistic Cleveland businessmen hanging on every word, and was broadcast live by the Mutual Broadcasting Company to its affiliates throughout the United States. Ayers remarked that it had been ten years since most Americans had enjoyed any degree of prosperity. He believed that affluence would return in 1939. Ayers predicted the auto industry would have a 30 to 50 percent increase in output along with higher factory pay. He forecast record results for electric power input and the tobacco industry, allowing folks to turn on the lights, break out the cigars and pipes, and smoke away.

An additional study revealed that Americans were buying sporting goods at a record pace, with manufacturers now enjoying sales of 44 million, a 27.5 percent gain from 1935. This translated to a stronger interest in sports than ever before. Baseball remained the number one attraction, meaning that a good portion of the sales likely consisted of baseball equipment. With all the forecasts and hard statistics, the 1939 season figured to be a healthy one for Bradley and the rest of the league owners.

In early February the Indians met with Cleveland mayor Harold Burton to chat about financing for the stadium lighting. The mayor reminded Bradley that the ballpark belonged to the city and arrangements needed to be made for its ownership of the new addition. City council would have a say in the final agreement before any construction could begin. Burton advised that the lease deal and the lighting were separate issues and would be dealt with in that manner.

The 1939 Cleveland baseball season officially kicked off on February 8 with the Ribs and Roast Dinner at the Hollenden Hotel. The local sportswriters came up with the idea of making fun of the Cleveland sports teams along with honoring the Indians and American League MVP. Fans could buy tickets for only five dollars, enjoy a first-class meal, and hear the writers "roast" the Cleveland sports owners and players.

The dinner commenced with five hundred people in attendance. There were skits and songs mocking the Indians, the football Cleveland Rams, and the Cleveland Barons of the American Hockey League. The baseball players took most of the hits, including a new song parodying the popular tune "Pocket Full of Dreams."

> We're no hitting terrors and we make a lot of errors,
> But we've got a lot of pennant dreams.
> We don't worry and we're never in a hurry,
> But we've got a lot of pennant dreams.
> Oh, the Yanks are king on Wall Street and the Cubs may
>   rule the west,
> But on Euclid Ave. we are the best.
> Don't you stew and fret, cause there ain't no pennant yet,
> For we'll win the pennant in our dreams.

Another skit made sport of Bob Feller, who had just received an eighty-seven-dollar fine for excessive speeding somewhere near Van Meter. The writer, playing Feller, pleaded with the judge for a receipt so he could bring it to Cleveland and sell for it big dollars to the Higbee Company. The spoof was an obvious dig at Alva and

Chuck Bradley for selling Johnny Allen's tattered sweatshirt to Higbee's during the 1938 season.

On the serious side, Mel Harder accepted an award for being the Indians' most valuable player. He did not have the hot start Johnny Allen did, or Feller's excellent September, but Harder remained the most dependable pitcher on the roster. For his efforts, the writers presented him with a handsome new movie camera. For his selection as the American League MVP, Jimmie Foxx of the Red Sox received a classy humidor packed with expensive cigars. The Ribs and Roast banquet went over big with the Indians fans, so much so that it would become an institution in Cleveland for the next several decades.

With all the unbridled optimism, something had to go wrong for the Indians, as it always seemed to do. At the end of February, rumors floated that Earl Averill had quit on the team in late September. The story that let slip was that he needed to hit .325 after 125 games to receive his usual bonus. Since Averill easily reached his goal and the club was out of the race, the word on the street was that he asked to leave the team and go home early. The gossip likely came from the Cleveland front office, particularly one Alva Bradley. A new contract with a $4,000 salary cut had been sent to Averill, despite his batting .330 for the 1938 season. Bradley remarked to the *Plain Dealer,* "Averill is a risky gamble at age thirty-six."

It might have been the customary posturing utilized by most owners when it came to salary negotiations; however, the charges that he had quit deeply stung the Cleveland center fielder. As one would expect, Averill strongly denied the rumors. He balked at the proposed salary cut, asking to be traded, preferably to the steadily improving Detroit Tigers.

Averill went three for twenty from September 10 through 15. He was out of the lineup in the second game of a September 15 doubleheader, appeared as a pinch-hitter on the 16th, then did not return until September 23. Averill claimed illness forced him out of the lineup, but Bradley maintained his outfielder sat because he had the bonus secured and did not care to play. This was all conjecture on Bradley's part, again probably to gain leverage in contract negotiations. Regardless, it put Averill in a negative light and on the defensive with the fans who had greatly admired him throughout his long career.

It is unlikely that Averill was guilty of any of the charges. The baseball season is long, especially for those who in their mid- to late thirties who no longer have that youthful vitality to draw on. He probably had his share of the bumps and bruises that any ballplayer experiences at the end of a rigorous schedule. Alva Bradley had gone too far with his accusations, resulting in a dispute that meant Averill was apt to be traded or released, ending his remarkable career in Cleveland.

The start of spring training came and went without an appearance by the sullen outfielder. On March 15 Averill issued a statement to the *Plain Dealer:* "I am ready to forget the club's action in slashing my salary and give the Indians the best I have in me if the management sends me a fair contract." He indicated that he would be fine with a trade to any club in the American League other than the struggling Philadelphia Athletics or the cellar-dwelling St. Louis Browns. The contract on the table called for a salary of $10,000 plus a performance bonus for playing at least 125 games. Averill wanted a higher salary without any type of bonus attached.

Almost a week later the Indians business office announced Averill had appeared in Cleveland, indicating he was ready to sign his contract. On the evening of March 21 he arrived at the League Park office and signed for a reported $13,000 with no bonus offered. Averill told the writers he had no objection to moving to right field if the team wanted him to do so. He claimed to be only five pounds above his playing weight, requiring only a week or two to shed the pounds and ready himself to play ball. Earl began his eleventh season with the Indians, though the papers continued printing trade rumors almost every day.

On the slightly bizarre side of spring training, catcher Frankie Pytlak cleaned out his locker and disappeared from New Orleans. Few people had any clues as to why the little man walked out of camp. The next day Pytlak returned for a long meeting with Cy Slapnicka and Oscar Vitt. According to those in attendance, Pytlak wanted more playing time than he had been getting and thought the one-day walkout would emphasize his point. Throughout spring training Rollie Hemsley got the majority of time behind the plate when Bob Feller pitched. Pytlak thought he could catch Feller as well or better than Hemsley, and demanded he be in the lineup more often. Frankie may have had an inkling that Hemsley had already passed him for the starting catcher's job, thus leading to the walkout. If so, he was correct. When the regular season began, Hemsley trotted out behind home plate while Pytlak sat on the bench. Slapnicka and Vitt remained perplexed by the catcher's actions, realizing they had another problem child on the Indians roster.

One of the most interesting prospects in camp was an aspiring relief pitcher named Bill Zuber. He had the distinction of being a member of the Amana Colony, a religious organization located in the heartland of Iowa. The founders came from Germany in the 1840s, eventually building a colony divided into seven villages. The colony grew to own 26,000 acres, including their own railroad station a few miles away in Homestead. The children went to a grammar school until age thirteen, then were recruited for a particular trade. Bill's father was a farm manager in Middle Amana, while Bill toiled in the fields as a laborer. All types of sports were forbidden, but the elder Zuber bought a baseball and gave it to his son. Bill grew to be six foot two and weigh nearly two hundred pounds, and could throw the ball at an uncanny speed. The colony elders greatly frowned upon it, but Zuber temporarily left home to play semipro baseball.

The colony shunned the outside world until the mid-1930s, when, at almost the same time, a fire destroyed their single mill and the effects of the Great Depression reached them. The group had few alternatives other than starting a for-profit corporation and distributing products in Iowa and the Midwest. This new venture gave Zuber some leverage in furthering his baseball career. Cy Slapnicka maintained a wide net around the state, allowing him to find the pitching prospect. In due course he moved him to Cleveland. In the offseason Zuber returned to the colony and drove a tractor for various farms.

Other than the Averill controversy and the Pytlak protest, spring training continued mostly in an orderly fashion. The players found a new form of entertainment when Ben Chapman brought a portable phonograph to camp. He had a number of well-liked Bing

Crosby records that he played for the guys after practice. Soon Mel Harder and Jeff Heath went shopping and bought their own records featuring the popular crooners of the day. They gave the discs to Chapman, who served as disc jockey, taking after-dinner requests from his teammates. In a short time, several of the players bought radios that were small and light enough to carry around on road trips. In addition to books and newspapers, the ballplayers now had more possibilities for instant entertainment.

According to *Baseball Magazine,* the players of the 1930s were more sophisticated than their counterparts of ten years before. One of the areas of improvement was in the quality of the food eaten on the road. A good number of Major Leaguers were becoming more conscious of the meals they chose. An unofficial survey showed that the average player ate a good breakfast, a light lunch, then a big meal after the game. Steak dinners were at the top of the list, with salad, rolls, and some type of potato. Dessert usually featured ice cream and/or a slice of pie. A glass or two of a soft drink completed the dinner.

A lot of players loved seafood. They would knock back a shrimp cocktail, then lobster as the main course. Over the years, the guys had learned to order seafood in the eastern cities, where they could be reasonably assured the food was fresh. Seafood prepared in Boston or New York City was certainly quite different from that served in St. Louis or Chicago. For years players had experienced ptomaine poisoning from food that had sat at room temperature too long and became quite spoiled. They laughed off the uncomfortable illness as a rite of passage for a Major League ballplayer. Approaching the 1939 season, individual cases of food poisoning had significantly diminished.

Baseball Magazine cautioned that too much liquor could result in "beer legs" or "rye gut," affecting performance on the field. The magazine especially warned players over the age of thirty to be careful with their alcohol. Soft drinks were also warned against, as they contained a huge amount of sugar, which could quickly add on the weight. The story of pitcher Ivy Paul Andrews was related as a cautionary tale to those who guzzled down Coca-Colas or ginger ale. Andrews had great difficulty keeping his weight under control. Year after year he came to training camp five to ten pounds overweight. He spoke with the team doctor about how frustrated he was. He seemed to eat the right food and not go overboard on the ice cream and pies. The doctor asked Andrews if he drank any soda pop. The pitcher nodded his head and said he liked to drink about ten to twelve bottles a day.

Before the Indians left New Orleans, the front office announced a new affiliation with the AA Buffalo Bisons. In a twist on the old adage "Keep your friends close, your enemies closer," Bradley and Slapnicka hooked up once again with Steve O'Neill as manager of the Bisons. That thinking was in line with naming Roger Peckinpaugh manager of the New Orleans Pelicans. Manager O'Neill had been gone from Cleveland for less than two years, while "Peck" had been replaced as Indians manager by Walter Johnson in 1933. Bradley was not one to harbor a grudge, allowing his former managers to be valuable members of the Indians organization.

One of the important decisions to be made concerned the shortstops and second basemen to be farmed out for more seasoning. Peck favored Frank Scalzi at short and Jim Shilling at second, as they were believed to be almost Major League ready. O'Neill had been given two young infielders to bring with him to Buffalo. Each player was highly regarded, but judged to be a year or two away from the big leagues. The shortstop, Louis Boudreau, had attended the University of Illinois, while Ray Mack, the second baseman, had graduated from the Case School of Applied Sciences in Cleveland. They would have the benefit of learning under O'Neill, a patient teacher and one of the most knowledgeable ex–Major Leaguers still in the game. Their stay at Buffalo would turn out to be much shorter than team officials anticipated.

Chapter 9

FELLER REACHES THE TOP

O n April 1, yes, April Fool's day, Alva Bradley released the long-awaited seven-game night schedule. The Indians' first home contest under the lights would be June 30 against the St. Louis Browns. Two more games would follow in July, then three in August, and the last date would be September 6 against the Detroit Tigers. He had scheduled the New York Yankees for August 30, though Colonel Ruppert had not yet given his approval. Bradley announced that the night-game schedule came with an automatic day off the following afternoon. The owners feared their teams might be too exhausted to play a half day later and wanted to wait and see what their clubs showed at the next practice.

There were two bids for installing the lights, one from General Electric and one from Westinghouse. Both bids allowed three weeks for construction to begin plus two additional months for completion of the project. GE proposed installing six towers and 760 1,500-watt lights. Westinghouse believed eight towers were needed along with 800 1,500-watt lights. Both companies were capable of handling the project and delivering a top-notch system. Whichever one Bradley decided to go with. he would have little cause for concern.

In other news, Bradley acknowledged that he had worked out a satisfactory lease agreement with the city. For the 1939 season the Indians were on the hook for $12,000 in rent payments.

Additionally, the City of Cleveland stood to receive 3 percent of the gross receipts up to $400,000, and 5 percent if revenue topped that figure. Bradley favored this method over the arrangement in 1938, when he had to pay three cents per person whether they got in free or not. Under the new agreement, passes for the 1939 Ladies Days and schoolchildren would not count in the revenue sharing. The Indians' women fans ate up the free passes at a rate of eight to ten thousand for each Ladies Day. At Municipal Stadium, these passes increased the numbers while still leaving ample room for the paying customers. The women really hollered it up for the home team, giving the Indians players some needed incentive in the 80,000-seat park. As Frankie Pytlak would relate to *Baseball Magazine,* "It's good to see the women come out to the ballpark, especially on Ladies Day because they're always for the home team. They don't seem to be such wolves as some of the opposite sex are." Jeff Heath added, "Feminine fans are human in their devotion to a player and his problems."

The magazine had words of caution for thoughtless men attending games during the hot summer months. A number of them tended to take off their shirts when the temperature soared, regardless of their cleanliness. The editorial stated, "What self-respecting woman wants to sit next to some hairy, steaming stranger stripped to the waist for a couple of hours?"

The city had the obligation to pay the Indians $1,000 per year until the actual construction costs for the lighting were paid in full. Bradley retained the right to break the stadium lease on thirty days' notice and receive a cash settlement for the balance remaining on the light fixtures. Bradley revealed that the 1938 attendance for the eighteen games played at the stadium totaled 402,414, an average of 22,356. With these numbers and twenty-five dates scheduled, including the potential crowds for seven night games, the chances of the Indians abandoning their lease at the lake front seemed remote at best.

As the regular season approached, the Indians and Giants were closing up their annual southern barnstorming tour. On April 14 they were in Richmond, Virginia, for the second-to-last game of the money-making trip. Things started well in the first inning when Jeff Heath walloped a long home run. Several innings later Heath chased down a pop fly, then carelessly dropped it for a two-base error. When he came to the bench, manager Vitt advised him to go back to the locker room, get dressed, and head back toward the hotel. Puzzled, Heath asked if it was because he muffed the catch. Vitt shook his head, but added that he did not like it when the outfielder chuckled after he made the error. Later Vitt told the *Cleveland News* he might not start Heath for the season opener, going with Moose Solters instead.

Heath had been irritated with Vitt since the opening of training camp. After a great season in 1938, he expected to get most of the playing opportunities in left field. Vitt surprised him by trying several other players at the position while limiting Heath's time on the field. The anger started to fester with Heath and would escalate for the duration of the regular season.

When the game ended, both teams showered and caught the next train going east to New York. The players had dinner, visited for a while, then went to their berths for an early snooze. While others slept, Rollie Hemsley wandered around the train doing nothing in particular. At one of the cars he was intercepted by a friend of his on the Giants, who produced from a paper bag a bottle of bourbon for their relaxation. In no time at all the two men drained the contents. For most of spring training Hemsley had been a model citizen, but this time he could not resist the urge to get roaring drunk. Without any warning, he pulled open the door to Indians' sleeping car, lit several matches, and threw them into the berths. He kicked over the cigarette urn, tossed one of the cuspidors the length of the room, and, somehow having gotten a bucket of water, threw the contents at several of the bunks.

Manager Vitt was summoned to the car, where he tried to reason with his tanked-up catcher. It was well past 4:00 a.m. when Rollie finally quieted down and surrendered the matches. His madcap behavior resulted in Vitt ordering Rollie back to Cleveland when the train delivered them to New York City. The half-asleep manager vented his frustration to the *Cleveland News*. "I'm not in favor of being tough with Rollie. I feel sorry for the man. But last night was terrible. I just had to take some action."

Once again the newspapers were full of the wild adventure of the previous evening. Hemsley's actions were ill timed, since the regular season would begin in just a few days. Instead of speculating where the Indians were going to finish or who might be playing right field, the articles concentrated on whether a suspension or fine was coming and whether Rollie would be on the team for game one with St. Louis.

Ed McAuley of the *News* had a different slant. He wrote in his column, "Don't you think it is about time that all of us in Cleveland accept the Hemsley situation with the same mature calmness that we show toward much more serious departures from the code of temperate living? He's neither a psychopath case nor a vicious ingrate—not even the victim of an uncontrollable craving for whiskey." McAuley believed occasional trips off the wagon were not a good enough reason to condemn the catcher.

Rollie boarded the train back to Cleveland for an uncomfortable meeting with Cy Slapnicka. One of the issues on the table was Hemsley's contract for the 1939 season. Slapnicka, in an effort to control the errant catcher, had added a good-conduct clause. If no problems occurred through the summer schedule, an extra $5,000 would be paid out at the end of the year. Hemsley knew the additional money was already in serious doubt due to the railcar fiasco.

When Rollie arrived at the train station at the Terminal Tower, two polite gentlemen were waiting to speak with him. They quietly informed him they were from an organization, Alcoholics Anonymous, designed to help people with drinking problems. Alcoholics Anonymous had been founded just a few years prior by Bill Wilson, a businessman in New York, and Bob Smith, a surgeon. Both men were alcoholics and had struggled for many years before they found the proper help. In 1935 Wilson was traveling through Akron on a business trip that did not live up to expectations. Worried that he might drink again, Wilson checked around the city and found a kindred spirit in Dr. Smith. They visited one another and resolved to partner up and help people with similar problems locally and nationally.

Wilson later returned home to New York, but Dr. Smith now had a number of people committed to sobriety and willing to help others. Two of them were present at the Cleveland train station to meet with Rollie. The gentleman explained what their organization had to offer and urged him to attend a meeting in Akron with others like himself. Initially Rollie hesitated, then agreed to keep an open mind about the organization and take in a meeting soon.

Before traveling to Akron, Hemsley got a cab to League Park and met with Slapnicka. They went over the incident in detail, trying to figure out the best course of action. The Indians general manager elected to decline any fine or suspension. Whether Rollie's admission that he was seeking help had something to do with it never became public, but they did hash out a plan that would allow Rollie to take some days off, when he would secretly check into an Akron hospital to dry out and begin treatment. Rollie would either run out a ground ball, then pull up at first with a phantom ankle sprain, or if he hit a fly ball or struck out, he would jog back to the dugout and pretend to slip down the steps. Slapnicka would see to it that Rollie went to his apartment and stayed out of sight of the ball club. Once he got to the Akron hospital, he would remain for as long as he needed. At a suitable time the bogus injury would heal, allowing Rollie to rejoin the team. The only people who knew about the plan were Slapnicka and Hemsley. Possibly trainer Lefty Weisman and Oscar Vitt knew something as well, but their names did not come up when Rollie announced his sobriety a year later. The days of "Rollicking" Rollie came to an end when he attended his first meeting in Akron.

Meanwhile the Indians returned home on the seventeenth, ready to get their equipment together and board yet another train for St. Louis. The players modeled their new road uniforms, which closely resembled those of the New York Yankees. The jerseys and pants were light gray, without the familiar stripes of the last few seasons. The shirts had navy-blue lettering in the front and back along with the caps of the same color. Most of the players approved of the new look, happy to be rid of the stripes down the pants and on the socks.

The *Cleveland News* sponsored a contest for the best slogan to describe the upcoming season. The phrase had to be nine words or less and be inspiring, amusing, and of course interesting. The winner would receive two season tickets at League Park and Municipal Stadium. One of the judges was Tris Speaker, always staying active with the organization in one way or another. Thousands of entries poured in, and after a lengthy review the slogan chosen was "World's Fair in New York, World Series in Cleveland." With a slogan like that, the Indians were a shoo-in.

On the morning of the eighteenth, St. Louis woke up to heavy rain with occasional periods of freezing sleet covering the main roads. Few people had any expectation of baseball being played that day. Wednesday and Thursday were similar, wiping out the remaining two games of the series. The trip to St. Louis was a frustrating mess for both the fans and ballplayers eager to start the season. The Indians had little or no practice time before catching their train back to Cleveland.

The club landed in town at 11:30 p.m., cranky from the three straight rainouts and discouraged by the same conditions they had experienced in St. Louis. The Friday weather forecast called for occasional showers with a temperature around forty-eight degrees throughout the day. Ticket sales had been brisk, reaching around 30,000, then fallen off due to the likelihood of another postponement. Cy Slapnicka arrived at Municipal Stadium and stared out at the playing field, nervously waiting for the early morning rain to let up. He had a dilemma: should he cancel the opener and keep the fans out of the rain, or play it to accommodate the several thousand out-of-town customers?

Around lunchtime the rain finally stopped, allowing Slapnicka to give the go-ahead to play the game. The grounds crew slowly removed the heavy tarp, revealing that the infield was in much better shape than expected. Wheelbarrows of dirt were tossed around the rough spots, giving the Indians and Tigers a few minutes for ground balls and batting practice.

Jack Graney appeared in the WHK broadcast booth, prepared to start another season of play-by-play. For the first time, all the Major League teams were airing their games on radio, the Yankees and Giants having been the last holdouts. A number of ex-ballplayers were doing the broadcasts, including Graney, Waite Hoyt, Harry Heilmann, and Walter Johnson. The addition of a second man in the booth opened the door for a number of retired Major Leaguers yearning to stay around the game.

New to the WHK broadcast was *Dugout Interviews,* a live program sponsored by Atlas Appliance stores that ran thirty minutes before each game. Graney had his portable microphone near the

Indians bench, where he spent several minutes interviewing one of the key players. Each year radio increased its coverage of baseball, much to the delight of the listening public. Other stations in town started evening sports shows to report on the Indians games and other important contests around the American and National League. Now there were somewhat fewer band concerts aired in the evening and more baseball news and features.

With the bad weather, the pregame ceremonies were kept to a minimum. The flag raising was handled by recruiting officers from all the armed forces. The activity of the German army in Europe was enough to catch the attention of more and more Americans each day. The presence of the recruiters quietly spoke to the crowd about the search for able-bodied men to begin filling the ranks. U.S. forces were not at the levels needed to suitably defend the country here and overseas. President Roosevelt and Congress were hardly beating the war drums, but a nod to increasing the ranks of the army and navy had been initiated. In just a few weeks the German army would start plans to invade Poland, with the actual offensive to take place late in the summer. This action led to the beginning of World War II.

Moments before game time, an attractive young girl made her way to the owners' box just behind home plate. Alva Bradley had pulled a number of strings to hire sixteen-year-old Judy Garland to perform the national anthem. The star of stage and screen was appearing daily at the Loew's State Theatre, right in the heart of Playhouse Square. In her show, Miss Garland sang the popular ballads of the day and did promotion work for her new film, set to be released in August. *The Wizard of Oz* had every ingredient necessary to be a major success.

Prior to the anthem, Miss Garland gingerly walked to home plate. The grounds leading to the plate were mud covered, resulting in her open-toed heels collecting gobs of dirt and grime with each step. Even with several gentlemen in the area, nobody did the gallant thing and dropped his jacket for Judy to stand on. The newsmen noted with amusement that chivalry was dead, at least at Municipal Stadium.

The anthem began with Garland tightly holding her hands over her ears, trying to hear herself over the powerful loudspeakers.

The band playing the anthem stood in deep center field, adding to her challenge in staying in time with the music. In spite of the formidable obstacles, Judy Garland gave a dazzling rendition of "The Star-Spangled Banner." Fans were stunned at the beauty and clarity of her voice, which many of them had never heard before.

After a comical break where several fans attempted to deliver a floral doghouse to Rollie Hemsley, the game started. The Indians trotted out to the field with the following lineup:

> Jimmy Webb (shortstop)
> Ben Chapman (center field)
> Earl Averill (right field)
> Jeff Heath (left field)
> Hal Trosky (first base)
> Ken Keltner (third base)
> Frankie Pytlak (catcher)
> Jim Shilling (second base)
> Bob Feller (pitcher)

Some familiar names were missing from the starting lineup, including Lyn Lary, Bruce Campbell, and Sammy Hale. Lary had gotten on the bad side of Vitt and Slapnicka, resulting in loss of his spot in the lineup and eventual sale to Brooklyn in May. Hale languished on the bench, judged by Vitt at this point to be only a part-time player. Averill, though still playing, had moved to right field to make way for the faster legs of Ben Chapman. The shuffling of the outfielder left both Bruce Campbell and Roy Weatherly sitting in the dugout, their status unclear.

Jimmy "Skeeter" Webb won the shortstop job with an impressive spring training. Webb had languished in the minors for six years until Judge Landis made him a free agent, another victim of the atrocious covering-up practice. Jim Shilling was destined for an early trip back to New Orleans, but the Indians front office believed Hale had slipped enough to add the rookie to the Major League roster. Earl Averill stood on shaky ground; the move to right field took him one step closer to his exit from Cleveland. It appeared just a matter of time before a trade took place or he ingloriously wound up on waivers. The split between him and Alva Bradley had gone too far to be repaired.

The Indians easily won the home opener 5–1, behind Bob Feller's sparkling three-hit pitching. He picked up where he left off last October 2, when he fanned eighteen Tigers. This day he only struck out ten, but allowed merely two walks, a huge improvement for Feller. The lone Detroit run came on a home run by outfielder Barney McCosky. In the sixth inning, Feller hung a curveball and McCosky knocked it far into the seats. The home run should not have happened, as on the previous pitch McCosky lofted a high foul near the seats behind home plate. Frankie Pytlak whipped off his mask and sprinted to the railing. He had a play on the ball, but at the last instant a fan wearing a bright green hat reached over, interfering with the Indians catcher. The ball dropped. Pytlak said after the game that he yelled to the fan, "What the Hell, What the Hell? Why the push?" The greatly embarrassed fan replied, "I'm sorry, Frankie!" Accepting the apology, Pytlak told reporters, "A nice guy probably, and I ain't sore at him."

For the Indians, Skeeter Webb had a nice debut with three hits, Hal Trosky drove in two runs, and Jeff Heath contributed a single and an RBI. The cold weather and early rain kept the crowd at 22,957, meaning a little over 7,000 stayed home. Concession sales were nowhere near a record, but the fans now had more choices for drinks, including the popular sellers Black Forest Beer and Erin Brew.

The opening of the baseball season marked the hundredth anniversary of the game, believed to have been invented by General Abner Doubleday while attending prep school in Cooperstown, New York. Although no compelling evidence existed to prove Doubleday had thought up the game and then gone about introducing it to men and boys cavorting in the fields of the small village, that did not stop Major League Baseball from going ahead with a year-long celebration.

The origins of baseball were hotly debated in the early 1900s, resulting in the formation of the Mills Commission, a body of several gentleman associated with the game. Albert Spalding, a former player, executive, and founder of Spalding Sporting Goods, was the driving force behind the commission. Spalding, who desperately wanted baseball to be an American game, charged the commission with finding conclusive evidence to support his views.

Advertising appeared in newspapers around the country, seeking documentation that the game had nothing in common with primitive ball and batting games from England and several other countries. After months of waiting, a letter arrived at the commission's office. An elderly gentleman claimed to have been in Cooperstown in 1839 and witnessed Abner Doubleday laying out a diamond and explaining the rules. The members of the Mills Commission took the letter as irrefutable evidence and joyfully proclaimed baseball an American game. They overlooked several facts, such as that the letter writer was five years old when he allegedly witnessed the historic occasion and that Doubleday had already left Cooperstown for the military academy in West Point, New York.

The great majority of baseball officials and sportswriters took it for granted that Doubleday was the man; hence the 1939 festivities. In the past few years a fine museum and library had been built in Cooperstown, along with a Hall of Fame dedicated to the all-time greats of Major League Baseball. The first to go in were Ty Cobb, Christy Mathewson, Babe Ruth, Honus Wagner, and Walter Johnson. A small ballpark aptly named Doubleday Field rose up a short distance from the museum. The National Association of Professional Baseball Leagues donated volumes of records, documents, and books to the library. On June 12 the museum, with one-of-a-kind artifacts and memorabilia, would see its grand opening along with the highly publicized dedication.

The Indians made it two in a row when Willis Hudlin beat the Tigers 2–1. Hudlin, in the twilight of his long career, pitched effectively for seven and a third innings while scattering eight hits. Last year's relief ace, Johnny Humphries, went the rest of the way, including a couple of strikeouts. Cleveland scored twice in the first inning, while Hudlin set down Detroit without any problems. The remainder of the month showed an inconsistent team, playing well one day then falling apart the next. A problem developed in the pitching staff as Mel Harder and Johnny Allen were slowed by nagging arm injuries. That left the starting rotation with only two healthy bodies in Feller and Hudlin.

The lack of pitchers culminated on April 30 in a nasty 14–1 loss to the Tigers at Briggs Stadium. Manager Vitt, with no one else available, handed the start to Joe Dobson, normally a member of the bullpen crew. He lasted five innings, getting drilled for nine runs and thirteen hits while walking four. In the bottom of the sixth, pitcher Johnny Broaca, formerly of the Yankees, made his debut with the Indians. He had difficulty from the start, loading the bases for Charlie Gehringer. Before anyone could blink, the Tiger great clobbered a grand slam to make the score 13–1. In three innings of work Broaca, who always wore a pair of thick glasses, surrendered a total of six hits and five runs along with another three bases on balls.

Broaca had a wealth of pitching ability, though his demeanor left quite a few people cold, particularly the Yankees. He hailed from Lawrence, Massachusetts, the son of ordinary parents trying to make a home for their family. He grew up an intelligent young man, with grades high enough to be accepted by the elite Yale University, where he pitched for the baseball team, coached by former Boston and Cleveland player Joe Wood. He should have learned quite a bit from "Smoky" Joe; however, he ran afoul of his coach by failing to pitch when scheduled and insisting on saving his arm for the Major Leagues.

In 1933, after only two years with Yale, Broaca quit the team and signed with the New York Yankees. He reported to Newark, where he spent the remainder of the season. In 1934 he won a job on the starting rotation and averaged a respectable thirteen wins in his first three seasons. Broaca looked to be on his way to a decent career. Being a member of the Yankees meant the probability of World Series appearances and the opportunity to earn a good chunk of money with the postseason cash. Most players would have appreciated this practically guaranteed bonus, but apparently Johnny did not care.

In the middle of the 1937 season, Broaca abruptly left the ball club, offering no explanation for his absence. He never returned, leaving his teammates and front office baffled by his disappearance. Some thought he had a back or arm injury but could not explain his walking away without seeking help. The Yankees had no other recourse than to put him on the involuntary retired list and cut all ties.

After New York won the World Series, disturbing news about Broaca appeared in the newspapers. His wife, eight months pregnant, had filed for divorce in Barnstable, Massachusetts. Several allegations of cruelty and abusive treatment surfaced in the course of the divorce hearings. Though he denied everything, Mrs. Broaca described a cold winter night when her husband threw her out of the house in her nightclothes, letting her freeze for nearly two hours. On another occasion he supposedly belted Mrs. Broaca in the head, causing her severe pain. The Yankees front office, horrified by the allegations and publicity about their former player, sent Mrs. Broaca a World Series share of $1,000.

The hearing dragged on until just before Christmas of 1937, when the presiding judge granted Mrs. Broaca a divorce and full custody of three-month-old John Jr. The defendant had to pay weekly alimony of $18 and all of his ex-wife's court costs. He left the courtroom for parts unknown until the fall of 1938, when out of nowhere he asked the Yankees for reinstatement. The papers were filed with the league office, and the moment they were official, the team put him on waivers. On November 20, heads were turned when only one team, that being the Cleveland Indians, put in a claim.

John Lardner, in his syndicated column, weighed in on the recent events. He wrote, "Johnny Broaca who was graduated from Yale in 1934 and from the New York Yankees by fast train in 1936, has just become the newest problem child in Oscar Vitt's extensive, hand-carved collection." The article, though much of it tongue-in-cheek, really cut to the heart of the matter. The Indians at present had several players who needed constant watching. Why would they take on a player with the baggage of Broaca? The only plausible theory had to be that Broaca might still be able to pitch and he came cheaply off the waiver wire. They already had a group of malcontents on the roster, so what difference would one more make?

The month of May brought the return of Rollie Hemsley from the injured list. In his nearly two-week absence the Indians signed veteran Luke Sewell to act as the emergency catcher. This would be the second tour of duty with Cleveland for the thirty-eight-year-old brother of Joe Sewell, the one-time Indians shortstop. Sewell still had some ability behind the plate in the event Frankie Pytlak cleaned out his locker again or Hemsley came up lame with another mysterious sprained ankle.

Rollie and Cy Slapnicka managed to keep the writers in the dark concerning his participation in Alcoholics Anonymous. Whenever the Indians were home, Hemsley quietly went to Akron to attended meetings on Wednesday evenings. He kept to the strict requirements of the organization, even lending a helping hand to newer members. His teammates were probably surprised by Rollie being on time for batting practice and the absence of the black eyes they were used to observing. They did not complain when Rollie's batting and catching improved, enough to make another All-Star appearance.

On May 18 Alva Bradley released the confirmed schedule for the seven night games. Some changes were made, with Detroit chosen as the opponent for the inaugural contest on June 27. Judge Landis planned to attend, along with American League president Will Harridge and Ohio governor John Bricker. The Indians made 78,811 seats available in case most of the population of Cuyahoga County and beyond wanted in. Fans who intended to buy tickets were required to send a self-addressed envelope with a personal check enclosed. Telephone reservations were not accepted.

Even with the Indians expecting massive crowds for the night games, the League Park full-time office staff remained woefully undermanned. Besides Bradley and Slapnicka, there was a switchboard operator, two ticket salespeople, a bookkeeper, and a business manager. How they were going to handle tens of thousands of ticket requests went unexplained.

The ticket applications poured in despite the Indians failing to put together anything close to a winning streak. They muddled along through May, staying in fourth place with a record around the .500 mark. On the twenty-fifth, the Indians were at Fenway Park to take on the Red Sox. Bob Feller started the game against Elden Auker, always a tough customer for Cleveland. In the bottom of the second inning, Boston second baseman Bobby Doerr reached first base with a clean single. Feller did not allow another hit the rest of the way as the Indians routed Boston, 11–0. Though he did walk five batters, Feller breezed through the Red Sox lineup, fanning ten in the process. Ken Keltner led the offense with three consecutive solo home runs, each traveling more than 400 feet. In the top of the ninth, Bruce Campbell singled, then jogged home on Hal

Trosky's blast to deep right field. Keltner stepped up to face Emerson Dickman and unloaded his third round-tripper of the day, Cleveland's fourth homer off the shellshocked pitcher. The visitors collected fifteen hits in overwhelming the Sox. Feller raised his record to seven wins against two losses, staying on course for a twenty-win season.

The big victory over Boston seemed to inspire the Indians to pick up their game. Over the next several weeks they pushed over .500 and kept going upward. Johnny Allen threw a two-hit shutout, Mel Harder returned to the rotation, while seldom-used Al Milnar began to win his starts. Oscar Vitt tinkered with the lineup, moving Rollie Hemsley to the leadoff spot. Skeeter Webb dropped down in the order, while Bruce Campbell got considerable playing time in right field. The odd man out was Earl Averill, seeing more and more bench time while Campbell played in right.

On June 12 all the Major League teams had an off day in honor of the ceremonies being held at Cooperstown, New York. Each team provided several players to attend the dedication and then play a seven-inning All-Star game at Doubleday Field. Many of the game's brightest stars were there, including the American League's Hank Greenberg, Charlie Gehringer, and Lefty Grove. The Indians, in a questionable move, did not send any stars, only a sore-armed Johnny Allen and bench player Jim Shilling. The National League brought an array of talent, including Dizzy Dean, Carl Hubbell, Johnny Vander Meer, Mel Ott, and Joe Medwick. The two teams played a late afternoon game after two high school teams reenacted an 1839 baseball match.

As the Major League game moved along, a great clamor rose from the crowd, yelling for Babe Ruth, an interested spectator, to take an at bat. The noise got louder and louder until Babe nodded his head and walked onto the field. He picked out a bat and stepped up to the plate for a remarkable ovation. Babe took a mighty swing but popped the ball straight up to the catcher. Later he would claim that his arm was tired from signing so many autographs throughout the day.

With a great flourish, the National Baseball Museum opened its doors for all fans to observe the treasures of the national game. On the steps to the entrance stood the immortals, Ruth, Honus

Wagner, Walter Johnson, Grover Cleveland Alexander, Eddie Collins, and George Sisler. Cleveland had three recent inductees joining them in Cy Young, Napoleon Lajoie, and Tris Speaker. Visitors stood silently at attention while a lone bugle played "Taps" in honor of the late members Christy Mathewson and Willie Keeler of the old Baltimore Orioles. Handling the speaking chores at the dedication were a gracious Ty Cobb and Commissioner Landis. Spectators filled the streets in the early morning and kept coming all day, leading to an estimated 15,000 folks crowding the main roads of Cooperstown.

Ford Frick, president of the National League, gave an eloquent quote to all the newspapers. "It is a glamorous story this epic of ten decades past. First the village green of Cooperstown, in the upstate New York, where boys scampering about with a stick and a ball learned a game with sound principles in its mechanics and rules that brought order and meaning to their exertions."

President Franklin Roosevelt sent a right and proper message to the proceedings. "It is most fitting," he wrote, "that the history of our perennially popular sport should be immortalized in the National Baseball Museum at Cooperstown where the game originated and where the first diamond was devised a hundred years ago."

Few if any people who attended that fine day had any inkling that the man honored, General Abner Doubleday, really did not invent the game. Many years later, historians found zero evidence that the general had anything to do with the invention of baseball. His papers said naught of the game, while Doubleday himself was nothing of an outdoorsman. Who, then, invented baseball? Many theories hold it came from an assortment of games such as rounders and town ball and several others. These primitive matches featured batters and fielders and running around bases. Throwing the ball at base runners was an accepted part of the rules. Over the years the games became more refined until the modern game emerged, probably in the mid-1840s. Regardless of the findings, there is no greater thrill for a baseball fan than to walk the streets of Cooperstown and take a long visit inside the Hall of Fame Museum.

While the dedication took place, Cy Slapnicka spent much time on the telephone with the Detroit front office. His objective, dictated by Alva Bradley, was to send Earl Averill to the Tigers for anything he could get. Over the winter Slapnicka had talked with numerous teams about a possible trade, but none of the players mentioned were of equal value to Averill. By early June the order came about to get rid once and for all of the "Earl of Snohomish." Slapnicka worked diligently, yet the only deal offered by the Tigers consisted of pitcher Harry Eisenstat and some cash. In his four years with Brooklyn and Detroit, Eisenstat had compiled an underwhelming record of 13–12.

The deal sent an unfortunate message to Averill about his worth as a member of the Indians. A future Hall of Fame player, Earl had to accept the move to the Tigers knowing he brought virtually nothing in return. The only positive for him was going to a better ball club, one that would shortly unseat the Yankees. Averill had a tremendous career in Cleveland, and is still mentioned today as one of the best Indians center fielders of all time. Owner Bradley is open to criticism for holding a grudge and letting a superb ballplayer go rather than letting him finish his career where he started.

With the Averill trade behind them, the Indians eagerly looked ahead to their June 27 debut under the Municipal Stadium light towers. Construction pushed ahead of schedule, allowing the club to make preparations without any contingencies. The evening before the historic game, players and officials from the Indians and Tigers paid a visit to the stadium. As all in attendance watched, the 712 lights were switched on, blanketing the grounds with enough illumination to allow fielders to handle ground balls and high flies above the outfield. After a short time the lights were switched off to demonstrate the vast difference between the artificial light and the few lightbulbs from the stadium concourse.

Ticket sales advanced into the 50,000 range, with estimates close to 60,000 by the first pitch. As expected, Bob Feller would start this game, trying for his twelfth win of the season. Game day brought massive excitement in Cleveland, with several thousand fans huddling outside the gates at 6:30 p.m. Many in the crowd were families with mom, dad, and all the kids. Alva Bradley had labored hard to clear the way for the entire clan to take in a weekday game. At this moment he was about to cash in on his ambitious new vision.

At approximately 8:25 the lights went on, to a tremendous ovation from the grandstand. The players, especially the outfielders, ran onto the field, anxious to learn the new technique of judging fly balls under the powerful lighting. Early on, the Tigers new outfielder, Earl Averill, misplayed a sinking line drive, taking the baseball squarely on the wrist. He survived, as did the other outfielders, who quickly fashioned adjustments and began to haul in fly balls without any missteps.

The ball game started promptly at 9:00 p.m. Feller blanked the Tigers in the top of the first inning. Rollie Hemsley led off the home half with a booming triple off Detroit starter Buck Newsom. Bruce Campbell walked, then Ben Chapman singled for the first-ever run under the lights in Cleveland. Hal Trosky lifted a sacrifice fly to make the score 2–0. The Indians doubled the score to 4–0 in the second when first-year infielder Oscar Grimes singled and Skeeter Webb beat out a well-placed bunt. The throw to first was wild, allowing Grimes to reach third. Feller struck out, but Hemsley sacrificed, permitting Grimes to cross the plate. Bruce Campbell singled to score Webb, giving Feller and the Indians a comfortable advantage.

After three full innings, Feller had recorded six strikeouts. The twenty-year-old flamethrower had the Tigers back on their heels, almost swinging in self-defense. Feller had developed something of a sidearm fastball or crossfire that he liked to unleash when he had two strikes on the batter. On this night it had a devastating effect on the Detroit hitters, helping him keep them without a hit through five innings.

Along with the writers in the press box sat old-time New York Giants catcher Roger Bresnahan. He was not ready to compare Feller with Christy Mathewson, whom he caught for many years, but he offered some genuine praise of the Indians right-hander. Bresnahan remarked to the *Cleveland Press,* "Couple of years from now that boy is going to be one of the greatest of all. He's easily 100 per cent better pitcher than he was when I saw him two years ago." A kind tribute from a man who had caught or played against many of the game's most talented pitchers.

Moving into the top of the sixth inning, the Indians led 5–0. The disoriented Tigers were still trying to find their first hit of the ball game. With two outs, up to the plate came former Indian Earl Averill, to a colossal ovation. He swung at a fastball and lined it to center field for a base hit. Feller suddenly could not find the plate, walking the next two batters to load the bases. Hank Greenberg strolled to the batter's box, presenting the Cleveland fans with their first anxious moment of the night. Feller rose to the occasion, swiftly fanning the Tigers star and ending the rally. Neither team provided any thrills over the next two innings, setting the stage for the Tigers' last go-round in the ninth. With one out, Hank Greenberg stepped to the plate. Feller had already struck out the first baseman twice. The count was one ball and two strikes when Feller reached back and unleashed a tremendous fastball that Greenberg could only wave at. Birdie Tebbetts ended the game with a routine fly ball to Chapman, and the Indians won their first home night game in style, 5–0. In addition to his second one-hitter of the season, Feller overpowered the Tigers with thirteen strikeouts. Barney McCosky whiffed four straight times, while Greenberg, one of the best hitters in either league, went down on strikes in three of his four at bats.

After the game, Feller told the *Cleveland News* about his third strikeout of Greenberg, "That pitch just snapped out of my hand like a bullet. Nobody could have seen enough of that one to have hit it." Rollie Hemsley agreed the pitch was unhittable, leaving one to ponder, could he have topped one hundred miles per hour on that pitch? Regardless, Feller displayed blinding speed throughout the night, thrilling the 55,305 fans in attendance.

If Bob Feller did not provide enough excitement, a Cleveland youngster gave the fans one last bit of rousing entertainment. Earlier in the game, a foul ball arched over home plate and got stuck in the protective screen directly below the press box, on the second tier. As the game ended, the boy sprang out of his seat and started a dangerous climb up the screen to grab the wedged-in ball. He made it fifty feet up, then another twenty sideways, and snared the baseball. When he looked down, he spotted four annoyed policemen waiting for him to descend. At that moment, several sportswriters motioned to him to continue up to the press box. He scampered up, climbed over the railing, then dashed to a side door and into the upper-deck concourse. The police could only shake their heads and let the little felon go.

Will Harridge had several flattering comments for reporters about the game he had just witnessed. "This is the most beautiful spectacle I've ever seen. But do you know what impressed me more than this marvelous lighting equipment? It's the carnival spirit of the fan." Speaking for those fans, a Cleveland man, Tony Maresh, said, "As far as I am concerned as an average fan, I like it much better at night. It's much cooler in the stands and it's much easier for a working man to get to a game."

The *Cleveland Press* recorded random comments from the crowd as they were departing the stadium for home. Several ladies were convinced night games enhanced their beauty. "Noses do not shine by moonlight and the face does not have to be repaired nearly so often as in the boiling sun of afternoon." From the men's department, "Trousers don't stick to the seats, cooled by night lake breezes. Stadium was warm but would have been an oven during an afternoon game."

Probably the best comment came from a fan right before the first pitch from Feller. A reporter asked the gentleman what his impressions were of the new lights. The man looked up and said, "Are they all on yet?" That observation aside, the evening went smoothly, just as Alva Bradley had anticipated. The fans and players both gave the night lights a thumbs up, eager to see more of night ball as the season progressed.

Two weeks later, the second night game took place between the Indians and the streaking Boston Red Sox. The Sox had won eight games in a row and ten of their last eleven. They had a record of 43–25 good for a distant second place behind the Yankees. Once again Bob Feller started the game. His opponent was Jack Wilson, who outside of Lefty Grove had the best fastball on the Red Sox staff. This game was a real test for the 41,210 fans, as the temperature remained at an uncomfortable ninety-one degrees. Feller waltzed through the first three innings, seemingly on his way to a repeat performance of June 27. In the top of the fourth, Feller retired one batter, then the Red Sox tagged him for six straight hits and five runs. Johnny Broaca came in to relieve and retired the side without any further harm.

Jack Wilson pitched effectively, blanking the Indians hitters through eight innings. In the bottom of the ninth, Jeff Heath opened the inning with a base hit. Ken Keltner walked, and Wilson's night was over. Emerson Dickman entered the game, the same reliever who earlier in the season gave up three straight home runs to Keltner and a bomb to Hal Trosky. Dickman walked Oscar Grimes to fill the bases, bringing Sammy Hale to bat. The crowd began getting their things together and finishing their beers when Hale fanned. Moose Solters, in a rare appearance, topped a slow roller down the third-base line. Jim Tabor came racing in, picked up the ball, and sidearmed it past first baseman Jimmie Foxx into right field. Two runs scored, with Grimes taking third and Solters second. Up to the plate came Rollie Hemsley, enjoying an excellent season. The Red Sox looked for Hemsley to pull the ball toward left field, but Rollie surprised everybody by dropping a perfect bunt that rolled between the pitcher's mound and third base. Tabor had no play on the ball as Grimes scored and Solters reached third.

As the crowd settled back in their seats and raised a disturbance that could be heard at Public Square, Roy Weatherly strode up to the batter's box. Weatherly set off a near riot when he lined a single to make the score 5–4. That brought Joe Heving into the game for the Sox. Chapman bounced a high chopper to the third-base side of the mound. Heving grabbed the ball and chucked it to the plate, but not in time to catch the speeding Hemsley. The Indians had come all the way back from five runs down to tie up the game. Heving got the side out, but the teams were now in extra innings.

Manager Vitt brought Mel Harder out to pitch the tenth, but the veteran did not have his good stuff and allowed one run to score. The Indians could not answer in the bottom of the tenth, and Boston held on for their ninth win in a row, 6–5. Even with the loss, the Cleveland fans had seen two spectacular night games at Municipal Stadium. Attendance for the games totaled over 96,000 spectators, making it already a successful experiment for the City of Cleveland and Alva Bradley. Owners around the American League took notice of the figures, scrambling to get their own plans for lighting. Clark Griffith, an early opponent night baseball, now favored a schedule of only evening games from June 15 to September 1. The race for lights in every Major League stadium began in earnest.

On July 18 the Indians hosted Connie Mack and his Philadelphia Athletics for game number three under the lights. The A's were already seventeen games below .500 and sinking fast. They did have Wally Moses and Bob Johnson, two good hitters, in the outfield, but not much else to brag about. This game attracted little interest from the fan base, as fewer than 10,000 people attended. Johnny Allen started for Cleveland, lasting only three and a third innings with three runs allowed before giving way to Joe Dobson. The Indians scored early, then added two insurance runs in the late innings. With three hits and three runs scored by Roy Weatherly, the home team rolled to a painless 6–3 win. Dobson pitched the remaining five and two-thirds innings, yielding only three scattered hits.

With a night game record of 2–1, the Indians looked forward to the August 7 matchup with the St. Louis Browns. Bradley and Slapnicka knew that most fans would not be excited to see the hapless Browns, preferring to listen to the radio play-by-play and get to bed earlier. The two execs had a plan to spur some interest in the otherwise ho-hum ball game. The middle of the Cleveland infield needed big-time help, and two young, promising ballplayers with the Buffalo Bisons were just about ready to make the leap up to the Major Leagues. The front office agreed to make the call and bring up Lou Boudreau and Ray Mack in time to make their season debut against the Browns.

Chapter 10

THE NEW GUYS ARRIVE

In recalling Mack and Boudreau, the Indians were ad-dressing attendance issues and attempting to light a fire under the ball club. Both were well-spoken college graduates, and they were developing into a first-class double play combination. The last time Cleveland had above-average shortstops and second basemen was all the way back in the early 1920s with Joe Sewell and Bill Wamby. Sewell stepped in to replace the excellent shortstop Ray Chapman, killed in August 1920 by a Carl Mays fastball. The Indians were counting on the two young men to strengthen the interior defense and provide some timely hits as well.

Ray Mack (Mlckovsky) was a native Clevelander, born to Joseph and Rose on August 31, 1916. He first made a name for himself at John Adams High School, doing extremely well at the sports of-fered. A big guy at six foot two and two hundred pounds, Ray had few peers on the football field.

Upon graduation from high school Ray enrolled at the Case School of Applied Sciences to study for a degree in engineering. The school had no varsity baseball team, and Mack had some res-ervations about playing college football. Later he would tell report-ers, "I never cared to play football. Baseball was the sport I really loved. Why did I play football? I had the size, was fairly fast and could take it." Could take it indeed, as Mack would go on to All-Ohio status three years in a row. Ray starred as a bone-crushing fullback, knocking over defensive lineman as if they were bowling pins. Occasionally he shifted to halfback, where he could turn the corner and outrun the linebackers. If the situation demanded it, he could pull up and loft passes to receivers sprinting deep down the field. On defense he lined up in the secondary while returning punts and kicks. Football ran in the family, with younger brother Howard playing halfback at Kent State.

In Cleveland the "Big Four" colleges were Case, Western Reserve University, Baldwin-Wallace College, and John Carroll University. All of them had strong football programs, bashing heads on a regular basis. The most intense rivalry among them was between the schools located next to each other, Case and Western Reserve. Their battles were always scheduled for the last game of the season and usually played at League Park. In 1936 15,000 fans watched Western Reserve drub the Rough Riders 32–3, a great disappointment for Ray and his teammates.

The following year, Ray became team captain and led Case to a winning season. In a 19–0 victory over John Carroll, Ray, wearing number 83, returned a punt thirty yards to set up a score, then later picked off a pass and raced forty yards for a touchdown. Jack Graney, covering college football for WHK, had Mack in the studio for a live interview. There was no debate that Ray was the best football player in all of northeast Ohio. In 1938 Ray was drafted by the NFL's Chicago Bears in the eleventh round. Despite the allure of pro football, he did not sign a contract, preferring to put all his energies into baseball.

Mack graduated college in the spring of 1937. He received a Bachelor of Arts degree in science with a senior thesis titled "Study of a Modulated Combustion Control for a Warm Air Furnace." Probably not a popular read, but no doubt a compelling effort. Additionally, he received the honor medal awarded to students who earned three varsity letters.

With classes behind him, Ray turned his attention to baseball. He joined the Poschke Barbecues in the Class A League, the city's top amateur organization. He hit over .400, and at a game at Brookside Park he blasted one of the longest home runs ever seen there. Brookside Park was the long-time site of the best amateur baseball played in Cleveland. From the turn of the century through

Mack's time and after, some of the most competitive baseball in the country took place at the grounds. An amateur game in the early 1900s drew a crowd estimated at 100,000. The park sat in a valley with a sloping hillside for fans to park themselves in great numbers. To excel there greatly enhanced your chances of being seen by scouts from the minor or Major Leagues. Ray's tape-measure home run and his all-around play did not go unnoticed.

In 1938 Mack put his name on a contract to play for Fargo-Moorhead of the Northern League, an affiliate of the Cleveland Indians. Over ninety-four games he dominated the league, batting .378 with 24 home runs and 96 RBIs. To help out the league scorers, he officially shortened his last name from Mlckovsky to Mack. The family was on board with the change, making it their legal name a few years later.

His terrific performance at Fargo earned him an invite to the Indians' 1939 training camp. He roomed with Lou Boudreau in New Orleans, two guys trying to make an impression with the big club. They became fast friends, noted for sleeping in until noon, having a quick lunch, and hurrying to practice. Though both were eventually farmed out to Buffalo, they became the number one priority of manager Steve O'Neill. In several months they developed into the smoothest double-play combination in quite some years. Mack had the great range needed for a second baseman, along with a strong, accurate throwing arm to make the pivot at second and complete the double play. His large frame made it difficult for sliding base runners to knock him off stride. It soon turned into a matter of when the Indians would make the call. In early August Ray got the word. He had a brief celebration, started up the car, and reported to the Indians as the new starting second baseman.

Mack had a familiar companion with him on the trip from Buffalo to Cleveland. Lou Boudreau climbed aboard and sat with Mack on the ride west through the northwestern part of New York and Pennsylvania. They had to be on cloud nine, knowing they had a chance to play side by side for many years ahead.

Lou Boudreau was born in Harvey, Illinois, on July 17, 1917. As a young boy he learned his reading and writing at nearby Whittier Elementary School. Before and after dinner Lou and his father, Louis Sr., a former semipro third baseman, practiced hitting and fielding. The elder Boudreau wanted his son to follow in his footsteps, while Lou had his mind made up to catch. After a number of father-son talks, the determination to park himself behind home plate vanished. Third base it would be.

At Thornton Township High School, Lou helped lead the basketball team to three state championship appearances, including 1933, when they won it all. He was an All-State forward, not the swiftest on the court, but one of the best all-around players in Illinois. Thornton did not have a baseball program, allowing Lou to do some high jumping on the track team. In the summers he played amateur ball for the North Harvey Merchants. Though showing loads of talent as a baseball player, he gladly accepted a basketball scholarship starting in 1935 at the University of Illinois.

The scholarship did not quite pay all the bills, forcing Lou to take a job as a handyman at his fraternity, Phi Sigma Kappa. His parents had divorced when he was seven, and neither had the money to support him throughout his college years. Without any regrets, he mowed the lawn at the frat house and worked in the kitchen. When time permitted, he earned fifty cents an hour as one of the ticket-takers at the Illini football games. With all the extra work, he managed to stay out of debt and concentrate on his studies and athletics.

Lou appreciated the side benefits of playing basketball, particularly the travel, which let him explore different restaurants and relax at fine hotels. His basketball skills were elevated to a national level by a game story in the *New York Daily News*, written after Illinois defeated St. John's University. "A veritable basketball hurricane hit the Garden last night as a streamlined Illinois University quintet headed by a positively brilliant little Frenchman named Lou Boudreau wrecked St. John's 60–45."

In addition to starring at basketball, Lou played third base for the varsity baseball team. He played well enough to achieve All-Big Ten status for two years, earning him tryouts with the Cubs and White Sox. The Cubs liked what they saw, telling Lou to come back and talk after his college graduation. Remarkably, the White Sox were not impressed at all, offering no words of encouragement. After the tryouts, Lou prepared for another school year and the 1937–38 basketball season. He had no idea of the disaster waiting to happen.

Lou's baseball ability attracted attention beyond the Chicago professional teams. The Indians and scout Harold Irelan had been watching Illinois baseball, specifically Boudreau. In the final game of the season, Lou had a big afternoon, banging out three hits, including a bases-loaded triple. Irelan got an introduction from the Illinois coach and got right to the point; he wanted Lou to play baseball for Cleveland. Eager to be a professional baseball player, he listened carefully to what Irelan had to say. The only sticking point concerned college eligibility. Lou wanted to stay in school and play more basketball and baseball while getting his degree. Irelan (remember his boss was Cy Slapnicka) assured Lou there was a way to work out an agreement and still remain college-eligible. The scout proposed a $1,000 bonus to be paid equally to his parents and $100 a month stipend to be sent regularly to Lou's mother until he graduated. (As it happened, Louis Sr. took most of the money he received and, being a great dad, bought a used car for his son to commute with.)

To complete the arrangement, Lou had to promise Irelan he would play for Cleveland after graduation and not entertain offers from any other ball club. If he stayed with the Indians organization for at least thirty days, another bonus of $2,200 would be paid out.

Lou had several important things to consider. The most critical was that his mother and father were struggling to pay their bills and really needed the money. Secondly, he wanted to be absolutely certain the agreement had no bearing on his athletic eligibility. The last point probably had the most pull of all: Lou really wanted to be a Cleveland Indian.

Scout Irelan must have convinced Lou that the transaction would in no way jeopardize his standing at Illinois. He agreed to the pact, then went home for the summer, where he got a job at Magic Chef, one of the largest manufacturers of stoves in the United States. He played baseball with the Grove Street Colts, earning five dollars a game for expenses. When time permitted he worked at a shoe store to earn a few extra bucks.

Once again the wayward Indians were playing fast and loose with the rules. Cy Slapnicka, as we know, nearly lost Bob Feller through tampering with the high school student, then did lose Tommy Henrich for covering up. It is hard to believe that a year later he still thought he could bend the rules and get away with it. College athletes with eligibility remaining were off limits to professional teams. If a student athlete chose to sign a pro sports contract while still pursuing a college degree, his days as an amateur were finished. The Indians front office likely thought they were the smartest guys in the room for acquiring Boudreau. They did not have his signature on a contract, and technically were not even paying him any type of salary. But they should have known better than to approach Lou or any undergrad unless the individual wanted to leave school and start a career in professional baseball. "Sly" Slapnicka was playing with fire one more time, although he was not the one about to suffer the consequences.

In the early part of the Illinois basketball season, Wendell Wilson, the school's athletic director, informed Lou that a letter had arrived at the office of Major John L. Griffith, the Big Ten athletic commissioner, claiming he had signed a contract with Cleveland. If true, a review by the Big Ten athletic board would take place and his eligibility would possibly be suspended. Lou explained truthfully that he had not signed anything and the money went directly to his father and mother. He had merely promised the Indians first choice when he graduated. Boudreau was probably unaware of a Big Ten rule printed in the *Daily Illini*, the student newspaper, that read, "A Big Ten athlete cannot use his athletic prowess as a means towards gaining compensation." When the athletic board met to debate the issue, the vote came in tied 3–3. The final decision went to Major Griffith.

Rather than break the tie himself, Griffith asked all the Big Ten athletic directors to cast a vote. In the first week of February 1938, the unsympathetic directors voted Boudreau ineligible for his junior year. In an effort to save face, Slapnicka sent a telegram to the Big Ten offices, saying he was willing to renounce all claims on Lou if the directors restored his amateur status. In a vain attempt to get the decision reversed, he sent another telegram to the University of Illinois, which the *Daily Illini* published on February 5. It read, "I, as vice-president of the Cleveland club instruct Harold Irelan Cleveland club scout as representative to visit the Illinois athletic authorities at Champaign, Illinois immediately and make every effort to bring about the reinstatement of student Lou

Boudreau." A well-worded telegram, but Slapnicka does not admit any guilt at all. If anything, the words demonstrate support for Boudreau and little else.

Arch Ward of the *Chicago Tribune* wrote a column defending Lou, while Major Griffith ripped Major League Baseball teams for approaching college athletes before they graduated. The *Daily Illini* editorial page chastised the Indians front office for the "conscience-less tactics it use[d] in its efforts to attain talent for its team."

All the support withstanding, the Big Ten did not change its ruling, and three weeks later made Lou permanently ineligible for supposedly not revealing all the facts. A devastated Boudreau weighed an offer to take a role in a Hollywood movie titled *Campus Confessions* with Hank Luisetti, the brilliant star of the Stanford basketball team. Luisetti had revolutionized the game by launching one-handed jump shots rather than the traditional two-handed set shot. Lou decided instead to sign with a professional basketball team from Hammond, Indiana. He played the entire season but did not quit school, still on track to get his diploma.

When the college term ended, he received a call from Slapnicka, carefully inquiring if Lou still wanted to play for the Indians. The general manager had no inkling whether Boudreau would say yes or slam the phone down in his ear. Besides, he was a free agent, able to entertain offers from any club in either Major League. Being a better man than most, Lou had no ill feelings toward Cleveland and agreed to sign a minor league deal. Slapnicka sent him to Springfield, Missouri, for Class C ball; however, Judge Landis issued a new ruling that any player from the Big Ten had to start at Class B or higher. Whether this had to do with Boudreau, the wily commissioner would not say.

Sent to Cedar Rapids of the Three-I-League, Lou played third base and hit an acceptable .290. As a show of appreciation and with no lawsuits pending, the Indians called him up in late September 1938. Lou got into one game at third base, playing four innings and earning a base on balls in two plate appearances. This set the stage for his invitation to New Orleans in 1939. Starting the season with Buffalo, he made the transition to shortstop, where he teamed up with second baseman and pal Ray Mack. In his abbreviated stint with the Bisons, Lou batted .331 with 17 home runs. In a weekend series against Rochester at the end of June, he hit for the cycle on Saturday, then followed that up on Sunday with four more hits, including a homer and three doubles. For the two games he went nine for eleven with two home runs, a triple, four doubles, and two measly singles. His remaining time with Buffalo was just about completed.

When Mack and Boudreau arrived at Municipal Stadium, they did not quite receive a hero's welcome. To make room for the new shortstop, Skeeter Webb, who had started most of the regular games, got a demotion to Buffalo. Some of the veterans grumbled about the move, wondering why Webb was not benched rather than sent packing. When Mack asked Ken Keltner for a bat to borrow, the third baseman refused to give one up. The Cleveland photographers motioned Ray to stand at home plate and pose for some pictures scheduled for the next day's editions. After a few shots, a number of his new teammates came out of the dugout and chased him away.

Since the beginning of Major League Baseball, veterans had made a practice of harassing rookies until they proved themselves both on and off the field. What happened to Mack here probably fell under that category; however, there was something else going on that may have contributed to the less than friendly welcome.

Oscar Vitt had become the target of animosity from a group of his regular players. This situation had carried over from last season, when Vitt started to pop off to anyone in general about the prowess of his baseball team. Earlier in the current year, though not reported in the daily newspapers, Jeff Heath had threatened to punch his manager's lights out. For his actions Heath got a stern lecture and a $50 fine. Moose Solters became angry with Vitt when the outfielder picked up a huge fine of $250 for violating club rules, though this did not appear in print at the time. Controversy and rumors began to plague Vitt, and soon the Cleveland papers started questioning whether the manager would return for the 1940 season.

With all the team-building stuff, going on the Indians prepared for the night game with St. Louis. The front office, probably Cy Slapnicka, had set up entertainment before the game, featuring vaudeville antics with heavyweight boxer "Two Ton" Tony Galento. At the end of June Galento had fought champion Joe Louis for the world heavyweight crown. He held his own early, even landing a few shots in the opening rounds, but Louis quickly took care of business, unloading some crushing blows and stopping the bloody fight in four rounds. Why the Indians thought of hiring Galento to entertain the crowd remains a mystery to this day. To some mild applause, he came bouncing out of the home dugout wearing a Cleveland uniform and started clowning around with the umpires. That appeared to be the extent of the program.

A moment later, a striking young woman drove a new automobile onto the diamond to hand Ray Mack a commemorative plaque. It turned out to be an advertising ploy for the release of the highly anticipated film *Wizard of Oz*. Supposedly the plaque was a gift from Judy Garland. The presenter called Mack a wizard, which got major laughs from the Browns bench. Mercifully, the presentation ended and the game could begin.

Willis Hudlin started for Cleveland, facing Lefty Mills for St. Louis. Hudlin collapsed in the top of the sixth inning, when the Browns scored twice to jump ahead, 5–3. One of Cleveland's three runs came on a two-out triple by Lou Boudreau. While he was perched at third, Mills uncorked a wild pitch, permitting Lou to trot home with his first run as an Indian.

In the bottom of the eighth, Cleveland rallied for three additional runs. Ben Chapman led off with a single and advanced to second on Hal Trosky's ground out. Jeff Heath lined a base hit to score Chapman, closing the gap to 5–4. Ken Keltner added to the cause with another hit, sending Heath to third. That brought Ray Mack to the plate, hitless in three tries. He grounded to short, starting what looked to be a double play. The relay came quickly to first but Mack, running as hard as he could, barely beat the throw while Heath scored from third. Two more singles from Rollie Hemsley and Roy Weatherly scored Mack, putting Cleveland out in front, 6–5. Al Milnar closed out the game, and the Indians had won another night game. Attendance for the evening totaled a sparse 16,467. While the debuts of Mack and Boudreau added to the numbers, trying to draw a crowd for the 29–70 Browns confirmed the difficulty of prying fans away from their radios.

After the game, sportswriters crowded around the Indians' new players. Mack regretted not being able to get a base hit, while Boudreau tried to temper his excitement. He told the *Plain Dealer*, "I don't want to appear cocky but I think I can make the grade. I am not worried about my fielding but I have been a little scared about not being able to hit big league pitching."

Four days after the St. Louis game, Alva Bradley announced he had signed Oscar Vitt to manage again in 1940. This revelation came as a surprise since Bradley rarely renewed a manager before the end of a season. His decision was undoubtedly meant to quell the ill feelings some of the players harbored for Vitt. Bradley informed the *Plain Dealer*, "They've got to know who is the boss and they may as well know now that Vitt will be giving orders again next season. Naturally I will back him up in whatever action he may see fit to take to maintain discipline."

Bradley's message spoke loudly enough to the dissatisfied Cleveland players. They would have to listen to their manager or the road out of town would remain open. To this point, the only known players to have a grudge against their manager were Jeff Heath and Moose Solters, and Solters had recently been sent away to purgatory with the St. Louis Browns. It is hard to believe that Heath remained the only player on the club not loyal to his manager. There had to have been at least several other disgruntled teammates who wanted Vitt relieved of his duties, but if there were, their names were kept out of the papers.

On August 22 Cleveland won another night game, beating the Washington Senators 6–4. Bob Feller earned his eighteenth victory, allowing only one walk. To ensure the triumph, the Indians scored six runs in the bottom of the sixth, the big hit a two-run double by Hal Trosky. The victory broke Feller's career-high mark of seventeen wins, set the year before. With more than a month left in the season, he was certain to top the twenty-game plateau for the first time.

Whether or not the addition of Boudreau and Mack was the catalyst, Feller's victory began a seven-game winning streak. The offense jelled to the point where it began to record football-like scores. On August 24 the outmanned Athletics were at League Park for a doubleheader. The A's had pitcher Lee Ross, with a dismal mark of 5–11, to start game one. The Indians hitters probably salivated when they saw Ross walk to the mound and take his warmup throws. Both teams had already scored two runs in the first when Cleveland came to bat in the bottom of the second inning. Ross fell completely apart, giving up seven earned runs and walking three batters in his total outing of just one and a third innings. The big blows came from the bat of Hal Trosky, who clouted a two-run homer in the first inning, then a solo shot off reliever Nels Potter in the fourth. For the game he had three hits, three RBIs, and four runs scored. Ken Keltner chipped with four hits, while most of the starting lineup had at least one base hit apiece.

In game two the Indians held a 4–2 lead going into the bottom of the sixth. The Athletics began with Jim Reninger on the mound, a veteran of only five starts in the Major Leagues. Against a hot-hitting club like Cleveland, an inexperienced pitcher such as Reninger had the word "disaster" written all over him. The A's hurler lasted a grand total of four and a third innings, allowing four runs and four walks before giving way to reliever Chubby Dean. Just two years before the lefty was playing first base for Philadelphia, but Connie Mack thought he had potential coming out of the bullpen. The Cleveland batters showed no mercy, pounding Dean all over the lot for seven more runs. The pitcher walked three batters in two-thirds of an inning to go with the seven tallies.

The final score for the second game was 17–2, making the total score for both games 27–4. Trosky, having a great afternoon, picked up three more RBIs in game two, as did Jeff Heath. Lou Boudreau had an outstanding game with three hits, two RBIs, and three runs scored from his leadoff position. Al Milnar got the win, pacing himself over the full nine innings as if it was an exhibition contest. The two lopsided wins put the Indians' record at 61–54, their best mark for the season. They had no chance of overtaking the Yankees or challenging Boston for second place, but had a fair chance to catch Chicago and reach third place. After the less-than-inspired ball the Indians had played for the bulk of the season, the current streak won them back a number of fans.

Three days later the Red Sox came to town for a four-game series, starting with a Sunday doubleheader at Municipal Stadium. Bob Feller started the first game, with former Indian Denny Galehouse on the hill for Boston. In the bottom half of the second inning, Jeff Heath came to the plate. With two strikes he took a tremendous swing off Galehouse, getting nothing but air for strike three. Heath walked toward the home dugout and, in a fit of indignation, hurled his bat at the Cleveland bench. The bat took a bounce, landed on top of the dugout, then flew into the stands, grazing *Cleveland Press* editor Louis Seltzer on the shoulder. Heath, boiling with anger, watched the flight of the bat as he kept walking to the Indians bench. Johnny Broaca, who had been quiet all year, greeted Heath with several loud comments. The two players faced off and Broaca flipped away his glasses, initiating a heavyweight battle right in front of their fellow players. Heath was a big, strong guy, while Broaca had boxed in his years at Yale. Thunderous punches went back and forth until manager Vitt and coach Oscar Melillo dared to step between them. Each got several bruises on their arms before stopping the fight.

Vitt strongly warned both players to cut out the nonsense or face a heavy fine. He banished them to the clubhouse, where Heath had to go anyway, having been ejected from the game. The odd part of the whole incident (other than the bat throwing) was that Heath and Broaca were fairly good friends. They usually sat together on the long train rides and talked for hours. The two players were the most unlikely pair to come to blows, but they did so right at the Cleveland bench. Due to the intensity of the fight, the sportswriters were careful in their questions to either of the warriors. Heath sat in the press box for most of the second game, looking contrite. For a moment, things seemed to have calmed down.

Back on the diamond, Feller and Galehouse were locked in a scoreless pitcher's battle through seven innings. In the bottom of the eighth, Feller led off with a walk but was forced out at second on Boudreau's ground ball. Bruce Campbell came to bat and sent the ball deep between the outfielders for a triple that scored Boudreau. The clutch hit proved to be the difference maker as Feller retired the Sox in the top of the ninth for win number nineteen. The crowd of 23,540 stood on their feet, roaring their approval of Feller's gem. He scattered four hits, struck out six while walking four, a great accomplishment for an already superb season.

In game two Cleveland started Willis Hudlin against Boston's Fritz Ostermueller. The two pitchers dueled for six innings with the game tied at 1–1. In the bottom of the seventh, Ray Mack broke the tie with his first home run as an Indian, making the score 2–1. The Red Sox once again evened things in the top of the eighth with Bobby Doerr's sacrifice fly. The score remained tied just momentarily. In the home half of the eighth, Hal Trosky came to bat with two base runners on and, in his customary style, bashed a long homer to make the score 5–2. Joe Vosmik homered for Boston in the ninth, but Hudlin finished the game without any further trouble. In one of their elite performances of the season, Cleveland had swept a doubleheader from Boston.

The next day the local papers were filled with stories and commentary about the important wins along with the shocking exploits of Jeff Heath. Ed McAuley devoted an entire column to the bat throwing and fight. He wrote, "Fortunately no damage was done but one needn't let his imagination run wild to conjure up a ghastly picture of what might have happened if that crazily-jumping bat had struck a child in the head."

McAuley revealed that he knew of at least two separate incidents where Heath had broken bats in the dugout and purposely knocked over the bat rack. At age twenty-three, Heath needed to show some real maturity fast, while keeping his emotions under control. The Indians were playing good ball at the moment and did not want any distractions like bat throwing and dugout fights. Unfortunately, Heath was just getting started.

On Monday both teams assembled at League Park for game three of the series. The stands were practically empty, with 2,000 fans scattered around the park. The many vacant seats in the lower deck permitted a leather-lunged gentleman to sit close to the infield and voice all kinds of scorn at the Indians players. His actions made little sense because the home team was still in the midst of a hot streak, playing excellent ball each day. Regardless, his taunts increased in venom as the game progressed. Mel Harder had the Indians comfortably leading 3–1 after six innings. In the top of the seventh the Red Sox put a run on the board, cutting the deficit to a single tally. In the bottom half streaking Hal Trosky continued his home run spree, this time a two-run blast to right field. Going into the eighth inning, Cleveland had a relatively safe lead, 5–2.

Boston's young outfielder Ted Williams had been unusually quiet thus far in the series. After Jimmie Foxx singled in a run, he suddenly woke up with a huge three-run shot over the right-center-field wall to put the Sox up 6–5. Williams now had raised his RBIs to 112, good enough to lead the entire American League.

In the bottom of the ninth the Indians made a last-ditch rally. With runners on first and third, the center of attention, Jeff Heath, came to bat. He had the count at 3–0 when he took a swing and hit a weak foul pop for out number two. Later Oscar Vitt would tell reporters he had flashed Heath the take sign but the outfielder paid no attention. As the fuming player shuffled to the dugout, the daring heckler ran all the way to the first row of seats. He carelessly leaned over the stands, calling Heath a bum and several other choice words. Heath had obviously not learned his lesson from the previous day's fiasco. As he walked past the dugout, he confronted the fan and punched him in the chest. The fan fell down in a heap while several policemen hurried down to the lower stands. They hustled the man way before Heath could launch any other blows.

The incident occurred so rapidly that hardly anyone in the seats or on the field saw it happen. The umpires were not aware of it, thus preventing them from filing a report to Judge Landis. Vitt did not see it, Alva Bradley, sitting several rows from the heckler, claimed he saw nothing. Incredibly, the lack of witnesses on the field meant that Heath faced no discipline. He also benefitted from a technicality in the rules: had he jumped into the stands, rather than staying on the field, punishment would certainly have resulted. After the game, word spread to the press box, but hardly anyone would condemn Heath for throwing the punch. Many commented that the fan had gone too far and deserved what he got. For the newspapers, Heath reluctantly admitted that he had crossed the line. He told the *Plain Dealer,* "It's just another mistake in a season full of them, but that guy was pretty abusive of everybody." Of course, the papers ran several more columns, scolding the Indians left fielder for punching a fan, no matter what was said.

Even with Heath's awful behavior, it turned out to be an exciting weekend for Cleveland baseball. Though they wound up splitting the tough series with Boston, the exciting play on the field breathed life into the franchise, setting up a terrific run in September. But first the Yankees were coming to town.

Despite New York having a twelve-game lead over Boston and a twenty-game lead over the Indians, the August 30 night game had a World Series atmosphere. Over 35,000 fans entered Municipal Stadium, bringing enough energy and excitement to light up the entire city. Al Milnar started the game against Yankees vet Lefty Gomez. In the top of the first, Red Rolfe singled, then rode home on Joe DiMaggio's ringing double. The Indians did not threaten until the bottom of the fourth inning. Ben Chapman reached first, then jogged home when Hal Trosky walloped yet another home run into the right-field seats. The Cleveland fans threw straw hats and bags of peanuts onto the field while Trosky circled the bases.

The Indians, behind Milnar's effective pitching, held the 2–1 lead into the top of the seventh. Joe Gordon walked for the Yanks, went to second on an error, then reached third on a Lefty Gomez sacrifice. The fans groaned when Milnar uncorked a wild pitch, allowing Gordon to tie the game at two. The next inning Red Rolfe sent a line drive to deep right center field. Bruce Campbell made a nice run, speared the ball, then dropped it for a costly three-base error. Charlie Keller singled to give New York the lead again, 3–2.

Jeff Heath, who had already struck out three times, led off the bottom of the ninth with a badly needed base hit. The home crowd rose to its feet when Ken Keltner lined a single to right field, Heath stopping at second. Both runners moved up on Ray Mack's long fly out. Manager Joe McCarthy chose to intentionally walk Sammy Hale and let Gomez pitch to Oscar Grimes. With fans screaming on every pitch, Gomez could not find the plate, walking Grimes to score Heath with the tying run. Johnny Murphy replaced Gomez, getting Lou Boudreau to hit into a double play, sending the game to extra innings.

Joe Dobson started the tenth inning for Cleveland. He walked Red Rolfe, the first batter, prompting manager Vitt to give Dobson the hook and bring in Harry Eisenstat. He held the Yankees without a score, setting up a dramatic finish in the bottom of the tenth. With one out, Ben Chapman drew a walk. Chapman then tagged up and went to second on a deep fly ball by Hal Trosky. Once again Joe McCarthy signaled for an intentional walk, this time to

Jeff Heath. The Yankees were playing for the double play, but Ken Keltner ruined their strategy by driving another single to left field. Chapman still had the speed, flying around third and scoring the game winner. The Indians won a thrilling ball game, 4–3. The fans were beside themselves, hurling seat cushions, more bags of peanuts, and dozens of straw hats all over the playing field. The hat throwers did not care, as Labor Day was right around the corner, meaning no more straw hats would be worn until next summer.

The Indians filed into the clubhouse, somewhat restrained in spite of the nail-biting victory. Earlier in the game, rumors spread from the Yankee dugout that Germany had invaded Poland. Oscar Vitt, coaching third base, got the upsetting news from McCarthy and circulated the story to his ballplayers. Vitt remarked to the *Plain Dealer*, "I think I said something about the irony of thousands of people here watching a ball game while thousands of others in Europe were being slaughtered."

The news turned out to be false, but the players on both sides were a bit shaken that the brink of war might have been reached. They knew if the United States got involved in the fighting, eligible men from the ages of about eighteen to thirty would be called to serve. That age group included the majority of players in the American and National Leagues and a large number of minor league players as well. The uncertainty of it all alarmed the men, who were not anxious to change uniforms, exchange their bats for rifles, and sail across the Atlantic to Europe. Many of the guys started to hover around any available radio and listen for the latest news from overseas.

On a brighter note, away from the war news, the six night games, with one remaining against the White Sox on September 4, had drawn a total attendance of 172,331, for an average of 28,721 per contest. The numbers were not spectacular, but they were good enough to further convince the remaining owners to hurry up and get those lights ready. A new era of baseball had been ushered in, one that would become the best way to play as the years went by.

Just two days after the Indians' victory, Germany did indeed invade Poland. On Sunday, September 3, England and France quickly responded by declaring war on Germany. President Roosevelt waited a few days before calling a press conference where he announced a limited national emergency. Plans were revealed to bulk up the army, navy, and marines by 46,000 enlisted men. This call was voluntary, but essential given the escalating war in Europe and American security at stake. The army currently had 200,000 troops, with an increase targeted at 227,000. The navy had 131,485 sailors and was authorized to add 14,000 more. The marines, with 19,800 troops, were asked to increase the number to 25,000. Few ballplayers answered the call, but the idea of a peacetime draft had to be on the minds of most citizens. A draft would not spare professional baseball.

While the important war news at the beginning of September overshadowed the baseball season, there was still nearly a full month of games to be played. On September 8 Bob Feller picked up his twentieth win, beating the St. Louis Browns 12–1. Before the end of the year, he won four additional starts to finish the season at a sparkling twenty-four wins versus only nine losses. He would lead the American League in wins, strikeouts with 246, and innings pitched with 292 2/3, tie for the lead in complete games with 24, and finish third in ERA at 2.85. Feller also led the league in bases on balls with 142, but all things considered, he had a fabulous year. He was by far the top pitcher in the A.L. and one of the overall best.

Cleveland eventually caught the White Sox, finishing in third place with eighty-eight wins. They had an excellent August and September, winning thirty-eight games against twenty-four losses. Part of the reason for their success in those last two months was Lou Boudreau and Ray Mack. They played outstanding defense, tightening the Indians infield to a level not seen in many years. Boudreau hit well in the leadoff spot, batting a respectable .255. The prospects for 1940 were looking sunny, with a great pitcher in Feller along with young talent in Keltner, Heath, Boudreau and Mack. A few pieces were still needed, but on paper the team was strong at most positions, with room for improvement. An exciting yet tumultuous year loomed ahead.

Chapter 11

FELLER IN THE RECORD BOOKS

The 1939 off-season had almost zilch happening until days before the annual meetings. At the end of November Alva Bradley announced he was severing relations with New Orleans, their long-time partner and the site of their spring training camp for the last twelve years. Cleveland had sustained an association with the Pelicans going back to the days of Charlie Somers, the original owner of the Indians franchise. Somers, a capable baseball executive, had the foresight to purchase several minor league clubs before it was in fashion. He signed players then sent them to his farm teams, where he could keep a close eye on their development. In 1915 Somers, hemorrhaging from severe financial problems, had no recourse other than to permit his bankers to sell the ball club. He did not leave baseball completely, retaining his ownership of New Orleans until his death in 1934. Over the years, the Indians bought dozens of players from New Orleans and placed them on their big league roster.

Though the team did not train at the Pelicans facilities until 1928, they usually stopped in New Orleans, playing exhibition games before heading north toward Cleveland. Bradley had a friendly relationship with Governor Huey Long, which eventually led to the Indians making their spring home in New Orleans. Long was a consummate dealmaker, offering Bradley and several of his shareholders the honorary rank of colonel in the Louisiana militia. In addition, Long agreed with a plan giving Alva and Chuck Bradley concessions for the Missouri Pacific Railroad, in which the brothers had a significant financial interest. The trains, carrying freight and passengers, did business in and around New Orleans and parts west. In return, the governor acquired shares of stock in the Cleveland franchise, which he held until his assassination in September of 1935.

Without Governor Long around to smooth over relations, glitches occurred between the Indians front office and that of the Pelicans. The conflict came to a head in the spring of 1939, when Boudreau and Mack were shifted to Buffalo. The Pelicans had a dismal season and blamed the Indians for their troubles. They were quite annoyed that the two highly regarded prospects were leading the Bisons to a pennant the shortstop and second baseman promised to them had been little help. The second baseman, Jim Shilling, went with the Indians when the season started, while the shortstop Frank Scalzi had been declared a free agent and left New Orleans for the New York Giants.

Bradley and Slapnicka did not want to hear the escalating complaints. Without their friend Huey Long to iron out any difficulties, they could not find a compelling reason to stay put. Soon the decision was made to end their entire relationship with the Pelicans and the city of New Orleans. Cy Slapnicka immediately went south to visit Miami and Fort Myers, Florida, to select one of those locations for the 1940 spring training camp. Within a short time Fort Myers got the nod to be the winter headquarters of the Cleveland Indians. The Philadelphia Athletics had trained there for some time, but left the site vacant four years earlier. Cy Slapnicka ordered his grounds crew chief, Harold Bossard, to take some of his men to Fort Myers and prepare the facilities, which had fallen into disrepair, for use in late February. Mardi Gras time had ended for the Indians ballplayers.

At the same time as the New Orleans declaration, a national story broke that a member of the Cleveland team had filed for unemployment compensation. If the claim was approved, the player stood to receive $15 weekly until the start of spring training. The article provoked a great deal of criticism from people who were angry that a well-paid, selfish ballplayer would consider taking money away from the thousands of U.S. citizens who were still on relief, even near the end of the Great Depression. The criticism was somewhat unfair, since relief and unemployment compensation were actually separate entities. But if the name of the player came to light, he would be vilified regardless. Unfortunately for Ken Keltner, somebody in the media spilled the beans.

The whole sad story began while Keltner was relaxing at his winter home in Milwaukee. He went bowling with friends, moaning about his lack of money until the baseball season started. One of his buddies told him if things were so bad, he should file for unemployment. While everybody laughed, Keltner considered the idea and without really thinking went ahead and filed. The claim was reviewed by the Ohio Unemployment Compensation Bureau and subsequently rejected. The reason given was that Keltner technically had yearly employment with the Indians and at no time was separated from his job.

Keltner realized he had made a mistake and attempted to withdraw the claim before word got out. He would later tell the papers, "It was the worst error of my life. I only hope the fans in Cleveland will give me a chance to live it down." Once the season started, he made amends locally by working with sandlot kids to help them with the fine points of the game. The Cleveland fans gave him the benefit of the doubt, but on early spring road trips the crowds in American League parks gave him the business.

In the first part of December, Stanley Frank, writing for *Collier's Magazine,* insisted that in 1934 Alva Bradley had refused a deal sending Mel Harder and Hal Trosky to the New York Yankees in exchange for Lou Gehrig. Yes, Lou Gehrig! The opening lines of the story read, "There will be hell to pay when the clients in Cleveland learn that a trade for Lou Gehrig was rejected when the Iron Horse was in his prime and Bradley ostensibly was in his right mind." Frank argued that the Indians could have won a pennant or two with Gehrig at first, blasting home runs over the high wall at League Park. He believed the presence of Gehrig would have significantly boosted attendance figures, enabling Cleveland to spend the extra cash on more quality players.

Gehrig playing regularly at League Park almost certainly would have had fifty to fifty-five homers a year. The right-field wall, standing only 299 feet from home plate, might have been smashed to pieces from Lou's bat. That being said, who would have replaced Mel Harder as the ace of the Indians pitching staff? He usually accounted for fifteen to twenty victories each season. The acquisition of Gehrig would have added tremendous power to the offense, but it would have detracted too many wins from the pitching staff. All things considered, Bradley probably made the right decision to nix the deal. After the story was published, the anticipated hundreds of angry letters from Cleveland fans never materialized at his League Park offices.

Before the start of the winter meetings, Lee McPhail, the general manager of the Brooklyn Dodgers, introduced a plan for postseason interleague games. Along with the World Series, he wanted the second-place American League team to play the second-place National League team, third place to play third place, and so on all the way down to the last-place teams. Most of the owners were strongly against the idea, believing fans were not interested in paying money to watch seventh- and eighth-place teams fight it out to see who was worse. In addition, they were concerned the games might take attention away from the World Series and diminish its importance. Clark Griffith had no interest in McPhail's plan. He told a reporter, "Just say for me McPhail is nuts. Somebody proposed this a long time ago and it was just as silly then as it is now." A year earlier Alva Bradley had recommended interleague play to take place in midseason. This was a plausible idea, yet Bradley's fellow owners voted it down. Today interleague play is a standard part of the Major League schedule, with friendly and unfriendly rivals for fans to see. Why the owners were against the Cleveland owner's proposition is somewhat puzzling.

On the heels of the *Collier's* article, Bob Feller traveled to Cleveland to sign his 1940 contract. Coming to the table as one of baseball's shining stars, he had all the bargaining chips a player could want in his negotiations. The two sides met briefly, agreeing on a contract believed to be worth $23,000. The money put Feller in the company of the highest-paid players in the game, including Joe DiMaggio of the Yankees and Joe Cronin of Boston. He would now receive the highest salary in the history of Cleveland baseball, surpassing even Tris Speaker, who earned extra dollars as player-manager. The sportswriters asked Feller what he would do with all the greenbacks. Feller said, "I'm socking my dough away some in annuities, some insurance some other things. All my eggs aren't in one basket." Ever the businessman, he had a diversified portfolio that would put him on solid ground.

The winter meetings were scheduled for Cincinnati as the final part of the hundredth-year celebration. The Reds were the first professional team in 1869, and lobbied for the meetings as a way to recognize the history of the franchise. Of course, the Red Stockings were not playing ball in 1839; nonetheless, the owners went for it, leaving behind the bright lights of New York City or Chicago.

The main themes to be hashed out involved reducing the power of Judge Landis and dominance of the Yankees. The minor league owners, at their individual meeting, wanted to be less dependent on the Majors and further away from the Judge's influence. They introduced a number of new rules that would thwart Landis and his ongoing efforts to guard the rights of the players. The key rule stated that farm clubs owned by a Major League team could act independently of one another. In that manner they and their Major League owner could legally move players around at will and make the covering-up practice a nonissue. Some Major League owners (mainly in the National League) agreed with the plan yet were hesitant to vote against Landis. After all, he had saved baseball when the 1919 Chicago White Sox turned into the Black Sox and nearly ruined the integrity of the game. Many owners had bought their franchises years later and did not have the allegiance to Landis that long-term bosses like Connie Mack and Clark Griffith did. In the end the American League owners stood with the Judge, voting against the new rules and allowing him to retain his broad powers.

The Yankees owned five minor league teams and had working agreements with twelve others. That fact alone kept them far ahead of their American League rivals. The other owners came up with an idea to ban New York from trading with any American League team. As crazy as that sounds, the owners believed the new rule would slow down the World Series champs while closing the gap with the other franchises. The new scheme actually applied to all American League teams in that whoever was champion could not trade until they gave up the crown. All the same, everybody who followed baseball knew the plan came about because of the Yankees.

The proposal went to a vote, and the results were seven for the rule and zero against. To make it unanimous, the Yankee representatives voted yes. The rule did not reflect democracy at its best. Still, it became law, and all New York could do in 1940 was attempt to acquire players through waivers in either league. The playing field may have been leveled to some degree, but New York had DiMaggio, Keller, Rolfe, Selkirk, Dickey, and Ruffing, while the other clubs did not.

In the middle of January, Judge Landis showed all the cynics from the winter meetings he still had all the power he needed. In a devastating move against the Tigers, Landis declared that ninety-one players in the Detroit minor league system were now free agents, able to bargain with any team of their choosing. He fined the Tigers $47,250 for various offenses against a number of the players in his ruling. His actions effectively ruined Detroit's farm system for at least several years. The judge warned all the other clubs that they were subject to the same treatment if found to be manipulating the rules. Landis now favored a clearinghouse system where Major League Baseball would have no ownership or affiliation in any minor league team. In his proposal, clubs had to equally subsidize the teams and buy and sell in a free-market system.

His rulings and ideas created quite a stir among the surprised Major League owners. Alva Bradley, when asked to comment, shared his own touch of frustration. He remembered that when he bought the Indians, outgoing president Ernest Barnard warned him to stay away from farm-system baseball. Bradley intended to follow that advice, but observed his fellow owners buying minor league teams to such an extent that he had no choice but to do the same.

Bradley had little time to worry about the everlasting fight between Judge Landis and the farm systems. In February the Indians owner met with Mayor Burton, the police department, and the parks department to establish a plan to relieve traffic flow around Municipal Stadium. A new larger pedestrian ramp was suggested that would be off-limits to taxis. A widening of East 9th Street had everybody in agreement, as well as connecting the West 3rd Street

Bridge to the Main Avenue Bridge. That would make it easier for autos to get to the stadium parking lots and exit faster. Bradley anticipated larger crowds in 1940 and wanted the paying customers to have an easier time getting to and from the lakefront.

As February came to a close, the Indians made preparations for their initial trip to Fort Myers, Florida. Located in Lee County in the southwest part of the state and near the Gulf of Mexico, Fort Myers was a popular vacation spot. Each winter a fair number of northerners boarded trains for relief in the much warmer climate. Thomas Edison and Henry Ford were among the elite who built spacious winter homes in Fort Myers. Folks who preferred to rent, and could afford it, stayed at the historic Royal Palms Hotel.

The city, with a population of 10,604 residents, had two movie theaters, a country club with a golf course, and choice spots for fishing. The newspapers labeled Fort Myers a "nine o'clock town," meaning there was little or no entertainment in the evenings. It would be a stark contrast to the nightclubs and restaurants of Bourbon Street, but this may have been Alva Bradley's intention all along.

On February 24 the advance party of players and coaches were bid farewell at the annual luncheon thrown by the Cleveland Chamber of Commerce. Ed Bang, the sports editor of the *Cleveland News,* served as toastmaster. He presented the players with a bat said to have belonged to Tris Speaker during the 1920 championship season, when he batted a spectacular .388. The hope was the magic in the club might rub off on the players. Bang then produced a bright new pennant with the words "World Champions, 1940." To applause and best wishes, the Indians party said goodbye and left for the train station.

Spring training would be different this year in that the guys would be allowed to bring their wives and children along with them. Some of the group took advantage, including Al Milnar, Mel Harder, Harry Eisenstat, and Ben Chapman. After practice the families headed to the white, sandy beaches to relax or do some sightseeing up the coast. The only caveat was the players had to spend the night at the team hotel, while the spouses and children were housed at various rental properties close to the practice field.

The Sporting News, in an editorial, took a dim view of the wives accompanying their husbands at spring training. "It [the training season] is one time when all of a player's thoughts should be directed strictly to the game. One doesn't have to be a graybeard to hark back to training camp in which players literally ate, drank, and slept baseball."

Gordon Cobbledick, writing from Fort Myers, completely disagreed with the *Sporting News* assessment. The *Plain Dealer* reporter thought it was much better for couples to play bridge after practice than for the guys to be smoking and drinking until the early morning hours. He judged that the ballplayers now thought of baseball as their job and did not live it twenty-four hours a day.

The Indians train took several long days and nights to arrive in Fort Myers. Greeting them at the station were Mayor Sam Fitzsimmons, who was a transplanted northerner, public officials, a high school band in full uniform, and a large group of local citizens, who offered them rides to the Royal Palms. The men were eager to drop off their suitcases and hit the golf course or find a good place to fish. The downtown spots were not like New Orleans, but on a first impression all seemed good with the players.

On March 3 the team reported to camp, with the exception of Johnny Allen and Frankie Pytlak. As usual, both men were unhappy with their contracts. Allen, who had been struggling with arm problems since 1938, had virtually no leverage in squeezing more money from the club. Even so, the thirty-five-year-old pitcher refused to report, thinking he still could find a way to pitch effectively.

Jeff Heath drove all the way from Seattle directly to Fort Myers. He brought his traveling companion with him, a friendly springer spaniel named Wally. All through camp folks could watch Heath and Johnny Broaca stroll the grounds at Terry Field with Wally trailing behind them. The camp had a more relaxed feeling around it, showing signs of a veteran team possibly coming together.

A highlight of the camp was a new sliding pit, something that had been missing while the team trained in New Orleans. The pit was fifteen feet long and contained a base of sawdust to keep the players from getting cuts and bruises on their legs. Manager Vitt believed the team had poor sliding habits. Better technique, he felt, could mean another victory or two, so each day the players flung themselves in to the pit, practicing various kinds of slides.

For some reason Ken Keltner was the worst slider on the team, so he took personal instruction from Ben Chapman, who had great expertise at stealing bases.

New faces in training camp included veteran lefty pitcher Al Smith, acquired from the Buffalo Bisons. Smith had had a couple of good years with the New York Giants, and pitched in the 1936 and 1937 World Series. The Indians were seeking another lefty starter and hoped Smith might recapture the form he'd had several years before. In late January, Cleveland traded outfielder Bruce Campbell to Detroit for right fielder Roy "Beau" Bell. The two newly acquired players were similar in that their best years looked to be behind them. Bell had two great seasons with the St. Louis Browns, being named to the All-Star Team in 1937, when he batted .340 and led the American League with 218 hits and fifty-one doubles. Just two years later he hit a combined .235 with St. Louis and the Tigers. Apparently the Indians coveted more right-handed hitting in the outfield and, as with the Al Smith signing, were thinking in terms of miracles.

Another big addition in every sense of the word was rookie Mike Naymick, who stood six foot seven. On the trip south to Florida, the rail line had to remove the wooden partition between two berths, which gave Naymick enough room to stretch out. While doing morning calisthenics, Naymick shot a large leg out and nearly kicked Oscar Vitt in the head. His contributions for the year would be minimal, but his large dimensions got him an unusual amount of attention.

Spring camp in Florida meant there was a sufficient number of major and minor league teams training in the general area. The Indians had at least nine clubs a short train ride away to play exhibitions with. There were a number of activities taking place in the vicinity, including a March 17 all-star exhibition in Tampa for the Finnish Relief Fund. In 1939 the brief Winter War between Finland and the much larger Soviet Union resulted in the Finns being compelled to turn over extensive territory to the victors, leaving thousands of people homeless. In a true humanitarian effort, ex-president Herbert Hoover organized the relief fund, raising nearly three million dollars to send overseas. Major League Baseball got involved by creating the all-star game, with the proceeds going to help the

Finnish people. Sportswriters were asked to cast votes for players to be selected for the game. The Indians had four players on the A.L. squad: Bob Feller, Rollie Hemsley, Ken Keltner, and Hal Trosky. Other outstanding players selected included Jimmie Foxx, Joe DiMaggio, Ted Williams, Joe Gordon, Hank Greenberg, and Lefty Grove. Among the National League stars were Johnny Mize, Mel Ott, Enos Slaughter, and Terry Moore.

The American League starting lineup featured six Yankees and three Red Sox. Red Ruffing was in the box for the Americans against Cincinnati's Paul Derringer for the Nationals. The game quickly revealed that the pitchers were far ahead of the hitters at this point in spring training. All the big guns failed to display any of their great batting skills, managing only a few singles here and there.

The score was tied at one run apiece in the last of the ninth. Bob Feller was on the mound, wowing the Tampa crowd with his high-powered fastball. National League catcher Al Lopez led off with a single to center field. Terry Moore bunted to advance the runner, but Hal Trosky dropped the throw, colliding with Moore in the process. Lopez raced all the way to third, then scored on another base hit to win the game for the Nationals 2–1. A crowd of 13,180 watched the exhibition, and the proceeds of $20,000 went to the Finnish Relief Fund. Major League Baseball had done its part, at least for now.

The Indians soon broke camp and undertook their usual schedule of exhibition games while gradually moving north. On April 4 they stopped in Augusta, Georgia, to face the Giants, with Feller going against Carl Hubbell. In the first inning, Ben Chapman homered over the left-field wall for the only run of the entire game. Feller pitched seven shutout innings, giving up six hits and striking out five. In the course of spring training the Indians right-hander had pitched twenty-two innings, yielding just one run while striking out twenty-two. He looked to be headed for another dazzling season, possibly better than 1939.

The next day Alva Bradley published the home schedule for Municipal Stadium. The Indians would play thirty-seven games at the downtown facility, including seven night games, Memorial Day and Labor Day doubleheaders, and, interestingly, twelve games in September. Maybe the team knew something nobody else did.

Playing all those September games at the stadium implied Cleveland might be planning to do more than just to slide into third place again. Bradley, for whatever reason, thought his club had a legitimate chance at a pennant run.

What was different this year? They had a surefire ace in the person of Bob Feller. Hal Trosky and Ken Keltner could hit the long homers and drive in runs. Rollie Hemsley called a good game and hit well for a catcher. The rest of the club had question marks surrounding them, though. The outfield no longer had an Earl Averill or even a Bruce Campbell. Jeff Heath had had a down year in 1939; Ben Chapman, Roy Weatherly, and Beau Bell were not going to be All-Stars. That left a lot of faith in Lou Boudreau and Ray Mack. They had each played less than a half season, yet were being counted on to have breakout years. Combine that with a pitching staff, after Feller, of Al Milnar, Johnny Allen, Mel Harder with arm issues, and retread Al Smith. The Indians, regardless of the front office's enthusiasm, had a lot to demonstrate before being labeled a contender to knock off the Yankees.

Ed McAuley had a good take on why the Indians were going to have a special season. He believed the players now appreciated and followed orders from manager Oscar Vitt. McAuley wrote in his *Cleveland News* column, "Vitt's contribution to the general air of well-being has been two in number. He has shown toward his men the respect and loyalty which the boss in any field owes to his hirelings, and he has made his decisions without apology or explanation to anyone."

Maybe McAuley's statement had some truth to it. Nevertheless, Vitt had to show his new attitude and keep it once the regular season took off. He did relinquish his third-base coaching job to Luke Sewell in an effort to keep his emotions inside the dugout. To win a pennant or even challenge for one, both manager and team had to be on the same page. In a few days the baseball world would find out.

The Indians pulled into a bitterly cold Chicago for the April 16 opener. The weather was really more suited for a Bears-Packers game than the White Sox and Indians. At game time the temperature hovered at a chilly forty-two degrees, with a touch of sunlight peeking through the clouds. Eddie Smith was on the mound for

Chicago, facing Bob Feller. In the bottom of the second the White Sox loaded the bases with two outs on an error and two walks. Rollie Hemsley called time and trotted to the mound for an important conference. When he returned home, Feller took his time, then struck out the hitter, Bob Kennedy, to end the threat.

The innings rolled by with neither team able to mount any kind of offense. Then, in the top of the fourth, Jeff Heath singled. With two outs, Rollie Hemsley shot one between the outfielders and hustled all the way to third as Heath scored the game's first run. Smith retired the side without allowing any more runs.

On the Cleveland bench, Jeff Heath realized Feller had not permitted any hits. He started to mention it out loud, but Harry Eisenstat jumped off his seat to quiet Heath down. A photographer attempted to take Feller's picture on the bench, but Lefty Weisman jumped in front of the lens, blocking the shot. In the top of the eighth, first base coach Oscar Melillo walked toward his familiar spot near the bag. Umpire Bill McGowan, always a thorn in the Indians' side, commented on Feller's possible no-hitter. Melillo later said, "If I had a bat in my hand I'd have killed him, the dumb this-and-that." The Indians had eliminated all the jinxes; now it became Feller's turn to finish out the pitching gem.

Mike Kreevich led off for the White Sox in the home half of the ninth. The sparse crowd of 14,000 stood up, urging somebody to break the string. Kreevich swung hard but lifted an easy pop fly to Ray Mack. Moose Solters, now playing left field for Chicago, hit a routine ground ball to Lou Boudreau for the second out. With the anticipation building on both sides, shortstop Luke Appling came to bat, tough for any pitcher to retire. Feller got the count to three balls and two strikes, then watched as Appling fouled off three straight pitches before drawing a walk. Taffy Wright was next. He let the first pitch go by for ball one. Feller delivered the next offering, and Wright hit a smash between first and second. Ray Mack moved quickly to his left and speared the ball on the outfield grass. He righted himself and threw a strike to Hal Trosky for out number three. After several near misses, Feller had pitched his first no-hitter, and the first ever on opening day. He had retired twenty straight batters before Appling's walk in the ninth. Feller's masterpiece was the first in the American League since Monte Pearson's back on August 27, 1938, and the first by an Indian since Wes Ferrell's on April 29, 1931.

The Cleveland players, coaches, and reporters mobbed Feller in the clubhouse. Trosky shoved his way past the horde to place the game ball tightly in his pitcher's hands. With everyone in the clubhouse hollering at once, the winning pitcher remarked to the writers, "You just have to pitch as well as you can and take what's coming. I've had three one-hitters in the Major Leagues and they weren't much different from this one. Luck has a lot to do with it."

Within minutes, telegrams arrived from Cleveland mayor Harold Burton congratulating Feller, Bradley, and the team for the outstanding feat. Word quickly spread around Cleveland that a grand celebration was in process, to be held in the Terminal Tower rail station the moment Feller and his teammates got off the train. All the civic groups would attend, along with the mayor and the always willing Tris Speaker.

The local papers devoted a sizable amount of print to in-depth stories regarding the historic no-hitter. They noted that Feller's parents and sisters were at the game with twenty or thirty friends from Van Meter, Iowa. The *Cleveland Press* reporters went around the city getting together comments from the average fan. One in particular from Dave at the gas station really stood out. In Dave's words, "I was sitting with my ear to the radio and I got so excited I didn't even hear a man drive over the signal bell line. Finally he opened the door and walked in." Rather than get up and help, Dave told the customer what was going on and the gentleman sat down to listen. Before long there were six or seven men crouched around the radio with their cars temporarily abandoned at the gas pumps. Similar accounts came from all parts of downtown, including a soda shop where the high school kids clustered around the store radio, uncaring that their dinners were waiting at home.

One of the papers ran a silly poem the following day:

> The Yanks can have DiMag and Keller
> We'll string along with Robert Feller.

Lost in all the merriment concerning the no-hitter was Rollie Hemsley's statement to the press about his membership in Alcoholics Anonymous. He had reached his one-year anniversary, certainly a milestone for him on the long road to recovery. Rollie freely talked about his misadventures of the past, relating several stories that nearly cost him his career in baseball. Recently, Rollie's teammates, being the supportive friends they were, resolved to test his sobriety. One evening while they were having dinner Hemsley left the table to use the restroom. While he was away, several of his pals poured liquor into his glass of Coca-Cola. Rollie reappeared, sat down, and reached for his drink. He took a gulp, then spit out the contents all over the table. Eventually the players bought into Rollie's commitment and tried no further tricks. He never stopped going to the nightclubs and bars, but at no time did he take a drink of alcohol again.

The Indians had played just one game in 1940, but produced enough excitement to light up the entire city. The Wednesday contest against Chicago had to be canceled due to the freezing weather. The postponement let the team board their passenger train early for a run to Cleveland. With this in mind, the date of the celebration was changed to Wednesday evening at approximately 8:30 p.m. The fans started lining up at 7:00, oblivious to the incoming trains and the difficulty the passengers had removing themselves from the platform. At 8:28 a shout of "Here they come!" rang through the station. With only twelve policemen on duty, the crowd surged forward to meet the incoming train. By conservative estimates, 5,000 folks packed the area, hoping to shake Feller's hand or get an autograph. Alva Bradley and most of his stockholders stood on the temporary stage, trying in vain to get the fans to back up. The scene was not quite pandemonium, yet with the shortage of police the chances for people getting trampled increased by the minute.

The train slowed to a stop, with Jeff Heath the first Indian to step off. He and his teammates quickly figured out the crowd wanted Feller. They cautiously made a path to the nearby restaurants and disappeared from sight, leaving Feller and Vitt to fend for themselves. After a few words from the manager, the star of the evening fought his way to the stage. A band played and the crowd screamed their appreciation while Feller took his place in front of the microphones. Most of what he said was drowned out by the fans, but sportswriters were able to jot down a few words. Feller said, "We're very glad to be back and I want to thank you for myself and also the Cleveland players for this welcome. We will give you all we got and we want you to stay behind us."

He remained on stage posing for photographers and signing a number of autographs. When the crowd thinned out, he managed to step down and find a route to safety. If the season kept on like this, Feller and the rest of the team might be requiring police escorts.

While the accolades continued to pour in throughout the evening and into Thursday, Feller accepted a much-wanted gift of an English springer spaniel from a Cleveland breeder. Fred Hadley presented the eight-month-old puppy to its proud owner, who would work with the dog in Cleveland, then take him home after the season to Van Meter. The two new friends would spend the winter months hunting rabbits, quail, and squirrels. The Indians players had a long tradition of acquiring Hadley's prized dogs and keeping them as hunting companions. Among the Indians with spaniels were Tris Speaker, Willis Hudlin, Mel Harder, Jeff Heath with Wally, and former team members Earl Averill and Bruce Campbell.

The home season opener was scheduled for Friday afternoon, April 19. The cold weather that had plagued the Indians in Chicago followed them the entire ride home. The early morning temperature was a wintry thirty-seven degrees downtown, and with the swirling winds already coming off Lake Erie, the wind chill likely put the stadium temperature at around twenty-five degrees.

The Indians and Tiger players dressed as if they were on an expedition to the North Pole. Many of them wore two or three sweaters for the pregame workouts. Ben Chapman, the old country boy from Alabama, wore three sweatshirts under his jersey. Some of the guys sported work gloves while taking batting practice, foreshadowing a trend that would take over baseball many years later. Rollie Hemsley and Luke Sewell wore gloves on both hands while taking practice tosses from the pitchers. Hank Greenberg, not one to shy away from difficult situations, instructed the batboy to store his bats in the clubhouse, keeping them warm until needed. He explained to reporters that his bats felt like heavy weights when they sat in the dugout in the cold.

Alva Bradley and Cy Slapnicka were not being callous about the weather conditions, but they had their reasons for wanting to go forward. If they postponed the game, they would have to give rain checks to about 30,000 fans. With Feller pitching the Sunday game, they knew the people with rain checks would want to be there. The problem was with the fans who had already purchased tickets for Sunday. How could everybody be accommodated without a massive number of duplicate tickets? The ideal situation would be to play the opener on Friday and not have to deal with any rain checks. The total attendance for the two games would then be 60,000–70,000, compared to one game with a number closer to 30,000 or 40,000. A number of the Major League teams earned the majority of their revenue from the home opener, Sundays, and holiday doubleheaders. To cancel any one of those would severely affect the bottom line. The opener, despite the near-arctic conditions, went on as scheduled.

Chapter 12

THE PLAYERS REVOLT

The Cleveland fans attending opening day came equipped with heavy winter coats, warm blankets, and thermos bottles or flasks. Some of them yelled, "What time is kick-off?" Writers covering the game had difficulty estimating the crowd because so many were standing in the tunnels and concourse to stay out of the biting wind. The official count eventually stood at 26,529 hardy souls.

The ceremonies before game time featured an appearance from the enchanting Mary Nell Porter, the reigning Maid of Cotton of the United States. Usually the players crowded around any good-looking lady on the field, but this time they stayed in the dugouts attempting to shield themselves from the cold. Oscar Vitt received his third straight ceremonial headdress from the cowboys and Indians in town for the annual rodeo. With that, the game began.

Johnny Allen, after pitching reasonably well in spring training, got the start for the Indians. He was matched up against the Tigers' Henry Pippen, a surprise starter with a lifetime record of only four wins and fourteen losses. Neither team mounted any scoring threats until the bottom of the sixth. With a run in and Chapman and Trosky on base, somehow Jeff Heath powered a ball through the frigid air and into the right-field stands. Allen had his best stuff going, pitching a three-hit shutout, 4–0.

The heavy rains came on Saturday, forcing the cancellation of game two of the series. Sunday's weather improved enough to play ball, though the thermometer barely inched over the forty-degree mark. Bob Feller was taking his warmups when another of Cleveland's great-looking ladies walked onto the field. She wanted to present Feller with a statuette courtesy of the Loew's Stillman Theatre on Playhouse Square. He had to have noticed, as the male fans were hooting and hollering, yet he gave no indication that he saw anything. Jack Graney spied the woman from the broadcasting booth and gallantly hurried over to assist. He accepted the award for Feller, who shyly kept on pitching while the woman walked back to the stands. As she prepared to leave, a fan shouted, "To hell with the trophy, give me the gal!"

Any hopes for back-to-back no-hitters faded immediately when the Tigers' Barney McCosky led off the game with a double. The Detroit hitters routed Feller for six hits and six runs through three innings. Bruce Campbell rapped two early doubles off his old teammate, aiding the Tigers in a 12–2 pasting. In the top of the third Feller pitched to McCosky, who lined a shot right back to the box. At the last instant he threw up his glove and deflected the ball away. Feller's teammates rushed to the mound, believing the hot liner had hit the pitcher flush in the face. The fans and players shook their heads in relief once they knew their star was still in one piece.

Despite the pasting from the Tigers, the Indians had an encouraging April, winning eight out of eleven games. As well as things were going, the atmosphere in the dugout and clubhouse was a completely different story. Now that manager Vitt confined himself to the bench rather than the coaching lines, the players started to become aggravated by his conduct. Each game Vitt would pace the floor, yell questionable comments about his team on the field, and overall make most of the guys on the bench quite agitated. At some point he shouted to anybody listening that he would rather have his 1937 Newark team on the field than the current Indians. The players remembered a game near the end of the 1939 season when the grounds were wet and the weather not suited for baseball. Hal Trosky off-handedly remarked he hoped he did not catch pneumonia. Vitt shot back that he hoped Trosky would because he was not helping the team anyway. Remarks like these stuck with the players and were intensified in the second extended road trip of June 1940.

To fan the flames a bit, Vitt several weeks before had benched veteran Ben Chapman for poor hitting. The former Yankee took the news badly, settling into one of his funks, which his teammates usually ignored. This time he did not attack the water cooler or throw any bats, but let the squad know he was furious at the manager. Since the players were already in a foul mood, Chapman's anger had an adverse effect on the situation.

The Indians stumbled a few times in May, yet had an overall record for the month of 15–10. On May 9 Bob Feller threw a 4–0 shutout against the Yankees, allowing three singles and fanning seven. Two days later, Johnny Allen beat Washington 1–0, the winning run scoring in the bottom of the ninth. Back at home on May 22, Mel Harder attempted to pitch with his arm still troubling him. He lasted only four and two-thirds innings, giving up five runs on twelve hits. In spite of this, Cleveland came out on top and Harder was awarded the victory, his first of the year. After the game Vitt allegedly said to Harder, "It's about time you won one with the money you're getting." That uncalled-for comment hit a nerve with a number of the Cleveland players. Mel Harder was a four-time All-Star, the winningest pitcher career-wise on the staff, and a great teammate. To criticize Harder, a player who was leaving it all on the field, came across as sacrilege.

Cleveland ended May with two wins against Chicago, leaving them one game out of first place. They would hop a train for Philadelphia to begin a four-team, twelve-day eastern swing. In Philadelphia and Washington the Indians played uninspired ball, splitting four games with each team. Next up were three games with New York, always a tough customer at Yankee Stadium. Cleveland dropped two out of three, the only bright spot a brilliant two-hit shutout by Al Milner. For the young season he had a sparkling record of 8–1.

After the Yankees series, Cleveland moved on to Boston, where Monday was an off day. The two games at Fenway Park had some significance, as both teams were tied for first place. With Feller pitching on Tuesday, the chances for a split were promising. While cooling their heels on the off day, most of the players gathered around the hotel lobby, listening quietly to an address from President

Roosevelt. The president announced a trade-in program for the army, in which old weapons would be replaced by new ordnance. The out-of-date rifles and big guns would be sold to the British armed forces. The Senate approved a 1.8-billion-dollar appropriations bill for adding soldiers, weapons, and the construction of war planes. The army had the go-ahead to recruit an additional 95,000 soldiers, while the navy had the authority to build an unspecified number of warships. Even the FBI received funding to hire 500 new agents to assist in vague national defense activities.

Ed McAuley sat with the players, gauging from their expressions how they were taking the news. He noticed Rollie Hemsley scowling throughout the broadcast and Beau Bell with a calm, expressionless face. Bell was not married; he would be subject to an early call should the United States eventually enter the war. In a somber column for the next day's *News*, McAuley reflected on what he saw. "The icy hand of war rests heavily on the shoulders of the Indians not as personal sorrow but as an instrument of depression suffocating into significance the normal lives of normal men." Some heavy prose there, but it illustrated that the ballplayers were acutely aware of the war in Europe and it indeed weighed on their thoughts. The clerk at the hotel noted that newspapers were scarce when the visiting clubs were in town, suggesting they were anxious to read about the happenings in Europe.

On Tuesday the Indians fell hard to Boston, 9–2. Feller pitched that game, surrendering five runs in the first five innings. In the bottom of the third, Joe Cronin touched him for a long two-run homer. Before the start of the sixth inning, Vitt yanked Feller from the game, replacing him with Joe Dobson. Several players in the Cleveland dugout heard Vitt say too loudly his opinion of Feller. "Look at him. He's supposed to be my ace. I'm supposed to win a pennant with that kind of pitching."

Vitt's outbursts came at a most inappropriate time in the season. Feller's losing effort left his record at eight wins and three losses, while the Indians had a mark of twenty-eight wins against twenty defeats. They were chasing the Red Sox for first place and still had well over half the season to play. If the team had been in fifth place and twelve games behind, Vitt's words might have been somewhat understandable. This fact had to be on the minds of the

Cleveland players as they ate dinner at a downtown restaurant and walked back to the hotel.

In his 1947 autobiography, *Bob Feller's Strikeout Story,* Feller discusses the impromptu player meetings. According to Feller, one of his teammates said what most were thinking about their manager: "I think we ought to see if we can get rid of him. We've got a chance to win the pennant, but not with him." Other guys chimed in and formulated a plan to enact when they arrived in Cleveland. For the moment they would wait just in case something exceptional happened, like a big victory in their final game of the trip.

The much-needed victory did not take place, as once again the Indians took a beating from the Sox, 9–5. Al Milnar started the game but ran into trouble in the bottom of the eighth inning. Mel Harder came in to relieve, but he could not stop the bleeding as Boston scored six runs. According to Feller's book, Vitt came to the mound and said to Harder, "When are you going to start earning your salary?" That was enough for the players, who decided to visit Alva Bradley when they arrived in Cleveland and demand Vitt's ouster. Rollie Hemsley and Ben Chapman privately talked with Boudreau and Mack, advising them to stay out of the dirty business. Even with their anger boiling, the guys wanted to make certain that if things went badly, the two young infielders would not take any blame. New team members Beau Bell and Al Smith got the same advice.

On the morning of June 13, a group of silent Indians marched into Alva Bradley's office. Mel Harder acted as the spokesperson, being the most respected member of the team and never a hothead. The identified players in the room with Harder were Jeff Heath, Rollie Hemsley, Ken Keltner, Al Milnar, Johnny Allen, Oscar Grimes, Johnny Humphries, Ben Chapman, and Bob Feller. Hal Trosky did not attend the meeting, as he had taken a plane home for his mother's funeral. Roy Weatherly was also not there. The group had approached him to take part, but he said he wanted more time to think it over. The players told him it was now or never. Never one to be pushed into anything, Weatherly refused to join his teammates.

Harder calmly explained to Bradley what the players thought about their manager and how important it was to make a change.

Several examples of Vitt's thoughtless comments and actions were brought forward. The players spared nothing in an attempt to boost their case.

For his part, Bradley, who had to be flabbergasted, kept his cool. He agreed to investigate the matter, yet strongly urged his team to keep quiet and stay away from the reporters. If word of their meeting reached the public, a firestorm of epic proportions would no doubt take place.

The players agreed to temporarily sit on the matter until they heard back from Bradley. They all had to be stunned when the Friday morning *Plain Dealer* had the complete story almost word for word. Someone had let the cat out of the bag for Gordon Cobbledick, who hurriedly compiled the devastating article for the front page. To this day it is still a mystery which player slipped the details of the meeting to Cobbledick. The sportswriter vowed to take the secret to his grave, and he did. One could speculate all day as to the likely player's identity; but it would be next to impossible to determine who had the biggest score to settle with Vitt.

Cobbledick's unforgettable story began, "In an act without known parallel in baseball history, the Indians yesterday presented to President Alva Bradley a demand that Oscar Vitt be removed as manager of the Cleveland baseball team."

The sportswriter then listed the claims presented to Bradley: "He has ridiculed his players in conversations with newspaper writers, fans, and opposing players and managers. He has undermined the confidence and spirit of individuals by sarcastic comments on their failures. He is a 'Wild Man' on the bench constantly storming up and down the dugout voicing caustic comments on the performance of the team and communicating his 'jitters' to the players."

The players did not hold anything back in their stinging criticism of Vitt. It took two years, but they had reached the point of no return in their relationship with their manager. Each participant wanted Bradley to fire Vitt and replace him with popular coach Luke Sewell. A calm presence on the field, Sewell was the complete opposite of the current manager. With him running the club, the players could go about their business of bringing home a pennant and not worry about innuendo or any double talk.

Within a day the *Cleveland News* and *Press* posted their stories and commentaries about the rebellion. Tommy Tucker of the *News* usually ran a humorous column filled with lighthearted banter and silly jokes. This time he left the hilarity behind. Tucker wrote, "Vitt may be a good baseball man. Feller and the others may be good ball players. But the combination of Vitt and the present team has obviously been loaded with dynamite. That dynamite occasionally explodes as this did, should be no surprise."

Vitt, with a day gone by, had a chance to defend himself via the *News*. He remarked, "The only men I spoke harshly to are Trosky and Harder. When Harder was knocked out in Boston the other day I made some crack to the effect it was about time a fellow getting his money would start winning. I was sorry as soon as I said it."

The incident involving Trosky happened at batting practice on the road. Vitt had a rookie prospect taking extra swings while the veterans waited their turn. Trosky complained and Vitt shot back, "Quiet Trosky! That kid may be our first baseman." Vitt's admissions were really damning evidence against him. In a roundabout way he had given support to the players' accusations while trying to explain himself. The dumbfounded Cleveland fans, who were reading everything in print, surely noted what the manager admitted.

With the local and now national sportswriters digging for more sensational material, Alva Bradley released a statement. "The whole thing is really a great surprise to me," he wrote. "I will not do anything until I have made an investigation. I know this—That 12 players couldn't have made up their minds in one day that they were not satisfied."

The admissions from the ballplayers, Bradley, and even Vitt confirmed that a major problem indeed existed on the club. The question remained, was it enough to fire the manager? In Major League Baseball there were managers who screamed at the players when they thought it necessary. Others waited after the game to bring a player in the office, close the door, and do their scolding. Still others treated the players like professionals, keeping the criticism to a minimum. Oscar Vitt fell into the none of the above categories. At any time or place he would pop off without thinking of the repercussions. He would run down his players without giving a thought to who was listening. Did this behavior warrant firing? Alva Bradley had a lot of things to consider.

With some time to reflect about the episode, Vitt had more to say to the newspapers. He stated, "It just knocked the socks right off me. I knew there were one or two fellows who didn't like me too well, but there were more than that—well I'm just overwhelmed." He went on to say he appreciated that Lou Boudreau and Ray Mack were not in the group that visited Bradley. Vitt had no knowledge the pair were advised not to participate.

What really knocked the manager for a loop was the realization that Bob Feller and Rollie Hemsley were part of the rebellion. He thought Feller looked to him as a father figure, while Hemsley trusted and respected him. After all, Vitt had done his best to help Rollie through his troubles with alcohol. That being said, both were team players, well aware of the controversy he had caused that hurt the ball club. When asked for comment, Feller pulled no punches. He said, "Sometimes it seems as if Oscar will drive us all nuts. It is a fact that his words and actions sometimes make the fellows so jittery they hardly know what they are doing."

The local sportswriters had mixed reactions to the player revolt. Most of them had seen Vitt in action but were reluctant to condemn him and call for his head. Editors such as Ed Bang and others had witnessed all types of rebellion throughout the years of Major League play.

In 1890 John Montgomery Ward, the New York Giants shortstop, had led a revolt that culminated in the Players' League. For one year another Major League was established with many of the game's finest players jumping to it. Many problems ensued, including low attendance and the eventual capitulation of the new league owners, who feared going head to head with both the American Association and the more savvy National League. A year later the Players' League folded.

In 1912 Dave Fultz, a former player and practicing attorney, started the Players' Fraternity, a fledging union for ballplayers. Fultz sought better treatment from the owners, who bitterly fought him at every turn. After an aborted player strike in spring training of 1917, the union collapsed and once again the Major League owners reigned supreme.

Sportswriters younger than Bang had seen the players fight for themselves only to be thrashed by the owners. Though sympathetic, those who covered baseball for a living did not go out of their way to buck management. They were in no way willing to suffer any consequences that could be dished out by the magnates. Thus, they weighed the incredibly volatile situation in Cleveland carefully.

It was Ed Bang who got to the heart of the matter. A player who asked to remain anonymous told him, "There isn't a man on the club who doesn't think we have the best team in the majors and we figure we will win the pennant if we are not subjected to ridicule and insults that should be no part of a ball club." Bang closed the column with some words of advice: "President Bradley will have to show the wisdom of several Solomons."

In the midst of all the controversy, the Indians still had to play a home game against Detroit. The well-played game went to extra innings, but Cleveland persevered, winning it in the tenth, 3–2. Al Smith boosted his record to six wins against only one loss. He scattered thirteen hits but maneuvered his way in and out of trouble for the victory. Just a season earlier, the veteran Smith had seemed to be at the end of the trail. While at Buffalo, he had worked with manager Steve O'Neill on developing a screwball. He learned the pitch well enough to earn him a ticket to the majors and some surprising triumphs.

Meanwhile, still reeling from the disturbing events, Vitt appeared in the dugout, but kept silent throughout the ball game. Maybe his composure had an effect, as the next day Cleveland buried the A's, 8–0. Johnny Allen had a no-hitter going through seven innings before yielding a single in the top of the eighth. He finished the game allowing only two base hits. Beau Bell had three hits and three RBIs to lead the team, while Ben Chapman, back in the lineup, had a triple and two runs batted in.

While the Indians got back to baseball and Bradley wrestled with a solution to the manager situation, the national sportswriters were quick to render opinions. Most of them had little empathy for the Cleveland ball club. Jack Conway, writing for the *Boston American,* said, "Baseball has disintegrated into the lollypop and kiddy-car stage. It will soon be necessary for managers to appear on the bench in formal dress, prove they know the answers in the book of etiquette." Dan Parker, sports editor of the *New York Mirror*, was blunter. "What his players say about Vitt's sharp tongue may be true, but since when has baseball become a game in which a manager had to pull his expletives when they weren't going right?"

The most important comments were those of the fans. They bought the tickets, ate the hot dogs and peanuts, and drank the beers. What they had to say surely had some influence on Bradley. Bradley acknowledged that he received an avalanche of letters and telegrams from the Cleveland fans, and the *Cleveland Press* published a number of letters to the paper. They were a mixed bag; some were in favor of Vitt, while others sided with the players. But they usually came straight to the point. One letter read, "Vitt never managed a major league club before he took over the Indians and probably never has learned how to handle mature players. If the players don't like Vitt, Bradley should let him go." Another read, "The players' word should certainly mean something to Bradley. In fact it should mean everything."

Two days later a nervous Oscar Vitt found himself summoned to Alva Bradley's office. Behind closed doors the two spoke at length. The previous August, when Vitt received his contract extension, Bradley advised him to stop flying off at the handle and cut down on the mistakes. He believed that if the manager calmed down, the team might just meet him halfway. Bradley knew his advice had not been heeded, causing an unprecedented rebellion right in front of him. If he sided with the players, the baseball hierarchy probably would excommunicate him. He might be accused of opening the door for other teams to start campaigns to oust their managers. Bradley had to think mighty carefully about his verdict.

After a painstaking session with Vitt, Bradley took the least controversial route out of trouble. He let the press know a firing would not happen; Vitt still managed the Cleveland Indians. Bradley may have believed or wanted to believe the players had spoken and were now intent on winning a pennant. He may have hedged on the assumption the manager had learned his lesson and would support the players while they fought for a chance to get to the World Series. Maybe the ball club would pull it off and everybody might put aside their animosity in winning a world championship. In that scenario Bradley had a win-win situation. He would have stuck with his manager through hard times and earned a World Series in the process. He could stress out about 1941 later.

The Indians wrapped up their series with the Athletics, winning three out of four over the weekend. After the doubleheader sweep on Sunday, Bradley stopped into the clubhouse to meet privately with his players. Whether they were forced or did it on their own initiative, the team delivered a signed statement withdrawing their demands for Oscar Vitt's removal. There were no photos of the guys hugging their manager or giving him a friendly slap on the back, but the revolt had apparently ended. The brief statement on Cleveland Baseball Company letterhead declared, "We the undersigned publicly declare to withdraw all statements referring to the resignation of Oscar Vitt. We feel this action is for the betterment of the Cleveland Baseball club."

Twenty-two members of the team put their signatures on the letter. The nonsigners included Jeff Heath, who was in the hospital with an abdominal strain, along with backup catcher Hank Helf, suffering from an intestinal ailment. Roy Weatherly walked out of the meeting claiming he had nothing to do with the whole matter.

It is easier said than done to determine who actually wrote the words. The players' signatures are quite legible, as is the statement. Since the declaration is only two sentences, there are just three capital letters, a W, a C, and a B. A close examination shows that each of the two sentences has different handwriting. Probably there are two separate authors of the document. All things considered, the team members likely wanted the sportswriters to keep guessing on the persons responsible.

Bradley left the clubhouse with a sense of relief and a small amount of optimism. He stated for the newspapers, "I'm glad the boys decided to call it off. But I still am considering the truth of a number of things. No, I am not ready to say we can forget the matter entirely." In his actions, Bradley threw a bone to the players by claiming the investigation would carry on. They may have been empty words of appeasement, yet the guys could take some solace that all was not in vain, or at least could hope so.

On the surface, the ball club seemed to have made their point. Now they went about the business of winning games. From June 13 through June 20 the Indians took seven out of eight games, vaulting them into first place. On Friday, June 21, the Red Sox came to League Park to begin a key four-game series. Cleveland had a one-game lead on Boston, and Detroit. A weekend sweep or three out of four would put the Indians well ahead of the Sox and allow them to concentrate on the Tigers alone.

Game one developed into a slugfest when, in the top of the third, Ted Williams drove a three-run homer over the right-center-field wall. Cleveland, with Al Milnar pitching, rallied to tie the game at 3–3 entering the top of the eighth inning. Jimmie Foxx came to bat and blasted a solo home run to give Boston the lead. In the bottom of the inning, the Indians tied the game at four apiece on a single by Rollie Hemsley. With Hal Trosky on first and Hemsley on second, Beau Bell ignited the crowd with a three-run homer of his own. The game ended 7–4, with Milnar picking up his tenth win of the year.

On Saturday a fine crowd of 12,000 watched Mel Harder handle the Red Sox for seven innings. He faltered in the top of the eighth, giving up two runs before Joe Dobson came on in relief. The game went to the top of the ninth with Cleveland still out in front, 7–5. Dobson had a daunting task in the ninth inning with Williams, Foxx, and Bobby Doerr scheduled to hit. In the Cleveland clubhouse, Mel Harder and Johnny Allen sat next to the radio, intently listening to Jack Graney's play-by-play. Ted Williams took a called third strike, but Jimmie Foxx singled to keep the Red Sox's hopes alive. Doerr grounded to Ken Keltner, who threw wildly to first, putting runners at second and third with still only one out. Dobson did not get any type of a break with Joe Cronin coming to the plate. While an edgy crowd squirmed in their seats, the relief pitcher got Cronin to lift a harmless pop fly to Hal Trosky. With two outs, third baseman Jim Tabor knocked a routine grounder to Keltner, who this time threw accurately to first, and the game was over, 7–5 in favor of Cleveland.

Joe Dobson had saved the day for the home team. By the time he entered the locker room there were shirts, towels, and caps flying around the room in celebration. Alva Bradley stopped by to shake hands with Dobson and offer his congratulations. Sunday would see a doubleheader at Municipal Stadium, and Boston surely had no intention of being swept. Al Smith and Johnny Allen would pitch the games, hoping to keep the winning streak, at seven games now, alive.

In game one Smith faced the aging Lefty Grove, still capable of reaching back in time and delivering an occasional gem. Heading into the bottom of the seventh inning, both pitchers were in control, allowing one run apiece. Ken Keltner electrified the Sunday crowd by slamming a long home run to left field, making the score 2–1. Then, in the bottom of the eighth, with a runner aboard, Ray Mack hit a shot up the gap to deep left center field. Williams and Doc Cramer, playing in center, desperately raced to intercept the ball. At the last instant the two outfielders slammed together in a horrific collision. Williams lay on the ground unconscious, while Cramer staggered to his feet and gamely attempted to retrieve the baseball. Mack easily circled the bases for an unusual inside-the-park home run and a 4–1 lead.

The action stopped for several minutes while the Red Sox trainer kneeled over Williams, trying to see how badly the young star had been hurt. Finally Williams rose to his feet and gingerly walked off the diamond. An ambulance transferred him to Lakeside Hospital, where X-rays were taken. No fractures were found, but Williams suffered a concussion, leaving him inactive for several days.

The rejuvenated Al Smith retired the side in the top of the ninth to finish an exceptional game. The win was his eighth of the season. The enormous crowd of nearly 56,000 shouted their approval as Smith walked slowly off the mound. The Cleveland fans put aside their concerns about the players' quarrel with manager Vitt and shook the rafters for the hottest team in the American League.

Game two started with Joe Dobson as an emergency replacement for a sore-armed Johnny Allen. Though he still pitched effectively at times, Allen never had any inkling when the arm would come up lame. Dobson, who had already pitched two strong innings of relief on Saturday, was called upon to match up with Boston's tough rookie, Herb Hash.

Once again Dobson pitched extremely well, permitting only two runs on solo clouts by Jim Tabor in the second and fifth innings. The Indian were unable to solve Hash, getting shut out for the first time this season, 2–0. The Red Sox narrowly avoided the sweep, but they departed Cleveland in third place, trailing in the standings by three full games. Detroit now had sole possession of second place, just one and a half games behind the Indians. The win streak had come to an end, yet the boys could enjoy themselves knowing they had the goods to bring home the elusive pennant. The season had not yet reached the halfway point, but the Indians, in spite of their recent troubles with Vitt, had a great shot to win it all. The oddsmakers updated their picks, giving Cleveland 3–1 odds as the favorite in the American League.

Chapter 13

THE PENNANT RACE IS ON

At the end of June, the Indians were sitting two games atop the American League standings. They owned a record of forty-two wins versus twenty-five losses for a winning percentage of .595. The Tigers held on to second with thirty-eight wins and twenty-five losses. The fading Red Sox had fallen to a distant third, while the Yankees shocked the world, managing to stay only one game above .500.

Cleveland had experienced a gamut of emotions in June, being about as low as possible early on, then swinging the opposite way to the uppermost spot in the league. They were the talk of the nation for the aborted mutiny as well as their stellar play on the field. The roller-coaster would continue in July.

Both leagues took a break for the July 9 All-Star game held in St. Louis. The Indians were well represented with six men on the roster. Feller and Hemsley were the only repeaters, joining first-timers Al Milnar, Ray Mack, Ken Keltner, and Lou Boudreau. None of the players were picked for the starting lineup, but Feller was scheduled to pitch at some point in the game. The Nationals, with some fine pitching of their own, rolled over their counterparts with well-earned 4–0 win. Feller pitched the seventh and eighth innings, yielding one run, hitting a batter, and fanning three. Milnar did not see the field, but the others all got a chance in the final innings, with Mack and Keltner striking out in their lone at bats.

Feller had now pitched a total of four and two-thirds All-Star innings, earning an important save in the previous year's game. Not just the American League but fans on a national level had witnessed the phenomenal twenty-one-year-old handle the best players in all of the National League. If there was any uncertainty regarding who was the number one pitcher in the game, Feller surely made a strong case.

After the All-Star break, the Indians remained on the road. Their next stop was in Philadelphia. After a Cleveland victory in the first game of the series, on July 12 the teams met for a night game. It was an unusually cold night, with the temperature in the thirties. While the small crowd shivered under the bright lights, Feller opposed the A's' Johnny Babich. In the visitor half of the third inning, Ben Chapman doubled and scored on Lou Boudreau's key hit for the first run of the game. Feller put on a stunning example of pitching, holding Philadelphia without a base hit for seven innings. During the top of the eighth, Feller walked over to Hemsley to show him a newly formed blister on his right middle finger. When the Indians trotted out for the home half, Hemsley determined to call for mostly fastballs to place as little stress as possible on the injured finger. Dick Siebert, a first-pitch hitter, stepped to the plate. Feller cut loose with a fastball and Siebert connected, driving the ball inches past Ray Mack's desperate lunge. Siebert had the A's' first hit, spoiling Feller's chances for his second no-hitter of the season. It would be the only hit Feller allowed in the 1–0 game, the fourth one-hitter of the Indians right-hander's career. He also had thirteen strikeouts and only two walks. He now had 151 K's for the season, far ahead of any other pitcher in the American League. A 300-strikeout season looked to be within reach.

Cleveland played inconsistent baseball throughout July, resulting in a first-place deadlock with Detroit at the end of the month. Several prominent hitters were experiencing subpar years including Ken Keltner and Jeff Heath. Many sportswriters assumed that Heath had lost his batting eye, the one that led him to second place in the 1938 title race with Jimmie Foxx. Sportswriters also believed Keltner's batting slump was caused by fan ridicule for the unemployment claim he filed over the winter, as crowds in the American League parks continued to throw insults at him. Keltner still played an excellent third base, the best in the American

League, but his batting skills were sorely needed to keep Cleveland in the pennant race.

On the positive side, Roy Weatherly led the club in hitting with a .322 average, six points ahead of Lou Boudreau. Hal Trosky had an average of .305 and led the Indians with 19 home runs and 68 RBIs. Bob Feller had a tremendous record of seventeen wins and only six losses, while Al Milnar had fourteen wins and five losses and Al Smith, though struggling in July, had a fine mark of 10–4. With the outstanding pitching, the Indians had a more than reasonable shot at a World Series date.

On July 31 the Red Sox were in Cleveland for a game at Municipal Stadium. The Sox wasted no time in pounding spot starter Joe Dobson for six runs in three innings. The home team came to bat in the bottom of the fourth behind 7–0. Playing like a team that believed in themselves, the Indians scored five big runs to cut the gap to 7–5. A struggling Ken Keltner led the charge with a mighty grand slam to the left-field seats.

Boston continued to add more runs, knocking around relief pitchers Harry Eisenstat and Johnny Humphries to extend the lead to 11–5. In the bottom of the seventh, Cleveland narrowed the gap to 11–8. That set the stage for a remarkable late comeback.

In the home half of the eighth, Roy Weatherly got things going with a base hit. With one out, Hal Trosky smacked a triple to score Weatherly and pull the Indians within two runs. The fans at the stadium let out a roar when a wild pitch with two outs allowed Trosky to cross home plate with the tenth run. Keltner lined a base hit, his fourth safety of the day, to keep the rally alive. Ray Mack stood at the plate representing the go-ahead run. The fans nearly went crazy when the second baseman clubbed a ground-rule double to the left-field corner. The Sox intentionally walked Rollie Hemsley to load the bases, setting up a force play. Bill Zuber, one of the many relief pitchers in the game, was due to hit next, but manager Vitt called time and sent utility man Russ Peters up to pinch hit. Joe Heving, the former Indian, broke off a curveball, which Peters lifted past the infield for a clutch single. Keltner scored the tying run with Mack racing around third with what would be the winning tally.

Cleveland had accomplished an incredible finish, staging a thrilling rally to erase a seven-run deficit for a 12–11 lead. Al Smith closed out the game, and the players celebrated on the field while the fans marveled at what they had just witnessed. This had to be the team destined to win the American League pennant. What could possibly stop them?

In the month of August the Tigers and Indians would face each other just two times, but the September schedule had the two front-runners playing nine games against each other, six in Detroit and three in Cleveland. The way both teams were performing, it appeared the head-to-head contests would determine the pennant winner. The Tigers had outstanding hitting, with an astounding six players batting over .300. Hank Greenberg and Rudy York were having prolific years, belting home runs and piling up RBIs, while thirty-seven-year-old Charlie Gehringer resembled a young man at second base. The pitching staff boasted three excellent starters in Buck Newsom, Tommy Bridges, and Lyman "Schoolboy" Rowe. Newsom was a good bet to win twenty games, along with an extremely high winning percentage. Rowe had struggled the past three seasons, but in 1940 proved he still had enough stuff to win regularly. The Tigers had the talent to win it all, but they had to overcome a determined adversary in Cleveland.

Before the Tigers visited Cleveland, the New York Yankees strolled into town for a three-game series. At the beginning of the first game, Yankee coaches Art Fletcher and Earle Combs embarked on a mission of throwing insults at the Indians players. Fletcher targeted Rollie Hemsley, calling him, among other things, "Whiskey Head" and "Crybaby." The latter was a reference to the Cleveland players trying to get Oscar Vitt fired back in June.

At first the catcher ignored the insults, but as the innings wore on, Rollie grew a trifle put out. He advised home plate umpire Cal Hubbard to do something or fight time was just around the corner. Oscar Vitt trotted out of the dugout, demanding that Hubbard stop the abuse or else his players would likely storm the field and lay into Fletcher. The umpire, tired of the misbehavior, walked to third base to warn Fletcher to shut up or leave the ballpark. That did the trick, at least for the rest of the game.

Before the finale of the series, Fletcher received a telegram from American League president Will Harridge, admonishing the coach for his excessive taunts and cautioning him about a possible suspension if the words did not cease. The telegram ended the hassle for the time being; still, the Indians had to travel to New York for one additional series. The odds of a repeat performance appeared better than even money.

The first two of the remaining eleven games between Detroit and the Indians were played on August 12 and 13 at League Park. On Monday Bob Feller was on the hill against a nineteen-year-old rookie named Hal Newhouser. Certainly a touch of déjà vu must have come to Feller, now the veteran against a young star in the making. To add to the situation, Feller woke up with a stiff neck and shoulder. He insisted on pitching, but could not throw the fastball like he wanted. In the bottom of the first, Hal Trosky and Beau Bell slammed back-to-back homers to stake Cleveland to a 3–0 lead. Newhouser did not get out of the inning, recording only two outs before being removed in favor of reliever Clay Smith.

In the top of the third, the Tigers put runners on first and second with nobody out. That left Feller to deal with the heart of Detroit's lineup, with McCosky, Greenberg, and York all coming to bat. Throwing mostly curveballs, he forced McCosky to hit a pop fly into short left field, where Lou Boudreau backtracked and made the catch for the first out. Feller stayed with the curve and Greenberg skied another pop fly, this time to Hal Trosky. With two outs Rudy York stepped into the batter's box, eager to get ahold of a pitch and send it deep to the stands. Feller, even with the soreness, reared back for several fastballs, striking out York to retire the side. A barrage of straw hats flew on the field, the first of many throughout the afternoon.

Roy Weatherly added a two-run home run in the fifth inning, raising the score to 7–1, and the Indians coasted to an 8–5 win. Feller, despite having great difficulty throughout the game with the bothersome stiff neck and shoulder, pitched well enough to post his twentieth victory of the campaign. Some big-time hitting from his teammates helped him to his second career twenty-game season.

Alva Bradley and Cy Slapnicka knew a Monday home game usually drew about 5,000 fans. Adding another 5,000 due to Feller pitching, they figured on attendance around 10,000. It came as a pleasant surprise when all the reserved seats were sold an hour before game time and the "Standing Room Only" sign had to be put out. In the end a total of 23,720 semidelirious fans attended the game, an all-time record for Monday attendance at League Park.

The second and final game featured Mel Harder versus another Tiger rookie, Johnny Gorsica. The game see-sawed back and forth all the way to the ninth inning, when the teams were tied at five runs apiece. Harder pitched well through six innings, yielding two runs on six hits. Oscar Vitt replaced him in the top of the seventh, calling for Johnny Humphries, the first of what would be a parade of Indians relievers. The relievers staggered through the last three innings, but kept the game tied into the bottom of the ninth.

Ray Mack led off with a single and advanced to second on Frankie Pytlak's sacrifice bunt. Harry Eisenstat, the last of the relievers, batted for himself and hit a high bouncer over the pitcher's mound. The ball never left the infield, but Eisenstat, racing to first, beat the throw from short. Mack had played it safe, holding at second while the throw was made. Ben Chapman stood at home plate with a chance to break the tie and send the Tigers home as losers. The pitch came and the leadoff batter hit a sharp ground ball to second. Dutch Meyer, filling in for an injured Charlie Gehringer, let the ball roll through his legs, permitting Ray Mack to use his football speed and race home with the winning run. The Indians had swept the two home games, and in the process opened a two-game lead on Detroit.

With the Indians in first place, several thousand World Series ticket application requests poured into the League Park box office. Fans were jumping on the bandwagon, convinced that the twenty-year drought was about to end. The team announced that fans were allowed to complete four applications per household for tickets ranging from $6.80 for box seats to $1.10 for bleachers. The four-application limit was a precaution against scalpers, who would buy large amounts and sell them for many times the face value. The tickets were to be red in color and large enough to keep as souvenirs.

Though the Indians were playing remarkable baseball, things in the locker room were not completely harmonious. Newspapers insisted that most of the Cleveland players still hated Vitt and were tuning him out. One account asserted that Rollie Hemsley and Hal Trosky were no longer speaking to their manager. Franklin Lewis of the *Cleveland Press* filed his opinion on the state of affairs. "The players, all but three of them who weren't around at the time, signed a truce with Vitt. But that truce, as far as most of the important members of the Indians are concerned isn't worth the paper it was written on." Lewis went on to say, "The Indians of 1940 are the most amazing, interesting, and intriguing team in baseball history."

The general consensus of the Cleveland reporters was that most of the team was playing for themselves while caring little for manager Vitt. The players were sending a message straight to Alva Bradley that what they revealed in their June meeting still held. As long as Vitt stayed out of their hair, a pennant could be attained without any help from the manager. It would be a rare thing for a team to win it all by thumbing their noses at the manager, but this club had been doing just that. A month and a half remained in the schedule, yet this group of ballplayers was fixed on accomplishing what they set out to do.

On August 22 the Indians were in New York for a three-game series at Yankee Stadium. Al Milnar went to pieces early on, the victim of a second-inning grand slam by Joe DiMaggio and two-run blast from Bill Dickey. Nine runs were scored before the side was retired. When Milnar walked off the mound, first-base coach Earle Combs allegedly yelled, "You're a yellow belly who doesn't have any guts!" The Indians pitcher and Combs had no love lost, going back to the early part of the season. Whenever Milnar took the mound against New York, Combs went out of his way to give him a hard time. Usually the coach yelled out loud the pitches he thought Milnar was about to throw. It irked Milnar to the point of losing his temper, and when Combs called him yellow, the pitcher went after him. Both dugouts emptied immediately, with Luke Sewell grabbing Milnar and pulling him away from the pushing and shoving. A moment later Sewell decided to tangle with Combs himself, but umpire Bill Summers got between them and stopped the near fight.

After several minutes both sides cooled down, the players gradually separating and walking back to their dugouts. The Yankees ended up the afternoon crushing the Indians by a score of 15–2. The next day, when the Cleveland players walked on the field for batting practice, they were greeted by Art Fletcher and several Yankees showing them the "choke" sign. The New Yorkers had their index fingers pushed against their own throats, the classic indication of falling apart under pressure or in sports terminology, choking. The Indians were not amused by the taunting, particularly when Fletcher advised them the only postseason money they would be getting would be for second or third place. Sick and tired of all the abuse, the Cleveland players shot back their own slurs at Fletcher and his cronies. It had been some years since the Yankees and Indians had been feuding, but on this day they were mortal enemies.

As the first-place team, the Indians were increasingly subject to all kinds of verbal abuse In New York and other American League cities, fans greeted them with catcalls, including the chant of "Crybabies," while the out-of-town sportswriters published sarcastic comments about the players and their attitude toward their manager. The team had a great deal of work ahead of them in keeping their composure and playing winning baseball.

The road trip moved on to Washington, then to Philadelphia. The players were met with rain and more rain, which eventually wiped out the whole series with the A's. While the Indians were biding their time in the hotel, several bags of mail arrived for the team. A large number of letters and telegrams addressed to everybody, including coaches, spilled out on the chairs and tables. With little to keep them occupied, the guys counted up the mailings to figure out who received the most. Bob Feller had 100 items, while Trosky, Harder, and Heath collected fifty apiece. Most of the items had phrases of encouragement, such as "You're the best in baseball" and "We're with you." Jeff Heath's fan club sent a telegram that read, "While there's Heath, there's hope!" The Cleveland faithful did their best to let the ball club know they had nothing but support back home. They were fully aware of the adversity the Indians faced on each road trip.

The worthiest support came as a telegram from Cleveland City Hall with signatures from over one hundred political, civic, and business leaders throughout northeast Ohio. The incredibly expensive cable message, written and sent by the Come-to-Cleveland Committee on behalf of the 1,200,000 residents of Cuyahoga County, read in part, "Cleveland has been thrilled by your efforts and accomplishments in this year's baseball season. Come on Indians, we're for you and with you. Keep up the good work may the pennant come to Cleveland." Some distinguished names on the wire included Mayor Burton, Safety Director Eliot Ness, Gordon Stouffer of the Stouffer Restaurants, Max Rosenblum, representing Cleveland Amateur Baseball, and a host of others, including the owners and executives of the Cleveland Rams football team and the Cleveland Barons hockey team, executives from Standard Oil, all the department stores, radio stations, and the three main newspapers.

The telegram demonstrated the passionate support the Indians enjoyed in their home city. The city and the fans, along with the ball club, had endured a long stretch without a championship banner flying over the stadium. In the thirty-nine years of American League membership, the Indians had but once brought home a pennant. They had five second-place finishes, good seasons but little solace for the players and fans. The Yankees had eleven pennants to their credit, Philadelphia nine, Boston six, Detroit five, the White Sox four, and Washington three. Only the St. Louis Browns had yet to score a single first-place finish.

The law of averages certainly had to be in Cleveland's favor; still, the effects of a difficult and emotional season worried the city enough to send a massive telegram to buck up their team. Surely every fan wanted to see happy faces and camaraderie on the ball club, but what they craved most of all was a championship, no matter how it came about.

On the last day of August, Cleveland faced Chicago at Comiskey Park. The White Sox scored two runs in the fourth and two more in the sixth to take a 4–0 lead, until the top of the ninth. The Indians staged a last-gasp rally, scoring three runs, then tying the game on Roy Weatherly's sacrifice fly. Johnny Allen, who had entered in the bottom of the ninth, retired Chicago to send the game to extra innings. In the top of the twelfth, Ray Mack singled with one out. With the hit-and-run signal on, Frankie Pytlak reached for a pitch wide of the plate, distracting catcher Mike Tresh for just an instant. The throw to second arrived a fraction late, allowing a hard-sliding Mack to make it safely. Pytlak swung at the next offering and lined a single to center. Mack hustled all the way home, beating the throw and giving the Indians the lead 5–4.

The White Sox threatened in the bottom of the twelfth when with nobody out Mike Kreevich hit a smash at second baseman Mack. The ball caromed off his shin and rolled into short center field. Kreevich never slowed down, motoring to second with an unusual double. Joe Kuhel then rapped a high bouncer near second. Boudreau fielded the ball, but his only play was to first. Kreevich stood at third, representing the tying run, with old friend Moose Solters the next hitter. Trying his best, Solters lifted a towering fly ball to medium center field. The Indians players were all in motion, with Boudreau racing to the mound for a possible relay throw and Allen running behind the plate to back up his catcher. Roy Weatherly set himself, made the catch, then threw a bullet toward home. Pytlak flung off his mask and moved a few steps to the left to position himself for the slightly off-line throw. Kreevich dashed toward the plate as the Indians catcher short-hopped the low toss. Pytlak, in one motion, gloved the ball, transferred it to his right hand, and dove headlong at the runner. The two players crashed together with a tremendous force heard throughout the stadium. In definitely one of the great plays of the Indians' season, Pytlak took the full impact, glove flying into the air, tagged Kreevich with his bare hand, and blocked the plate with his body. Even with solid blows to his wrist and arm and a spike wound in his thigh, Pytlak held the ball for the double play to end the incredible game. Cleveland had won a thriller, 5–4.

With the month of August in the books, the standings stood as follows:

Cleveland	74–50	
Detroit	72–53	2½ gb
New York	68–54	5 gb

The Yankees had come back from the dead, winning twenty out of thirty games to climb back into the pennant chase. With two games in Cleveland, followed by three in Detroit, they still had an opportunity to catch the leaders. But they would need to win at least four out of those five games.

The Indians' schedule for September looked favorable, as between the six road games in Detroit they had a long home stand of sixteen games. If Cleveland could break even with the Tigers and win big at home, the pennant would be theirs, and with it the signal to celebrate as if it was 1920 again.

The *Cleveland News* threw all objectivity away, starting a telegram campaign to the players still on the road. The first telegram went to Jeff Heath for his home run on August 30 in Chicago. Heath crashed the four-bagger in the first inning with two runners aboard. Staked to a three-run lead, Bob Feller had another masterful performance, effortlessly winning his twenty-fourth game of the year. Heath's telegram from the *News* the next day read,

> For that all-important home run that won the ball game last night. Cleveland today salutes, congratulates, and thanks you. Honor to you too for your refusal to let ill fortune, illness and unpleasant incidents get you down. Remember just one thing is important:
>
> CLEVELAND WANTS THAT PENNANT.

The reference to unpleasant incidents no doubt covered the bat-throwing and punching the fan in Cleveland. Regrettably, those two incidents were not the only unpleasantness Heath had experienced. A few weeks before at a home game with St. Louis, he was summoned to pinch hit in the bottom of the ninth inning. He came to the plate reluctantly, as he disliked entering a ball game for one at bat. Of course he struck out, and had a major meltdown when he returned to the dugout. Part of the anger went toward Vitt for making him pinch hit. They exchanged words over several minutes, resulting in a heavy fine for Heath.

That evening Cy Slapnicka, for some unstated reason, chose to intervene and rescind the fine. He called manager Vitt with his decision, then notified Heath that if he apologized the fine would disappear. The ballplayer did so, happy to see his manager overruled. The fine probably should have stuck, as most of the Indians in the dugout heard Heath say the next time he would take a bat and crack Vitt over the head with it.

Why did Slapnicka put himself in the middle of the situation? He may have wanted to help his players' morale by siding with his team rather than his manager. His action put Vitt in an awkward position, sending him a message to the effect of "Don't mess with my players!" If Vitt already believed his job was tenuous at best, this message surely added fuel to the fire.

With another win on September 1 over Chicago, the Indians rode home for a doubleheader with the seventh-place St. Louis Browns. Everything seemed to be going in the right direction for Cleveland, especially given another chance to beat up on the luckless St. Louis club. Veterans Mel Harder and Johnny Allen were slated to pitch against Vern Kennedy and Elden Auker. All four pitchers were well into their thirties and immune to any pressure, regardless of what was at stake for the home team. As expected, a pumped-up crowd of 52,000 spectators filed into Municipal Stadium, eager to witness the destruction of the Browns. When they passed Gate A, folks heard the loudspeaker send a warning to stay away from scalpers and only buy tickets at the office. Some of the scalpers apparently were circulating counterfeit passes to the game.

The afternoon unfolded with two unexpected pitchers' battles. In game one the journeyman Kennedy held the Indians in check. With the score at 1–0 in favor of the visitors, St. Louis got a runner on first base. The next batter grounded to Harder, who picked the ball clean, whirled, and threw to Boudreau. The shortstop touched second for the out, then fired the ball into the right-field stands. A base hit scored the second run. Kennedy staggered in the ninth inning, yielding one run, but with two outs retired Sammy Hale on a fly ball for the surprise win. The boisterous fans were stunned, expecting Cleveland to come back and win it. It was the St. Louis Browns, after all. How could the first-place Indians lose the ball game 2–1?

In game two Johnny Allen resembled the All-Star pitcher of the past, blanking the Browns through eight innings. He got the fans going by flashing his old form, including arguing with umpire Bill Grieve and hurling the rosin bag all over the infield. Unfortunately, Elden Auker had the same magic, holding the Indians without a run. In the bottom of the eighth, a hot-hitting Frankie Pytlak singled, then Johnny Allen got the crowd on its feet with a sharp base hit, sending Pytlak to third. Ben Chapman walked to the plate, ready to drive in the go-ahead run. Luke Sewell, coaching at third, asked for time to meet with his leadoff hitter. Manager Vitt had flashed the squeeze sign, and sent Sewell to make sure Chapman knew it was on. The Browns figured out during the lull what the

Indians were up to and smartly moved their infielders in. As Pytlak sprinted for home, Chapman bunted. The first baseman played the bunt perfectly, throwing in time to nail the runner and keep Cleveland from scoring. All sorts of catcalls rang down from the stands as the fans let Vitt know what they thought of his strategy.

St. Louis scored a run in the top of the ninth, sending Allen to the sidelines, complete with the obligatory furious toss of his glove into the dugout. He had pitched a whale of a game, holding the Browns to that one run and giving his team an excellent chance to pull out the game. With Allen in the clubhouse sipping a beer, the Browns scored twice more to win the game 3–0 and gain an appalling sweep of the doubleheader. The Indians managed only five singles off Auker.

In the locker room a heated Ben Chapman ranted about the ill-fated squeeze play. "I'll never do it again, never. I don't like that play. If I get 10 signals I won't. If I can't bat in a run what good am I?" Chapman had a valid reason for his outrage. A long-time Major League outfielder with good bat control, he probably should have been left to hit away. The situation called for a contact hitter to get the ball out of the infield, something Chapman could do. In effect, the bat was taken out of his hands, and the play backfired.

It helped slightly when the players received news of the Tigers dropping a doubleheader to the White Sox. Even though the Tigers has fallen, a golden opportunity for the Indians to increase their lead over Detroit went by the wayside. The stampeding Yankees split a doubleheader with the last-place Philadelphia Athletics to pull even with the Tigers in second place, trailing Cleveland by three and a half games.

As one might guess, the next day's newspapers were filled with analysis of what went wrong. It only validated what the fans at the stadium and those listening on radio already knew. James Doyle, in his Sporting Trail column for the *Plain Dealer*, rewrote the chorus of "Home on the Range." His parody went like this:

> Home, home on the fritz,
> Our poor Redskins were fresh out of hits.
> And such a soft touch,
> When it came to the clutch,
> That we all suffered fits just like Vitt's.

The comedy helped Cleveland fans laugh off the anguish they were dealing with. Detroit's having lost two to the White Sox relieved the Indians' distress some, but they had to be aware of the narrow margin for error remaining.

After a much-needed day off, the Indians boarded a train for their first of three series with Detroit. While everything was not on the line here, the three games were crucial to the stretch drive. For Cleveland to take command of the race, two wins were essential, one a must. The Tigers and their fans knew what had to be done: sweep the three games or win at least two.

On Wednesday afternoon, September 4, Bob Feller started for Cleveland, matching pitches with Schoolboy Rowe. He did not have his great stuff working, but labored along to give his offense a chance. In the second inning, with the Indians down 2–0, Hal Trosky socked a solo home run, his twenty-fourth of the year. Ray Mack tripled in a run in the top of the fourth, but Hank Greenberg answered in the Tigers' half with a solo shot to keep the Tigers ahead 3–2. The next inning, former Indian Bruce Campbell tormented his ex-teammates with a bases-empty homer. The easygoing Campbell did not hold any grudges, but he delighted in beating up on the Indians whenever he got the opportunity.

In the bottom of the seventh, Charlie Gehringer broke the game open with a three-run blast, raising the count to 7–2. Rowe set the Indians down the next two innings and Detroit had drawn first blood. To add to Cleveland's woes, Trosky pulled a muscle hustling on the bases and was doubtful for the next two games.

The Cleveland players knew they had to regroup and battle in game number two. They had to find a way to handle the fired-up Tigers plus their fans, who were firing insults at a rapid clip. The crowds in the American League cities were having a great time labeling the Indians as "crybabies" and quitters. The chants increased as the season reached September, often accompanied by baby dolls and bottles. Razzing Major League players had been a tactic since the nineteenth century, but the insults from the Tiger fans were outside the norm. The Cleveland players tried to shrug them off, but the taunts were having the intended effect of taking a part of their concentration away.

When the team attempted to have Oscar Vitt fired, they had no idea of the widespread abuse they were setting themselves up for.

They tried to tune the noise out, but it was next to impossible. The usually levelheaded Ed Bang, a strong believer in sportsmanship, wrote in his column that after the incidents in New York, and the way the Tiger fans were following the Yankees' lead, it was time for the Cleveland players and fans to give it back in kind. Bang stated his case simply: "Fight fire with fire."

The next day, Al Smith faced the Tigers' Tommy Bridges. Cleveland held a 3–2 lead going into the bottom of the sixth inning, when Rudy York clobbered a three-run homer for a 5–3 advantage. In the next inning Bruce Campbell stuck another arrow in the Indians' heart with an additional three-run shot to break the game wide open. Billy Sullivan further exasperated his ex-teammates by contributing a double and triple. The final score read 11–3, an embarrassing defeat in light of what was at stake.

In the concluding game, the Tigers battered Johnny Allen, Al Milnar, and the towering Mike Naymick for ten runs on fourteen hits. Hank Greenberg hit his twenty-eighth of the year, while Billy Sullivan had a two-run homer. The outcome was never in doubt; the final score was 10–5. The Detroit fans poured it on the "crybabies," promising to bring even more harassment in the next series.

The prior evening, some of the Cleveland players had met in their Detroit hotel to talk things over. They may have vented about how to circle the wagons and stop the then-four-game losing streak. Not everyone on the team was aware of the impromptu gathering and knew what was discussed. Whether deliberately leaked or not, stories about the meeting reached the papers, provoking various interpretations. The *Cleveland News* placed the story on page 1, signaling a major revelation. According to the article, a Cleveland player said the attendees vowed to ignore any signs from Oscar Vitt they disagreed with. He referred to the questionable squeeze play against St. Louis as the last straw. Another player said the opposite, that the team members went over things they could do to play better baseball. Nobody quite knew the truth, but it is possible there was a mini-rebellion once again to go around Vitt and ignore his game-day strategy.

The Cleveland club arrived back home on Saturday morning, just in time for "Homecoming Day," a hurriedly prepared rally at Public Square. A crowd of 7,000 exuberant supporters attended, intent on lifting the spirits of the home team. The event was broadcast live by WHK and WGAR radio. As the team sat on a temporary platform, Alva Bradley spoke, followed by Mayor Burton, urging the fans and players to keep fighting on. Then two local bands played "The Star-Spangled Banner" and "Don't Give up the Ship." The rally lasted a short time, but long enough for the ball club to hear the message that the city still had their backs. Every city in the Major League wanted a pennant, but the Cleveland fans more than wanted it. They had to have it this time.

The weekend series against the Chicago White Sox was another exercise in frustration. The Indians were losers in the first game and barely salvaged game two in extra innings, 5–4. Bob Feller relieved Al Milnar in the ninth inning with the score tied and pitched two scoreless frames. In the bottom of the tenth, Jeff Heath started things with a double off the wall in left field. With Ken Keltner up, a passed ball moved him to third. Keltner, who had already contributed a two-run homer, took a mighty swing but flied out. That brought Ray Mack to the plate. The White Sox called time to discuss walking him and Rollie Hemsley to load the bases, which would force Bob Feller to hit or Vitt to pinch hit for him. Ted Lyons, the starter, who was still in the game, wanted to pitch to Mack, and Manager Jimmy Dykes agreed. The infielders played in, but a determined Mack slapped the ball past them into the outfield for the win, 5–4.

After the games of September 9, the standings looked like this:

Detroit	77–57	
Cleveland	76–57	½ gb
New York	75–58	1½ gb

The Indians had held first place for four entire weeks until the series loss to the White Sox. The Yankees were now hot on Cleveland's tail, and were coming to town for two critical ball games. The animosity between the two clubs, plus everything that was at stake, would make for some compelling baseball at Municipal Stadium.

The Wednesday afternoon doubleheader versus New York attracted over 33,000 revved-up Cleveland fans. With the sky darkening and a threat of rain in the air, many were wearing overcoats. Among the out-for-blood fans was Mickey Rooney, the star of the immensely popular *Andy Hardy* movies, who was in town on a promotional tour for his latest film. The nineteen-year-old movie idol sat directly behind the Indians dugout, no doubt amazed at the fans' rowdy behavior. Between games Rooney visited the clubhouse, joking around with the Indians players.

When the Yankees came to bat in game one, it appeared the Indians faithful had taken advice from Ed Bang and were ready to fight fire with fire. They yelled, screamed, and taunted the Yankee players and third-base coach Art Fletcher. In the top of the fourth inning, as Joe DiMaggio approached the batter's box, without any warning a barrage of lemons, tomatoes, eggs, and bananas came flying out of the stands at Joe D. and coach Fletcher. Several of the missiles scored a direct hit on Fletcher's pants, while a single lemon plunked a photographer squarely in the back. Another lemon grazed the Yankees bat boy, causing little damage.

A fuming Joe McCarthy rushed out of the visitors' dugout, threatening to pull his team off the field and demanding all the fruit and vegetables be removed from the stands and the guilty parties be tossed out of the stadium. The umps said no and ordered McCarthy to take his place back in the dugout. The Cleveland fans stood and howled at the Yankee skipper as he walked across the field. Moments later several firecrackers went off, adding to the general hysteria.

Six members of the stadium grounds crew dashed onto the field to clear up all the accumulated debris. When they had finished their task, a single beer bottle soared out of the upper deck and landed just a few feet from the hated Art Fletcher. A dozen policemen climbed the ramps and converged on the area where the bottle appeared to have originated. Several fans pointed to a young man trying his best to look innocent. The police questioned him, but several other spectators claimed they had the wrong guy. No arrests were made, and thankfully no further bottles reached the playing field.

Lost in all the excitement was a tremendous performance from Yankee rookie Ernie Bonham. At one point the pitcher set down nineteen straight Cleveland batters. Bob Feller pitched a strong game, but his teammates could not generate any type of offense on his behalf, and the Yankees won by a score of 3–1.

Game two saw the Yankees take an early lead of 2–0 off Al Smith. But in the bottom of the third the Indians pounded Red Ruffing for five runs, the key blow a double by Beau Bell that scored Heath and Boudreau. New York added another run in the fourth. The teams were playing in a steady drizzle under blackening skies, and by the sixth inning the Cleveland infielders could not see the signs flashed by Frankie Pytlak from behind the plate. The umpires gathered for a few moments, then decided to call the game. The doubleheader ended in a split, leaving both teams exactly where they were at the start. Meanwhile, the Tigers beat Boston 11–7 to take a slim half-game lead. All three teams were still very much in contention as the season moved along to mid-September.

While the Indians' game results made front-page news, another article on page 1 got the attention of the entire nation. Congress announced that the votes were in place to pass the Conscription Act. The bill called for a peacetime draft, for which 16.5 million American males were eligible. Capitol Hill estimated that of that total, approximately 5 million would qualify for a year's service in the military. All those between the ages of twenty-one and thirty-five were required to register when the official dates became available. Of course, several exemptions applied, including men who had dependents, who were physically unfit, or who had jobs in agriculture or industry. The government figured the cost to set up the draft could go as high as a hefty 1 billion dollars.

By all indications, Major League ballplayers were not receiving any exemptions for the impending draft. Their eligibility seemed to be no different from that of any American male. Back in 1918, at the height of World War I, the Work or Fight Order obligated all ballplayers to take a job in the war industry or be drafted and sent overseas. The baseball season ended early, on September 1, speeding up the process of converting ballplayers to infantry soldiers. Fortunately, the war ended several months later, keeping the majority of the players stateside.

Since the United States had not entered World War II, those drafted would remain in the country training at various army and navy bases. The question of a baseball season for 1941 had yet to be answered. It hinged on how many players might be drafted before spring training and whether those who departed could be replaced by promising minor leaguers. The bachelors would suffer heavily here, but the married men with dependents were likely to avoid service and continue playing ball. The near future was muddy at best.

As the Conscription Act made headlines, the American League pennant race carried on. Boston traveled to Cleveland for their last appearance of the year. Mel Harder, counted on for his experience and leadership, got the nod in game 1. He accepted the challenge and then some, stopping the Red Sox on just three hits. Harder had his best curveball of the campaign, breaking sharply in on Ted Williams and the other lefties in the lineup. The Indians batted around in the fourth inning, plating seven big runs for an 8–1 victory.

The next day Al Milnar followed suit, pitching a nifty three-hit shutout, his best effort of the season. Cleveland scored the lone run in the fourth inning. Strangely, only 1,000 fans were on hand to witness the victory. Apparently local supporters were only interested in seeing the Yankees or Tigers and expected the Indians to thrash the lesser teams.

In the final game Boston shelled Johnny Allen for six runs in five and a third innings. The Cleveland bats went almost completely silent in the 6–1 loss. The standings after September 14:

Detroit	80–59	
Cleveland	79–59	½ gb
New York	77–60	2 gb

The Indians had sixteen games left to play in the season, compared to fifteen for Detroit. The way the teams were playing, the three remaining road games versus the Tigers might determine the American League championship.

Cleveland's homestand still had five games with Philadelphia and three more against Washington before the all-important showdown in Detroit. The matchup with the A's included two makeup games that resulted in the clubs playing back-to-back doubleheaders. The Indians swept the first one, 5–0 and 8–5. Feller threw a two-hit shutout in game one, fanning seven and not allowing a single base on balls for his twenty-fifth win.

The next day's twin bill started out with a relatively easy 8–3 win. Mel Harder had his second excellent outing in a row, holding

Philadelphia to three runs for his eleventh victory. Ray Mack crushed a grand slam homer to give Harder all the runs he needed. The Indians were in position to sweep again, but they came up short in the nightcap and lost the next day as well.

Cleveland may have been suffering from both physical and mental fatigue. They had played much of the year as the most hated team in the American League, with fans heckling them to no limit. The two doubleheaders on top of each other likely sapped their strength. Throw in the loss of the still-sidelined Trosky and you might lose a game or two you should have won. The box scores reveal the Indians chalking up a bunch of singles but few extra-base hits. If the pitching had not been first rate, the season might have been lost.

The Washington Senators arrived in Cleveland for the crazy third doubleheader in four days. The offense continued its lackluster form, but in game one Johnny Allen pitched beautifully, beating the Senators 3–1. Hal Trosky returned to the lineup but went hitless in four trips. In the second game, Washington started a fairly good hurler in Sid Hudson. Manager Vitt made the decision to counter with Bob Feller on only two days' rest. The Indians ace showed no ill effects from the last-minute start, winning his twenty-sixth game of the year, 2–1. In the sixth inning Roy Weatherly belted a rare Cleveland home run to tie up the game. The next inning Ray Mack doubled and Feller himself lined a single for what would prove the winning run. The next day Al Smith completed the much-needed sweep, again giving up one run in a 3–1 triumph.

In the series Indians batters totaled two doubles, no triples, and only Weatherly's home run. By contrast, as the Indians were finishing their series, the Tigers were hammering Philadelphia in a doubleheader by a combined score of 23–3. Rudy York and Hank Greenberg drove in five runs each in the first game, while York homered again in game two and added three more RBIs. Detroit recorded twenty-seven total hits, about as many as the Indians were getting in a week. Unless the Cleveland hitters found some pop in their bats, the decisive three games in the Motor City looked tilted in the Tigers' favor.

Chapter 14

UNCLE SAM WANTS YOU

O n the train ride to Detroit, the Indians had several important things to mull over. First and foremost, they had to think about the next three games in perhaps the most hostile environment they had ever encountered. The Tigers fans would be worked up to a frenzy and capable of all kinds of abuse, including physical. Every Cleveland player would have to find a means to ignore the taunts, insults, and flying objects. A daunting task, yet the team, in the midst of a stirring pennant race, could not let themselves be intimidated.

Another strong consideration was the bonus money for advancing to the World Series, $5,000–$6,000, by conservative estimates, for each participant. The Indians were competitors, but the lure of a sizable extra check for a long vacation or shiny new automobile surely weighed on their minds. In addition to their shares, the stars of the World Series could look forward to product endorsements and radio appearances. Winning a pennant did not happen every year, unless you were the Yankees. You had to grab the opportunity when it presented itself.

If that was not enough, each member of the club had to think about the approaching draft registration, slated for the middle of October. All males between twenty-one and thirty-five were man-dated to visit their local voting precinct and sign up. Local draft boards were forming in each ward, gathering applications and assigning serial numbers to the potential draftees. All numbers would be sent to Washington, where the national draft board had set up a lottery for the numbers. According to the *Cleveland News,* if the first number drawn happened to be, say, 430, all those with that number moved to first in line. A low or high serial number did not matter, as the random drawing set up the order of who got the initial calls.

The men who were in line early would receive draft questionnaires with multiple pages to complete. Among the questions were physical condition, dependents, income and property ownership, religious convictions, and ability to speak a foreign language. The draft classifications began with Class I-A, those who were fully qualified. Class I-B designated partial service due to physical limitations. The next class covered industrial and agricultural workers, whose jobs were considered essential to national defense. Those who had dependents, meaning wives, children, and parents, were next. The final class designated those completely unfit for military service.

For Major League ballplayers, the bachelors fit into Class A. The married men were in the dependent class, but a caveat existed for them. In the event of war with Germany, the likelihood of exemptions might rapidly decrease with the need for soldiers overseas. Eligible young men hoped the peacetime draft would stay as it was for the long term.

Thursday evening the Indians' train, carrying fifty-seven in the party (some wives were included), chugged into the downtown Detroit station. They were not surprised to witness about 1,000 Tiger fans waiting on the platform. The familiar chant of "Crybabies, crybabies" rang out from the crowd, along with tin horns and bells. A group of high school kids tossed a ripe batch of eggs and tomatoes at the visitors. With the exception of Lefty Weisman, who took an egg to the shoulder, everyone in the party successfully ducked into the cabs outside.

The team arrived safely at the Book-Cadillac Hotel, but was exasperated to find that not only had most of the unwelcoming crowd followed, but through some channel they knew which side of the hotel the players and coaches were staying at. Aided by megaphones, which they handled in shifts, the mob kept up the loud taunts for several hours. Several of the Indians retaliated by filling ice buckets with water and dumping the contents from several stories high. The opening salvos had been fired.

Late the following morning, when the Indians arrived at Briggs Stadium, they found eight policemen surrounding their dugout. A long afternoon was about to take place. Oscar Vitt let his pitchers and catchers know there might be Tiger spies in the outfield stands ready to pick off their signals and relay them to the Detroit bench. To thwart them, Vitt ordered his men to change signals every inning.

The fans filed in and slowly took their places in the grandstand, many of them carrying baby bottles and infant clothing. Here and there were clotheslines strung up with doll clothes and bottles, another attempt to rattle the visitors. When Ben Chapman led off for Cleveland, a fan jumped out of the lower stands and pushed a baby carriage to home plate. Minutes later, another well-meaning person leaned over the railing next to the Indians dugout and tried to dump a pile of baby clothes on the bench. The police moved in quickly to stop him. The Detroit fans had done their level best. Now it was time for their team to do the same.

The two clubs had identical records of eighty-five wins and sixty-one defeats. In Greenberg and York, the Tigers had two of the most prodigious sluggers in either league. The Indians had one home run hitter in Trosky, but their strength was a tremendous pitching staff. Bob Feller led all pitchers on the two teams, along with a great supporting cast of Milnar, Smith, and Harder. Good pitching against good hitting: an ideal matchup for the two finest clubs in the American League.

The Detroit weather cooperated, featuring sunny skies and short-sleeves weather for the 22,508 in attendance, including a thousand fans from Cleveland. Buck Newsom got the assignment for Detroit, facing the Indians' September ace Mel Harder. The game went scoreless until the top of the third inning. Roy Weatherly stroked a double, then crossed home plate on Lou Boudreau's RBI single. In the bottom of the fourth, the Tigers evened the score when Charlie Gehringer walked, Hank Greenberg singled, and Rudy York hit a sacrifice fly.

The Indians came right back in the top of the fifth with two more runs, bunching together three singles and a sacrifice fly from Boudreau to take the lead at 3–1. An inning later they made it 4–1 on Beau Bell's double and a ringing base hit by Ken Keltner. That ended Newsom's day, replaced by Clay Smith.

Using sharp-breaking curveballs that darted across the corner of the plate, Mel Harder kept the Detroit hitters baffled. They could nick him for only three singles through seven innings. After the game, Greenberg would tell the thirty-two sportswriters gathered from around the country that he never saw a better performance from a Major League pitcher. His teammates were attempting to blast Harder from the mound, he said, but they could not do so.

In the bottom of the eighth, Tigers pinch hitter Billy Sullivan grounded out. Barney McCosky then worked Harder for a walk, and Gehringer singled, bringing manager Vitt out to the mound for a conference. He talked things over with his pitcher, then signaled to the center-field bullpen for a righty. More than a few people were caught off guard when the gate opened and Bob Feller jogged onto the field, the same Bob Feller who had pitched complete games on Sunday and Wednesday. Vitt may have been in panic mode, calling for his ace with barely one day's rest. Of course, Feller was a gamer, ready and willing to pitch on a moment's notice. But the second-guessers had a field day, believing Feller could not possibly be ready to pitch well after throwing eighteen tough innings in four days.

While Greenberg waited for Feller to complete his warmup tosses, fans stood or moved to the edge of their seats. It was do-or-die time. The pennant could hinge on every pitch. Greenberg stepped in to the batter's box and took strike one from Feller. The Indians pitcher checked the runners, then delivered home once more. Greenberg took a big swing and lined the ball to center field for a base hit. McCosky scored and Gehringer sped around to third. Rudy York lined a single to right, scoring Gehringer. When outfielder Beau Bell fumbled the ball, Greenberg raced all the way home, and York to advanced to second. Pinky Higgins rapped the third base straight hit off Feller, scoring York with the go-ahead run. Out came Vitt, signaling for Joe Dobson to replace his best pitcher, who simply had nothing on the ball. The beleaguered manager had bet the house on Feller and come up empty, leaving him open to serious criticism that just might send him on a one-way ticket to California. The walls were closing in.

Dobson ran into trouble immediately, giving up two more hits, including a pinch hit single by none other than Bruce Campbell. The huge five-run inning ended with the Tigers now leading the ball game 6–4. Cleveland had one last chance in the ninth inning, but would have to beat up ace reliever Al Benton.

Ben Chapman led things off with a popup in foul territory for out number one. As he slowly walked back to the dugout, a Detroit fan taunted him. Chapman shouted back, escalating the confrontation enough for a policeman to vault into the lower stands and place the heckler back in his seat. Another moment or two and there might have been a terrific fight.

Roy Weatherly kept Cleveland's hopes alive by smashing a double, his third hit of the afternoon. Lou Boudreau came through with his third hit, driving home Weatherly and cutting the margin to one run. While the Detroit crowd held their collective breaths, Hal Trosky drilled a single to right field, sending Boudreau all the way to third. Hearts were pounding all around the stadium as Beau Bell stood at home plate. Bell had been a disappointment all season, never regaining his batting form from several years back. At this moment he had a chance to redeem himself and become an all-time Indians hero. Unfortunately, Al Benton's sixteen saves were not a fluke. He bore down on the Indians hitter, striking out Bell. With two outs, Ken Keltner represented the last gasp for Cleveland. He already had three hits and had driven in a run in the sixth inning. He made contact, but hit an easy grounder for out number three. The Tigers had rallied to take the first of three, 6–5.

The Indians quietly shuffled through the dugout on their way to the locker room. The umpires had to use the same route to reach their dressing room. Talk about being in the wrong place at the wrong time. Jeff Heath found himself shoulder to shoulder with home plate umpire Bill McGowan. Heath turned and berated the ump for some questionable calls against the Cleveland pitchers. The argument grew in intensity, resulting in umpire Bill Summers getting between the two and threatening Heath with a fine and suspension. One of the Tigers pulled the furious ballplayer away before he started throwing punches. Rumors later spread that Heath had indeed socked McGowan, but no witnesses were available to

BAD BOYS, BAD TIMES

comment. McGowan did file a report with the American League office, resulting in a fifty-dollar fine for Heath.

Inside the Indians locker room sportswriters noticed the complete silence. Nobody hummed in the shower or went around slapping backs. Mel Harder sat in front of his locker, head bowed, mumbling to himself. When reporters sought him out, Harder answered the questions diplomatically. He refused to place blame on his manager or anyone else for the backbreaking loss. Feller did much the same, telling reporters he did not have his usual stuff but tried his best to extinguish the big Tiger rally.

The Cleveland papers, as expected, were all over the story of the crucial defeat. Ed McAuley somewhat defended Oscar Vitt by insisting that if Feller had retired the side, the Cleveland fans would be nominating Ol' Os for manager of the year. He asserted that Vitt played the percentages in using his number one pitcher to get five outs and save the ball game. It backfired, but that was baseball.

McAuley later changed direction, asserting that if the Indians lost the pennant Vitt's move would be known as the "$500,000 bum guess." He added that Feller and Harder spoke well to the press, but were bitter about the moves made. Another player, who asked for his name to be withheld, said, "He [Vitt] had no business taking out a pitcher who had allowed only four hits in eight innings. As it turned out, Feller wasn't only wasted yesterday the work he did may take something away from his performance Sunday."

Gordon Cobbledick had much to articulate in his *Plain Dealer* column. Normally a sportswriter who examined all sides of an issue, he came down hard on Oscar Vitt. Cobbledick alluded to the June 12 player meeting with Alva Bradley. He reminded his readers that one of the team's grievances was the allegation their manager had no confidence in the players. This was revealed when Vitt pulled Harder out of the game even though he still had command and a three-run lead. It backed up what the club had been saying all along. Mel Harder was a four-time All-Star, one of the most dependable pitchers in all of baseball. Throughout September he had pitched extremely well, fully conscious of the importance of each game. For Vitt to make the move he did spoke volumes.

What did the losing manager have to say? While reporters crowded around him, Vitt, naturally, defended himself. "If I had the same situation to deal with tomorrow I'd do exactly the same thing." He insisted Harder was too tired and with Greenberg and York due up he could not gamble on his pitcher going any further. Vitt claimed he had nobody in the bullpen he thought enough of to handle such a precarious situation. He picked Feller, knowing the risk involved.

Tris Speaker had made the trip to Detroit with the ball club. Asked for his observations, he replied, "Bob seemed to be in good form but the Tigers just dug in and swung as if they knew what was coming with every pitch. It looked like batting practice." Though two games were left to play in the series, Cleveland writers and fans would remember this game for a long, long, time.

On Saturday Al Milnar faced off against Schoolboy Rowe. Through four quick innings neither side mounted any kind of a threat. The 42,320 Tiger fans generally behaved themselves, except for the usual "Crybaby" chants and some scattered lemons thrown at Frankie Pytlak. In the home half of the fifth, right fielder Pete Fox doubled and pitcher Rowe drove him in with a single for the first run of the game. A throwing error by Ken Keltner led to the second run. Detroit added two more in the sixth on another double by Fox, and a single by Birdie Tebbetts. Milnar finished the inning and went no further. The Indians never threatened, losing game two 5–0. Schoolboy Rowe allowed only five scattered hits in increasing the Tigers' lead to two games. Sunday loomed as the most pivotal game of the season. Cleveland would leave town either one or three games behind.

A massive crowd of 56,771, the third-largest in Detroit history, packed the stands for game three. The burning question was whether Bob Feller had enough left to stop the Tigers from sweeping. Tommy Bridges opened the game for Detroit, throwing a variety of soft stuff to keep the Indians off balance. It worked for an inning. Hal Trosky, leading off the second, had to dodge a barrage of lemons at home plate, but they didn't keep him from belting a home run off the top of the right-field foul pole. Frankie Pytlak capped off the inning with a double that scored two more runs for a 3–0 margin.

Cleveland increased the lead in the third when Roy Weatherly homered and Beau Bell doubled to score two more. Feller did not have his overpowering fastball, but pitched well enough to win his twenty-seventh game of the year, 10–5. All told, the Indians walloped five home runs, with additional solo shots from Chapman, Keltner, and Feller, his second clout of the season. A happy ball club rode the train back to Cleveland now a game out of first with five more to play. They had two games at home with St. Louis, then a rematch with the Tigers to determine the American League championship.

The Indians took a much-needed day off on Monday, recharging their batteries as much as possible. They had to be cautious not to look past the St. Louis Browns. The Browns were not going to lie down, starting Elden Auker and Vern Kennedy, the two pitchers who had shut down Cleveland in the Labor Day doubleheader. Mel Harder opposed Auker in the first game, which developed into another pitcher's battle. The score was tied 2–2 going into the Indians' half of the sixth. With two out and a runner on third, Vitt rolled the dice, sending Jeff Heath to the plate to pinch hit for Harder. He got his bat on the ball but grounded out to end the inning. Harry Eisenstat, pitching the top of the seventh, found himself in trouble from the get go. He allowed two important runs before retiring the side and giving way to Johnny Allen. St. Louis, led by outfielder Ray "Rip" Radcliffe, scored three more times against Allen to upset the Indians, 7–2. Auker, now being labeled a bona fide jinx by the Cleveland sportswriters, won his fifteenth game of the season, five of those wins against the Indians. With Detroit taking the day off, the Indians back another half game.

On Wednesday the Tigers played a doubleheader against the Chicago White Sox, while the Indians resumed play against the Browns. With their backs to the wall, the Indians managed to score four early runs to top the Browns 4–2 and stay in the race. At the end of the game the players raced to the clubhouse to catch the Detroit broadcast of the White Sox–Tigers doubleheader. They bunched up around the radio, sitting on the training tables and traveling trunks and leaning against the wall. The pitchers yelled out what to throw the Tiger hitters as if the White Sox hurlers could hear them.

The first game went to Detroit in extra innings 10–9. The nightcap stood at 2–1 Chicago heading to the bottom of the eighth. Up came Hank Greenberg, who bashed his forty-first home run, tying the game at two apiece. That blow completely knocked the enthusiasm out of the Indians clubhouse. The players listened silently as the Tigers scored one more time to put themselves two games ahead in the standings with three to play. To claim the pennant, Vitt and his team would have to sweep the series beginning on Friday.

Detroit had a special train booked to bring them into Cleveland on Thursday evening. Word got to the Tiger players about plans for a special greeting that would take place at the Terminal Tower moments after the train pulled in and the traveling party walked the steps to the concourse. Several hundred Cleveland fans had plotted to ambush the players with a variety of fruits and vegetables, payback for the Indians' reception a week ago in Detroit.

Cleveland civic leaders, Mayor Burton, and Alva Bradley all had messages printed in the newspapers urging fans to be good sports and leave all the edibles behind. The Come-to-Cleveland Committee issued a statement that read, "We think it would be a fine thing for a crowd to go to the terminal tonight, meet our friends from Detroit and give them a big hand." It seemed that the fans forgot to read the Thursday newspapers and were preparing to give the friends from a Detroit much more than a big hand.

The Tiger players hashed out a plan of their own. They would stop the train at the Linndale station, on the near west side of Cleveland, and take taxis to the Hotel Cleveland. In the end the team decided to ride into Cleveland and attempt to run the gauntlet.

Franklin Lewis rode with the Tigers, collecting material for a feature in the *Cleveland Press*. He observed that the Detroit club was loose and relaxed, primed to settle the pennant race and go on to face Cincinnati in the World Series. Lewis reported that as the train arrived, Schoolboy Rowe took it upon himself to disembark first, walk toward the concourse, and scout ahead. As he climbed up the steps leading to the main level, he spotted the large crowd with enough objects to pelt the entire team. He scurried back down the steps to warn his teammates and the Briggs family, who were traveling with them. Pete Fox, Buck Newsom, and Hank Greenberg defiantly climbed the steps, but were forced to fall back under heavy fire.

One of the railway workers let the team know that there was a freight elevator near their train, mostly hidden from view. Taking the elevator down would let them go farther underground and reach a tunnel that led to an escape two blocks from the hotel. The entire party crammed themselves into the elevator, down the tunnel, and away from the hostile crowd. They were able to reach the Hotel Cleveland safely.

The Friday game at Municipal Stadium drew an excellent afternoon crowd of 45,553 fans. To ensure a raucous crowd, Bradley declared the game Ladies Day, which brought 18,000 enthusiastic women ready to do their part to secure a victory. The ladies walked through Gate C bringing lunches along, including not only sandwiches but fruits and vegetables, which they had no intention of eating. As the ladies settled into their left-field seats, some of the Tiger players jogged to the outfield to loosen up their throwing arms. Within moments a random lemon or two arched from the stands in the general direction of Earl Averill and Hank Greenberg in shallow left field. Greenberg saw some humor in the debris, picking up a lemon and gently tossing it back to the seats. The ladies considered that an affront and littered the field with dozens of tomatoes and eggs.

The grounds crew used rakes and wheelbarrows to remove the smashed items in time for the game to start. As the cleanup was under way, Del Baker, the Tigers manager, called his veteran players together for a conference. He had Schoolboy Rowe ready to face Bob Feller, but was considering giving him another day's rest. He talked it over with his vets, who all agreed that they might not be able to beat Feller this afternoon. Even if they lost today, they still had two games to clinch the flag. Why not throw another pitcher to the wolves?

The meeting ended with the starting assignment going to Floyd Giebell, who had been recalled from Buffalo just two weeks before. He had fared well in his first start, against Philadelphia, earning him a chance to go against Cleveland. Baker was in effect conceding the game to Feller and the Indians, letting Rowe and Newsom rest their arms for Saturday and Sunday. The home team did not know they were facing Giebell until fifteen minutes before the game. They had the drawback of not being familiar with the obscure pitcher and having to learn what he threw when at bat.

On the positive side, Giebell had little Major League experience and might fold under pressure. In a few minutes the world would find out.

Feller retired the Tigers in the top of the first. In the home half Roy Weatherly lifted a lazy fly ball to left field. As Greenberg circled under it, a tremendous volley of fruit and vegetables plus remnants of lunches came soaring and landed at his feet. Apples, oranges, tomatoes, and eggs littered the field in a quantity never seen before in organized baseball. The game was stopped for the grounds crew to grab their rakes and wheelbarrows and again clean the field.

Home plate umpire Bill Summers went to the public address system and announced to the crowd, "Ladies and Gentlemen, the management of the Detroit ball club will remove their team from the field if the throwing does not stop. Every time a fly ball is hit and a Detroit player is interfered with the umpires will call the batter out." His words were partially drowned out by the booing from the crowd.

When the game resumed, the Indians were retired and took the field for the Tigers to come to bat. Meanwhile, an army of Cleveland police and plainclothes detectives scoured the stands in search of potential troublemakers. They did not see an individual or possibly several men in the left-field upper deck holding half a crate of tomatoes. The crate was tossed over the railing directly above the Tiger bullpen. In a million-to-one shot, it gathered speed and landed smack on the head of catcher Birdie Tebbetts, knocking him unconscious. The cops raced to the spot where the crate was tossed and arrested Carmen Guerra, a twenty-five-year-old neighborhood iceman. They hustled him around the concourse and past the players' entrances toward the locker rooms. For some unknown reason, the door to the Tigers locker room stood wide open. As the police and suspect passed by, one of the Detroit players yelled, causing several teammates, including a revived Tebbetts, to charge out the door and throw punches at Guerra. Several were landed before the police could restore order and get him outside to a patrol car.

That should have been the end of things. However, in the stands a Cleveland fan and a visitor from Detroit started an ugly fight that ended with a bottle smashed over the Tiger fan's skull. Police again intervened, breaking up the brawl and sending the heavily bleeding man to Charity Hospital. Sportswriters later wrote they had never seen such mayhem in all their years covering baseball. The game turned into a literal black eye for the city.

Meanwhile a ball game was still being played on the field. Leading off the bottom of the third inning, Ray Mack reached first on an error. Rollie Hemsley lined a single, sending Mack to third and setting up a grand opportunity to get a run home. With the pressure on, Floyd Giebell pitched like a seasoned veteran, striking out Feller to get the first out. That brought up Ben Chapman, needing just a base hit or a fly ball deep enough to score Mack. Again Giebell proved up to the task, fanning Chapman. He finished the inning by retiring Roy Weatherly on a fly out. The Indians' failure to get on the scoreboard gave the young Detroit hurler a big shot of confidence.

In the top of the fourth inning, the Tigers had a man aboard with two out and Rudy York coming to bat. Feller delivered, and the first baseman hit a high fly ball down the left-field foul line. Ben Chapman sped over to the corner, but the ball carried into the first row of the seats in fair territory, just 330 feet from the plate, barely out of Chapman's reach. The lazy fly ball turned into a clutch home run for Detroit, giving them a 2–0 lead. York's thirty-third homer put the Indians in come-from-behind mode with five innings yet to play.

In the fifth inning Cleveland had an excellent chance to get back in the ball game when Rollie Hemsley led off with a base hit and reached second on a wild pitch. Feller worked Giebell for a well-earned walk, setting the stage for the top of the order to even up the game. Once again Ben Chapman stood in the batter's box, facing a pitcher with almost no Major League experience. To the fans' utter disbelief, Chapman struck out for the second time. Roy Weatherly, enjoying a career season, had another shot to cut into the lead. Despite the deafening sound from the crowd, all the center fielder could muster was a medium fly ball for the second out. Lou Boudreau represented the last hope, but Giebell won the battle by fanning him and ending the promising inning.

The innings went by too quickly for the charged-up home crowd. They watched Feller mow down the Tigers, his only gaffe being the short Rudy York home run earlier in the game. In the Cleveland half of the seventh, Ray Mack hit a screaming line drive off Giebell's glove for an infield hit. Hemsley stroked a routine ground ball that Charlie Gehringer booted, putting runners at first and second. Feller dropped down a sacrifice bunt, moving both runners into scoring position with only one out. Ben Chapman had his third chance of the afternoon to bring the runners home. Giebell wound up and did his best Bob Feller imitation, unbelievably fanning Chapman a third straight time. Roy Weatherly had another opportunity to be a hero, but, as the fans clenched their fists and yelled encouragement, Stormy grounded out to third. The statistics later revealed that the Indians' first and second hitters between them left an incredible twelve men on base.

The bottom of the ninth rolled around, making thousands of hearts beat rapidly. Three outs to go for Giebell to pull off one of the great upsets in baseball history. Ray Mack batted first and hit a fly ball to McCosky in center field. Hemsley, who had hit the ball well all day, pounded a ground ball to Pinky Higgins for the second out. Manager Vitt called Feller back to the bench, sending Jeff Heath in to hit. The Cleveland players watched grimly, hoping for something good to happen. Giebell delivered and Heath hit a harmless ground ball to end the game.

In front of some 45,000 people in the most pressure-packed game of the entire season, little-known Floyd Giebell won his second start, propelling the Detroit Tigers to the World Series. The silence could be heard in every corner of massive Cleveland Stadium. The Indians were presented with an ideal scenario, needing only to win a game against a seldom-used pitcher whose only win had come against last-place Philadelphia. Even with the Tigers willing to concede the game, the Cleveland players failed to take advantage. The team could blame nobody but themselves for getting shut out at home, ending their quest for their first pennant in twenty years. The one consolation for the players was the second-place money of $1,500 per man. A nice bonus, yet far from the World Series money that had fallen just outside their grasp.

In analyzing the Indians' tumultuous season, a few notable things stand out. Lou Boudreau had an excellent year, batting .295 with 185 hits, 46 doubles, and 101 RBIs. His defense at shortstop bordered on spectacular, as he made plays other infielders could only dream about. Ray Mack hit well all season, ending with a .283 batting average, 12 home runs, and 69 RBIs. Together with Boudreau, he gave the Indians unbeatable defense up the middle. At third base, Ken Keltner had a good, not great year, hitting .254 along with 15 homers and 77 RBIs. These three young infielders had a huge role in keeping the Indians fighting for the pennant.

Bob Feller led American League pitchers in almost every category: wins, 27; ERA, 2.61; innings pitched, 320⅓; and strikeouts, 261. With the season on the line, on September 27 he pitched a complete game with two runs and three hits allowed. In most instances, that performance would have been enough to win.

The Indians finished 11–11 against Detroit, a good enough number, but had the same record against the St. Louis Browns. To split with a seventh-place team is a key example of not getting the job done. In September Cleveland lost three out of four to the Browns, including the Labor Day doubleheader. This fact alone went a long way to explaining why the Indians failed to grab first place. Of their last thirty games they could only win half, including three losses to St. Louis and a 3–6 record against Detroit. If one adds these things together, it is not difficult to see why the Indians had to settle for a second-place finish. They could not put the entire blame for their troubles directly on Oscar Vitt's shoulders. There were other shoulders available, including Ben Chapman, who fanned three times in the crucial game against Floyd Giebell; Jeff Heath, who had a dismal season, batting an anemic .219 with 14 home runs and only 50 RBIs; and Frankie Pytlak, who in part-time duty had a strong September but overall batted .141, by far a career low. The Indians bullpen showed inconsistency throughout the season, blowing too many leads during crunch time. The end came at the hands of a Detroit pitcher who would not win another game in his short-lived Major League career.

Chapter 15

GOODBYE TO OL' OS

At the end of a most trying season, the Cleveland play-ers packed their belongings and scattered to various parts of the country. Oscar Vitt loaded his automobile for the cross-country trip back to California. Before departing, he attempted to meet with Alva Bradley, hoping to learn about his status for 1941. Bradley had few words to say, letting his manager hang in limbo while he set off for a leisurely three-week vacation to an island off the Georgia coast. On Bradley's return he would schedule a meeting of his shareholders to sit down and determine Vitt's fate. Betting men likely had their cash riding on a new manager for the upcoming year. Vitt began his journey home anxious and unsure if he would ever see Cleveland again.

On October 16, while Vitt bided his time in California, National Registration Day began processing would-be soldiers throughout the United States. The draft offices opened at 7:00 a.m. and remained open until 9:00 p.m., allowing working men ample time to sign up. Bob Feller, after driving all night from Van Meter, proceeded immediately to the out-of-towners registration post on Euclid Avenue downtown. Feller, like every other eligible male, patiently stood in line waiting for his turn at the registration table. Photographers got his photo, wearing a well-tailored suit and later displaying his shiny new draft card for posterity. Mel Harder and former Indian Joe Vosmik reported to their assigned station in University Heights, a middle-class suburb on Cleveland's east side, though without a crowd, reporters, or photographers accompanying them. They and all the eligible ballplayers in the American and National League signed up, uncertain what the future would hold.

Major League owners combed over their rosters, struggling to figure out how many players were likely to don military uniforms in the coming months. After some study, they determined that the majority of their rosters were married men with dependents and thus should be spared from service. Among the bachelors, some of the important names included Hank Greenberg and Barney McCosky of Detroit, Jim Tabor of Boston, Hank Leiber of the Chicago Cubs, Max West of the Boston Bees, and of course Bob Feller. It would be up to the draft boards to decide, but in the case of Feller he had an ill father, a mother, and a younger sister to take care of, which probably indicated a deferment. The draft lottery was scheduled for October 29, and soon after that date a resolution of status would follow. At this point the Indians and Tigers had the most at risk.

On October 28, the contract of the beleaguered Oscar Vitt expired. With little fanfare, Alva Bradley met with the press and announced that Vitt's contract would not be renewed. A search for a new manager commenced immediately, with names such as Bucky Harris, Mickey Cochrane, and coach Luke Sewell bandied about. For his part, Vitt expressed no surprise. He had already had a strong feeling that his tenure had ended. Earlier in the month he had claimed that the front office, particularly Cy Slapnicka, did not have his back. He cited the argument with Jeff Heath during the St. Louis game and the interference from the general manager to stop any fine or suspension. Slapnicka strongly denied the allegation, but Vitt may have had a point. Regardless, the deed was done and Vitt's days in Cleveland were a memory.

While Oscar Vitt resumed managing in the minor leagues, at no time did he ever coach or manage again in the Major Leagues. That in itself strongly suggests that the Indians' players were correct in their assertion that Ol' Os was not the man for the job.

About two weeks later Alva Bradley hired Roger Peckinpaugh to manage Cleveland in 1941. "Peck" had been the first manager chosen by Bradley when he bought the club in late 1927. His tenure ran through the middle of the 1933, when the owner decided on a change, firing Peck to bring in Walter Johnson. The firing notwithstanding, Bradley and Peck remained friendly, staying in touch and often playing golf together on Cleveland's east side. Apparently Bradley now wanted a manager who supported the players and never criticized them in public.

Peck signed a two-year deal for $12,000 per year. The papers asked the new manager why he took the job for a second time. He succinctly replied, "Vitt is gone now so I don't see why a new manager would have any difficulties." Bradley later made sure Peck's statement held true by asking waivers on Johnny Allen, then sending him to St. Louis, far away from Cleveland. In the coming months, several more headaches would be traded, essentially giving Peck a clean slate.

Heading to the winter meetings, American League president Will Harridge proudly announced record attendance numbers for 1940. Total figures reached 5,443,791, up over 1,000,000 fans from 1939. Night games were an important factor in the approximately 25 percent increase. The Indians were second in average attendance for night games, with an impressive 30,159 over seven games. Only the Chicago White Sox had a slightly better number. In total attendance, Cleveland had great numbers, drawing 902,576, their highest total since 1920. Of course, the pennant race had brought extra fans to League Park and Municipal Stadium; however, Bradley had labored hard to spark more interest from fans. His plan to build lights for night baseball and his goodwill in promoting the game via Ladies Day certainly paid off in establishing a strong market for baseball.

Bradley and his front office traveled to Chicago to take part in the early December winter meetings. The first order of business was re-electing Commissioner Judge Landis to another term. Even with the recent dismantling of the Tigers farm system and various other rulings, the owners were unanimous in returning the Judge and his $47,000 salary.

A lively debate took place regarding the number of night games teams were allowed to schedule. Don Barnes of the Browns and Connie Mack of the Athletics proposed increasing the number from seven to fourteen. Both clubs were lagging behind in attendance and believed additional night games would help increase revenues. The owners were divided on the issue. The naysayers considered the games nothing more than novelties to pique fans' interest and maintained that playing more than seven times might result in poor attendance. Mack argued, as Bradley had done two years ago, that 90 percent of the population was available for night games, compared to just 10 percent for weekday afternoons. The vote tally was four votes yes (including Bradley) and four votes no. Judge Landis broke the tie by ruling that night games must remain at seven and no more. Bradley stated that his vote supported the Browns and A's owners, but he had no intention of adding more night contests even if approved.

The owners announced a continuation of the Hall of Fame exhibition game, planned for June 13 in Cooperstown. The Indians were selected to play against the Cincinnati Reds, the current World Series champs. Getting the thumbs down was the Finnish Relief Fund game, held the previous year in Florida. The owners reckoned that since some of the teams trained in California, it would be foolish to send representatives across the entire country and back again.

At the end of the meetings, the Indians completed a big six-player swap with the Boston Red Sox. Cleveland sent Frankie Pytlak, Joe Dobson, and Sammy Hale to Boston in exchange for catcher Gene Desautels, pitcher Jim Bagby Jr., and outfielder Gerry "Gee" Walker. Sending away perennial holdout Pytlak and aging vet Hale made the deal addition by subtraction. The Indians received a young prospect in Bagby Jr., the son of Jim Bagby, the pitching star of Cleveland's 1920 world champions. Desautels could handle himself behind the plate, and the team believed Walker would be an upgrade in right field.

To make room for Walker, the club sent Ben Chapman, a disappointment in his two years with the team, to Washington for pitcher Joe Krakauskas, a four-year veteran with a losing record. The Canadian hurler figured to be a spot starter at best. All the changes morphed the club into a quieter, gentler organization. Only one potential headache remained in Jeff Heath, but he would later announce at spring training a rededication to baseball and his teammates. Whether new manager Peckinpaugh could count on it remained to be seen.

The new year of 1941 helped the Cleveland ball club shake off the effects of the divisive episodes of the previous campaign. On January 21, Bob Feller visited the League Park offices to sign a new contract for $30,000, the highest salary ever handed to a pitcher, eclipsing the previous record of $27,500 paid out to Lefty Grove. Rollie Hemsley negotiated a contract calling for $16,000, the highest salary ever paid to an Indians catcher. The residual effects of a strong revenue season were apparent in that few of the returning players had any difficulty in accepting their contract offers. As spring training approached, a wealth of optimism seemed to surround the club.

The enthusiasm for the new season jumped tenfold when the news came regarding Feller's draft status. The Cleveland board announced that he would not receive his selective service questionnaire until at least July 4. Estimates on processing forms revealed that the chances of Feller being called before October appeared remote at best. Of the 3,866 men who registered in the pitcher's district, Feller ranked at 2,857, putting him in one of the final groups to be contacted. Hal Trosky and Rollie Hemsley were classified III-A, meaning an exemption for family men with one or more children at home. Several Indians had classifications of I-A, meaning immediately available for service, but other than Beau Bell, they did not figure prominently in the Indians' plans. Jim Hegan, a highly regarded young catcher in the Indians camp, had yet to reach his twenty-first birthday, leaving him completely out of the draft system. Manager Peckinpaugh had few worries about losing any of his vital players for the duration of the regular season.

At the end of February the pitchers and catchers reported to Fort Myers for their second preseason in the southern Florida city. Alva Bradley and Cy Slapnicka presented the club with a terrific perk, a three-day trip to Cuba to play exhibitions against the Brooklyn Dodgers. The trip was scheduled for the weekend of March 7 through March 9, and players would be allowed to bring along their wives and children. Lew Mumaw, the Indians' traveling secretary, handled all the arrangements. The team would take several chartered buses to Miami, then board a steamer for Havana. Due to the war in Europe, travel regulations had been tightened, resulting in a huge pile of paperwork being necessary for the entire party.

Forms needed to be completed for every person planning to take part, including birthplace of each individual, proof of citizenship, residence information, and a host of other details. The entire trip had to be cleared through Washington and even Canada, where Joe Krakauskas still maintained his residence. In addition, a total of fifty-seven Indians fans made the trip to Fort Myers, receiving permission to accompany the team to Cuba. Lou Mumaw labored overtime to get all the paperwork in order so the ball club could leave the country.

Jack Graney, Pinky Hunter, and several engineers boarded the ship, awaiting the completion of preparations to broadcast Saturday's game back to the United States and Canada. The plan was to have a live hookup from Havana's Tropical Stadium, from which a shortwave signal would be sent to an RCA station in Marblehead, Long Island, New York. The signal would then be relayed to Mutual Studios in New York City, where the broadcast would become available to 175 stations across the United States and 34 in Canada. On the shortwave band alone, stations in Europe and South America had the equipment necessary to pick up the game. Graney had done some national broadcasting previously, but sending a game from Cuba was a definite first.

On the trip south the Atlantic Ocean was calm, allowing players and wives to dance to the orchestra music under a beautiful moonlit night. Rollie Hemsley danced with his eleven-year-old daughter Joan for most of the evening. Adding to the thrill of taking a cruise to Cuba, there were no reported cases of seasickness.

On arrival the players reported to Tropical Stadium, where they underwent a demanding two-hour workout. Afterwards the players were free to ride back to the Hotel Presidente, gather their wives, and take in the sights. A group of players including Harder, Boudreau, and Keltner hailed a cab, looking for the nearest cigar factory. When they got there they were amused to find that the factory workers were only interested in meeting the great Bob Feller. The players loaded up on the much-preferred Havana cigars.

On Friday afternoon Cleveland met the Brooklyn Dodgers in the first of the three scheduled exhibition games. Clearly the Indians' minds were on other things, as they fell by a lopsided score of 15–0. The Cuban fans had to be disappointed by the lack of effort, but must have been buoyed by the knowledge that Feller would pitch part of Saturday's game.

After the defeat, the players dressed quickly, excited about an evening in downtown Havana. They had several choices for the night agenda, such as the Grand Casino Nacional, the spectacular Tropicana night club, or the aptly named Sloppy Joe's, where they could down the finest rum. They could worry about redeeming themselves the next day, when a tremendous crowd was anticipated.

Unfortunately, Saturday brought a fierce tropical storm, washing out the game and confining the Cleveland traveling party to their hotel. Along with the postponement went the worldwide broadcast of the afternoon exhibition. Graney and his staff had traveled all the way from Cleveland to Miami then on to Cuba only to see their historic broadcast canceled by the driving rain.

On Sunday the teams played a doubleheader, making up the rainout and giving the fans what they wanted; a closeup look at Bob Feller. A crowd of 15,000 watched Feller pitch three shaky innings, allowing three runs but striking out Joe Medwick with two outs and two runners on base. That seemed enough for the fans, who relished the rare chance to see the most talked-about pitcher in the Major Leagues. The Indians won the first game 8–4 behind the hard hitting of Jeff Heath and Ken Keltner. In game two Peck let all the second-stringers and camp invitees play, resulting in a surprisingly well-played 3–0 loss. The trip not only helped promote goodwill among the Cuban people but gave the Indians' traveling party a huge adventure. Sunday evening everybody boarded the steamer, immigration cards and souvenirs in hand, for the voyage north to Miami.

The team had barely unpacked their bags when out of the blue Alva Bradley issued a heated statement to the press. Though a new season loomed around the corner, several out-of-town writers and columnists were still publishing annoying references to the crybabies of 1940. Writers including Bob Considine, in a feature for *Esquire* magazine, Bill Dooley of the *Philadelphia Record,* and Roy Stockton of the *St. Louis Post-Dispatch* chastised the players for their actions of nearly a year ago. Bradley had heard enough. "There is an inside story which if told will convince the harshest critic of the Tribe that the ball players were absolutely justified in their meetings of rebellion. And if my team is ridden this season I am going to tell the inside story, regardless of anyone's feelings. Already I see signs that some of Oscar Vitt's friends among the non-Cleveland newspapermen aren't willing to forget."

In one of his columns, Ed McAuley revealed that a meeting had taken place among the players as far back as 1939. The unnamed team members thought about going public to air their complaints about Vitt, but their plans for bashing him were dropped when Jeff Heath prematurely spoke to writers about players "popping off." McAuley intimated that a certain player had received an offer of a bonus from Vitt for completing a task, then never collected anything for his efforts. A few more tidbits came to Bradley's attention in August 1939, but he, wanting to immediately quell the unrest, hired Vitt as his manager for at least one more year. Usually he waited till the end of the season to evaluate, but in this instance he acted out of character, thinking his players would get the message and concentrate on playing ball rather than fighting with their manager.

The *News* reporter and the other Cleveland writers now backed the players unequivocally. They circled the wagons, so to speak, resolved to protect the players from any out-of-town scorn. The outside instigators of Cleveland heckling must have gotten the message, as at no time did Bradley reveal the inside story.

In early April the Indians abandoned Fort Myers to begin their annual barnstorming north of Florida. As they moved through the cities, the team received some welcome visitors from the past. Former Cleveland players Joe Sewell and Jim Bagby Sr. wished the team well, followed by a surprise visit from all-time great Ty Cobb. The players eagerly listened to stories and anecdotes told by baseball's finest hitter. Several months later the somewhat mellowed Cobb would land in Cleveland to help raise money for amateur baseball. Visits completed, the rest of the tour went smoothly, helping the club ready themselves for the April 15 home opener.

Ticket sales for the initial game went far beyond normal expectations. Team officials forecast a crowd, weather permitting, of over 40,000 fans, which, if accurate, would break the all-time Cleveland record. Many writers, local and national, selected Cleveland to win the pennant over Detroit and New York. The Indians lacked the best hitters in the American League, but looked to have the top pitching staff and defense among their rivals. That alone, the writers thought, would bring the Indians the much sought-after pennant.

WHK Radio prepared for another year of play-by-play, introducing a new program and a partnership with P.O.C. Beer. The new program, titled *Home Runs and Haircuts*, featured a live broadcast three days a week at 12:45 p.m. from the Gibson and Reninger Barber Shop in the Terminal Tower. Jack Graney hosted the show, interviewing folks about their views concerning the Indians. The best answers won a free haircut, shave, and shoeshine, easily a fifty-cent value.

The arrangement with Pilsener Brewing Company offered fans a P.O.C. Radio Baseball Score Board to follow along with Graney's broadcasts. The cardboard gimmick had a diamond with bases and space to keep track of hits, runs, innings, outs, errors, plus balls and strikes, and even double plays. The price was fifteen cents, and it could be purchased only through the Pilsener Company local plant or the WHK offices. No doubt thousands of young boys cajoled their parents for the purchase price and a stamp.

Graney was now considered one of the crack play-by-play broadcasters in all of the Major Leagues. Over the years he had developed unique methods to greatly enhance his listeners' enjoyment of recreated games. Early in the regular season Graney followed the out-of-town weather reports. If he knew it was a cold day where the Indians were playing, at the beginning of his studio broadcast he would ask his engineer to bring an overcoat. In games where the Indians starting pitcher was being hit hard, he would ask partner Pinky Hunter to get the glasses and see who might be warming up in the bullpen. Then they would mention a name or two as they waited for the teletype to let them know if a relief pitcher had entered the game. If they were right, Graney would say, Yes, so-and-so is coming into the game. If wrong, he would correct himself by saying, for instance, that he thought it was Eisenstat, but it was actually Johnny Allen. All of this banter led fans to forget that Graney was sitting comfortably in the WHK studios downtown.

April 15, opening day, rolled around with balmy temperatures and high, if not disproportionate, expectations. The newspapers included a detailed map for those attending the game on where to park and walk to the stadium. Municipal lots on the east and west side of the facility had capacity for 2,350 autos, plus a lot just off East 9th had room for an additional 1,000. No cars were allowed to park on St. Clair Avenue south, Ontario Street running to Public Square, and West 3rd going south. Ramps on West 3rd and East 9th heading north were available to all pedestrians not using buses, cars, or taxis.

A record crowd of 46,064 piled into Municipal Stadium wearing Indian headdresses and an array of colorful hats. The Indians and White Sox, in clean new uniforms, trotted out of their dugouts to start their usual pregame routines. In the middle of batting practice, a long drive in the stands was collared by a young fan who gave the ball to his girlfriend for a souvenir. Park police climbed into the stands, demanding the ball be returned to the field. The couple reluctantly parted with the ball in the midst of boos from nearby fans. Edgar Smith, one of the Chicago pitchers, picked up the controversial ball and tossed it toward the batting cage, then grabbed another practice ball, gazed at the policemen, and flipped it back to the young couple in the stands. This time the police shrugged and did nothing.

The huge assembly included a gentleman from Lake County who had not missed a home opener since the Cleveland Spiders of 1894. In addition, Ettore Boiardi, the Cleveland spaghetti and sauce maker and soon-to-be household name as Chef Boyardee, brought twenty-five excited young boys from the Bellefaire Orphanage. A group of fans, without any prompting, started a rendition of "God Bless America," a gesture to the terrible events overseas. Just about everybody in the stadium joined in on the song, displaying their patriotism in a spontaneous manner. Moments later a new tradition commenced with all in attendance rising for the singing of the national anthem. The commissioner's office and Major League Baseball believed the time had come for all fans to honor their country before the first pitch. At the conclusion a male possessing a tremendous set of lungs bellowed, "To Hell with Hitler!" The crowd roared its approval, the reality of the war in Europe never far from their thoughts even at a sporting event such as baseball.

Bob Feller opened the game by plunking Bill Knickerbocker on the arm for the first base runner of the season. He struck out Luke

Appling on three pitches, but Joe Kuhel walked and Moose Solters singled to left field, sending home Chicago's first tally. Feller pitched like his old teenage self. He would end up issuing seven bases on balls, including walking the bases loaded in the sixth inning. And in the second he hit White Sox pitcher Bill Dietrich with a sizzling fastball. Dietrich took several minutes to recover, then walked slowly back to the Chicago bench. Manager Peckinpaugh, after conferring with the umpires, gave his okay for the pitcher to take a seat and then return to the mound after a pinch runner took his place on the bases. Dietrich cleared his head and was able to complete the game, leading the White Sox over the Indians 4–3. The last Indians run scored in the bottom of the eighth inning when Ray Mack walloped a home run well over 400 feet, deep into the left-field seats. By an unlikely coincidence, a former amateur teammate of his jumped to his feet and made the catch between groups of fans diving for cover.

The opener went into the books as a loss, but the players and fans shrugged it off, knowing there were 153 games left on the schedule before all was said and done. Cleveland came back and won the next two when Al Milnar and Al Smith threw consecutive shutouts at League Park. The Indians then went on the road, playing their next series at the unfriendly confines of Briggs Stadium. This time, thankfully, the Tiger fans had no doll carriages or tomatoes and eggs with them.

In a demonstration of first-class baseball, Cleveland won two out of three games at Detroit, with Feller and Mel Harder taking their first victories of the season. Early results appeared to be positive, especially the new outfield, with Gee Walker in left field and Jeff Heath in right. Both were rapping out extra-base hits, taking some of the burden away from Trosky and Keltner. At the end of April the Indians were in the midst of a winning streak, pushing them into first place ahead of the Tigers and Yankees. They were a happy lot, demonstrating a harmony that had been sorely missing over the past three years.

Cleveland would eventually reel off eleven wins in a row, raising their record to a gaudy 16–4 before a loss on May 6. A week later the Indians were on the road, stopping in New York to face the hard-hitting Yankees. After Feller won the first game of the series,

Mel Harder, off to a terrific start, raised his mark to 4–0 with a complete-game six-hitter. New catcher Gene Desautels and Gee Walker supported Harder by belting solo home runs. In the top of the eighth Lou Boudreau singled, then jogged home on utility outfielder Clarence "Soup" Campbell's first Major League home run. The final score read 4–1 in favor of the Indians.

Joe DiMaggio went hitless in three at bats against Harder, but the next afternoon "Joltin' Joe" got a clean base hit, starting an improbable batting streak that is still talked about in the twenty-first century. Cleveland played a role at the beginning of the streak and would gain national attention two months later when DiMaggio and the Yankees visited Municipal Stadium.

Throughout the month of May, the Indians remained in excellent position for another run at the pennant. Leading the charge were Bob Feller and the man with a new attitude, Jeff Heath. On Sunday, May 25, St. Louis was in town for an afternoon game at Municipal Stadium. Heath came to bat in the top of the fourth against a familiar face in Johnny Allen. The pitch came and the fans heard a tremendous crack of the bat as the baseball was propelled deep to right field, about ten feet inside the foul line. With 20,000 mouths wide open, the ball landed far back in the upper deck of the right-field stands, the first time anybody had reached it in nine years of baseball at the stadium. Heath's monstrous shot eclipsed anything hit by sluggers of the past, such as Babe Ruth, Lou Gehrig, and current star Rudy York. Allen watched in stunned silence as Heath circled the bases with the longest home run the Cleveland fans had ever seen. Ken Keltner followed with a single, which was the last straw for the embarrassed Browns pitcher. Ray Mack, batting next, had to hit the deck as the first pitch came right at his ear.

Feller struck out thirteen St. Louis hitters for his ninth win of the early season as the Indians coasted to a 6–0 win. Heath added an RBI triple and a base hit. The Cleveland slugger had nine home runs already, tying Rudy York for the American League lead. His batting average soared to .355. Heath was having his best season since his full-time debut in 1938. It did not take a genius to explain the about-face in his performance. A new manager letting him play his game made a world of difference to the right fielder. Happy days were here again.

On June 2 the baseball world and much of the United States mourned the loss of all-time great Lou Gehrig. One of the most loved and respected of all ballplayers, Gehrig succumbed to amyotrophic lateral sclerosis, which had forced him to retire two years earlier, ending his consecutive-game streak at 2,130.

Ed McAuley wrote a chilling column the day after, recalling a set of circumstances that happened on June 1, 1939. A month earlier Gehrig had voluntarily removed himself from the Yankee lineup, taking some time to rest and hopefully shake off the undiagnosed malady that prevented him from playing ball. He accompanied his team for their series with the Indians. At the same time, Yankees manager Joe McCarthy, who was scheduled to appear at a weekly luncheon attended by most of the Cleveland sportswriters, begged off, replaced by coach John Schulte. The *Plain Dealer* and *Cleveland Press* withdrew their reporters, but the *News* editor, unaware of the cancellation, sent Bob Kimball, a new writer. A question was asked about Gehrig's health, and Schulte candidly replied, "He's a sick man and he's going to the Mayo Clinic to find out what has been sapping his strength. We hope it's nothing serious although he doesn't look good now."

Kimball raced for a phone to call in the story to the paper. When McAuley arrived at the League Park press box a short time later, he got a message from his editor, probably Ed Bang, instructing him to get down on the field the moment New York completed batting practice and find out if the story was genuine. Gehrig was out in short right field, taking relay throws from the outfielders. McAuley scrambled to the Yankees dugout to wait for Gehrig to sit down. He cautiously approached the Iron Horse and gently asked if there was any truth to the story. Gehrig, without looking up, denied the account and said he felt fairly well.

Regardless, the *News* sent the story to the wire services, generating a small sensation around the country. The New York writers quickly refuted all the details, claiming the account was nothing but a bunch of rumors. The Yankees continued their road trip west, winding up in Chicago. Soon word came that Gehrig had indeed taken a flight to Minnesota for a thorough examination at the Mayo Clinic. Everything in the June 1 *Cleveland News* story was true.

In mid-June the Indians used a couple of days off for the annual Hall of Fame exhibition game at Cooperstown, New York. Peck started all the bench players, who played well enough for a 2–1 victory over the Cincinnati Reds. The diamond had been saturated throughout the morning, resulting in the game being halted after six mud-filled innings. The abbreviated exhibition was dedicated to the memory of Lou Gehrig, an appropriate gesture toward the man who had done so much for baseball. As the teams were ready to take the field, a musician played "Taps" in honor of Gehrig. His prominent Hall of Fame plaque had been draped over with black cloth. Though it was a somber occasion, a light moment took place when a small dog raced on the field, snagged the glove of Clarence Campbell, and took off for the countryside. A group of boys chased down the dog, which dropped the glove and raced away for parts unknown.

In the Indians' last game before they left for Cooperstown, they hosted the Washington Senators. In the bottom of the fourth inning, Senators pitcher Kendall Chase drilled Roy Weatherly with a fastball just above his ear. The fans clearly heard the sickening noise. Roy crumpled to the ground, unconscious for several frightening minutes. Rollie Hemsley and Oscar Grimes carried him off the field to the clubhouse, where help was waiting. After Weatherly eventually opened his eyes, he reported that he had seen a million shooting stars the second the baseball struck him above the ear. An ambulance transported him to Lakeside Hospital for X-rays. Dr. Castle, the Indians physician, saw nothing fractured, but diagnosed Weatherly with a severe concussion. He did not return to active duty for another nine days.

Manager Peckinpaugh informed the sportswriters he had planned to distribute batting helmets while the team practiced in Fort Meyers. Peck stated, "I really intended to get the helmets before the season opened. Larry McPhail the Dodgers president was strong for them when we were in Cuba this spring. Several players in our league are wearing them and the average spectator doesn't even notice the difference." Peck explained that the helmets were lightweight, worn on the inside of the player's cap. Some of the Dodgers and the Giants wore them, he said. In the American League a few Washington Senators also wore them, as did Lamar Newsome, a reserve infielder playing for Boston.

In the 1940 season Larry McPhail had watched helplessly as both Pee Wee Reese and Joe Medwick went down with serious beanballs to the head. Each player missed significant time recovering from concussion-like symptoms. Rather than write it off as part of the game, McPhail searched for an answer to this neglected problem. He located a doctor who was experimenting with a lightweight type of plastic capable of lessening the shock of blows to the cranium. McPhail invested in the contraption and swayed many of his reluctant players toward wearing the protection. The ballplayers' main concern was that opposing players would find out and they would be subjected to endless needling as "yellow." Hidden under the cap, the protection would be hard to detect.

Peck failed to explain why he never actually went ahead and ordered them himself. But at least the conversation was happening, even though the vast majority of Major League ballplayers still preferred no protection. That would not come until the late 1950s.

As the season went on, the Indians pitching staff, other than Feller, slowly fell apart, resulting in the team plunging in the standings. By July 4 they were in second place, trailing the Yankees by two and a half games. Cleveland had a spectacular Independence Day scheduled, with an afternoon doubleheader against St. Louis at the stadium followed in the evening by the much-heralded Festival of Freedom, which would feature a magnificent fireworks display. The afternoon got off to a rousing start when the hometown guys provided some dazzling fireworks of their own.

In game one the Browns had a comfortable 8–4 lead heading into the bottom of the ninth inning. With two men out and two aboard, Ken Keltner ripped a line drive home run into the left-field stands, cutting the gap to a single run. Relief pitcher Jack Kramer entered the game for St. Louis starter Johnny Niggeling. He walked Clarence Campbell, bringing Jeff Heath to the plate. Hitless in four at bats, Heath drove a base hit to right field. The ball got away for a two-base error, scoring Campbell and leaving Heath at third. Hal Trosky walked to the batter's box with a chance to knock in the fifth run of the inning and win the ball game. As Kramer delivered to the plate, Heath dashed fifteen feet down the base line, then put on the brakes. Harlond Clift, the third baseman, had already moved three or four steps toward shortstop, since Trosky, a lefty, rarely hit his way. Both Kramer and Clift paid little or no attention to Heath. Clift even yelled to the pitcher, "Work on the batter Jack, this guy ain't goin' nowhere." Rather than pitching from a stretch, Kramer went into his windup just as Heath raced for home and slid in safely ahead of the pitch. His audacious steal of home won the ball game 9–8. The Indians bench poured out of the dugout and pounded on Heath in celebration.

In game two Cleveland, behind Al Smith, was on top 1–0 after six innings. American League rules at the time prohibited any ball game from starting an inning after 5:30 p.m. The Browns hurried to bat at approximately 5:29, barely a minute before the curfew. They managed to score two runs, regaining the lead and forcing the Indians to score twice to win. The holiday crowd of 34,000 had seen one comeback and now urged the club for another. As if it was scripted, there were two men on base and two men out when Lou Boudreau dug in at the plate. He wasted no time, lashing the baseball off the left-field wall for a game-winning two-bagger. Cleveland had won the doubleheader the hard way, forging two thrilling come-from-behind victories with two outs in their last at bats.

The jovial fans filed out of the stadium, making way for the Festival of Freedom and its spectacular fireworks show at dusk. Over 70,000 people crowded into the stands, eager to see all the festivities, including, music, parades, patriotic floats, an army and coast guard demonstration, and, as a grand finale, the fireworks.

At the start of the extravaganza, several planes flew over the stadium, dropping American flags all over the park. Then came a live national address by President Roosevelt, heard clearly through the loudspeakers surrounding the interior of the stadium. The bands played "Yankee Doodle" and several other favorite tunes, followed by a parade of army cars being converted to weaponized half-tracks for overseas use. Soon darkness fell on the stadium and the fireworks began. The families in attendance cheered heartily as the rockets exploded high over the playing field. What a day for Cleveland! The Indians swept a doubleheader, and the city hosted over 100,000 people downtown. The festival served to whip up patriotic feelings among the local citizens, embedding in their thoughts the probability of war in the days ahead.

Major League Baseball had already seen a small number of players drafted into the service. Pitcher Hugh Mulcahy of the Philadelphia Phillies had left for boot camp several months ago.

In May Hank Greenberg entered the army, severely damaging the chances of the Tigers repeating as the American League champions. Buddy Lewis, the fine young Washington outfielder, received notice of his induction, which would take place immediately after the season's end. Several marginal players were also called, along with a significant group of minor league hopefuls.

Newspapers reported that Ted Williams might not finish the season, and that the same might be true for Bob Feller, although everyone in Cleveland knew that story was false. But with all the Major Leaguers registered, few people could be certain how many players' names would be called before the end of the season.

The Yankees were now in first place, but that news took second billing to Joe DiMaggio's fantastic hitting streak. The streak had commenced on May 15, and in the first week of July it was still going strong. The Yankees were on the road, drawing large crowds eager to see how long the streak would last. DiMaggio had easily surpassed Ty Cobb's mark of forty, accomplished in 1911, followed by George Sisler's modern and American League record of forty-one, set in 1922. Next was Bill Dahlen's total of forty-two games in 1894, and beyond that stood the all-time record of forty-four games, set by Hall of Famer Willie Keeler in 1897. With America keeping track, on July 2 Joe D. erased Keeler, then carried on through fifty games.

On Sunday, July 13, New York played a road doubleheader against the Chicago White Sox. An enormous crowd of 50,387 witnessed Joe extend the hitting streak to games fifty-two and fifty-three. The Yankees came east to Cleveland with DiMaggio at fifty-five games.

The two clubs met on July 16 at League Park. Despite it being a Wednesday matinee, 15,000 people poured into the park, more concerned with the streak than the outcome of the ball game. DiMaggio wasted no time in lifting the mark to fifty-six games, looping a single off the bat handle into center field. He picked up two more hits in the course of the game, including a double off the left-field wall. The Yankees, thanks to five RBIs from catcher Buddy Rosar, crushed the Indians 10–3. Lost in the excitement was that New York now led Cleveland by six games. Forget about DiMaggio's streak; another couple of losses would just about end the Indians' chances for 1941.

On Thursday evening, July 17, the two clubs met at Municipal Stadium for game two of the series. Cy Slapnicka announced that all 34,000 reserved seats were sold out, leaving only general admission tickets available at the box office. The seats went on sale at 5:30 p.m., drawing extensive lines of fans undeterred by all the prime locations having already been taken. Two hours later, ticket sales had soared to over 67,000, the largest crowd of any night game to date.

Al Smith, pitching on three days' rest, started the contest against an aging Lefty Gomez. Though his fastball had seen better days, Gomez, relying on off-speed pitches and knuckleballs, kept the Indians hitters guessing for much of the game. The Yankees scored in the first inning on a single by Red Rolfe, followed by he could have been an Indian Tommy Henrich's double. That brought DiMaggio to the plate. He lined a bullet down the third-base line. Ken Keltner made a tremendous lunge, backhanded the ball as it was going by, then righted himself and threw to first in time to get the speeding DiMaggio. Cleveland evened the score in the fourth inning when Gee Walker belted a drive to deep left center field that rolled to the wall, far enough for Walker to hustle around the bases for an inside-the-park home run.

The game stayed knotted up at 1–1 until the top of the seventh inning. After drawing a walk in the fourth, DiMaggio was up to bat again. Once again he smashed a drive at Keltner, who managed to knock the ball down, recover, and fire to first ahead of Joe D. The fans had mixed emotions. They were thrilled by Keltner's brilliant play, yet worried DiMaggio might not get another chance to extend the streak. As the crowd buzzed about what had happened, Joe Gordon homered to give New York the lead, 2–1.

In the Yankees' half of the eighth, Charlie Keller rapped a line shot to straightaway center field. Roy Weatherly sprinted in, attempting to catch the ball off his shoetops, but the ball skipped by and rolled all the way toward the bleachers. Keller raced to third with a gift triple courtesy of Weatherly's faulty judgment. The Indians pulled the infield in, attempting to cut off any ground ball and hold Keller at third. Lefty Gomez surprised everybody by lofting a soft pop fly over the infield, scoring Keller with New York's third run of the day. First baseman Johnny Sturm singled, moving Gomez to second. Red Rolfe lined a double, bringing home the huffing and puffing Gomez. Tommy Henrich drew a base on balls off new pitcher Jim Bagby Jr., bringing DiMaggio to the plate with the bases loaded. What a scenario! DiMaggio at bat with three runners aboard for one last chance to keep the streak alive.

Bagby leaned toward home, intent on getting his name in the record books by retiring the Yankee great. With most of the Cleveland fans standing and shouting, Bagby delivered the pitch. DiMaggio swung, bouncing one to shortstop Lou Boudreau. At the last instant the ball took a weird hop, but Boudreau seized the baseball in his bare hand and flipped it underhand toward second base. Ray Mack collected the toss, stepped on the bag, then threw to first ahead of the resolute DiMaggio. Unless the game went to extra innings, the spectacular hitting streak had ended at fifty-six games. Superior infield play had done the job.

The Indians added to the drama in the last half of the ninth. Pinch hitter Larry Rosenthal belted a triple past the outfielders, scoring two runs. Rosenthal stood on third, representing the tying run with nobody out. Hal Trosky rolled a ground ball to first, not deep enough to score the runner. Clarence Campbell was next. He scorched a line drive off relief pitcher Johnny Murphy's leg. The ball landed a short distance from the mound, and Rosenthal, who had committed himself to running, was trapped in a rundown between home and third. Campbell should have been able to take second, but for some unexplained reason stood on the right-field foul line, watching as Rosenthal was eventually tagged out. This error in judgment let Johnny Sturm stand in front of first as Weatherly batted, preventing Campbell from taking any kind of a lead. Weatherly represented the last hope, but he drove a hard ground ball right at Sturm, who made the pickup, ending the game with a victory for New York and closing the books on DiMaggio's fifty-six-game streak.

In the visitors' clubhouse, writers made their way, pencils and notepads ready, to where DiMaggio sat quietly in front of his locker. "I can't say that I am glad it's over," DiMaggio said. "Of course I wanted to go on as long as I could. The guy who turned the trick was Keltner. He was rough on me." Ironically, on June 1 in New York, in game 2 of a doubleheader, DiMaggio whistled a shot down the third base line. Keltner knocked the ball down but threw low and wide to first. After a moment the official scorer ruled a base hit rather than an error, allowing the streak to reach eighteen games. A month and a half later, on two similar balls hit to him, Keltner made perfect throws to end a phenomenal feat that may never be topped. For his part, Keltner had little to say to writers. He did comment, "He hit the ball hard but was unfortunate enough to hit where it could be fielded."

In the course of the streak, DiMaggio batted .408 with 91 hits in 223 at bats. He accounted for 55 runs batted in while hitting 15 home runs and 4 triples. It was the Indians who figured heavily in the beginning and end of the magnificent streak.

The summer months of 1941 greatly benefited from Joe DiMaggio's implausible performance. Fans all around the country raced to snatch the morning paper, hoping the streak continued. Anyone talking baseball had to include at least a few sentences about the Yankee star. In a time of uncertainty about the future of the entire world, DiMaggio brought relief to thousands of people.

In all the talk about the game at Municipal Stadium, not many folks paid attention to the staggering numbers recorded by the Cleveland Concession Company. Fans were super-hungry and mighty thirsty, eating 124,000 hot dogs and 12,200 bags of peanuts and popcorn and guzzling 248,000 bottles of Coca-Cola and 12,000 bottles of beer. Anticipating a big night of food consumption, 350 vendors walked the grandstand while 22 vendor stands were open. Total attendance for the night game at the stadium plus the July 16 game at League Park reached 82,000 customers. Even with the Indians faltering, another big year at the box office was ensured.

Chapter 16

ANOTHER PLAYER-MANAGER

B eyond the excitement of halting the DiMaggio streak, things went steadily downhill for the Indians. Mel Harder developed bone chips in his pitching elbow, while Hal Trosky suffered from agonizing migraine headaches. Feller, recently named the *Sporting News* player of the year for 1940, pitched reasonably well, but the rest of the staff fell off considerably. Thoughts of winning the pennant grew more distant with each passing day.

Nonetheless, fans all around Cleveland perked up with the news of the Sunday, July 27, Amateur Day at Cleveland Stadium. Max Rosenblum, the man behind the event, scored an extraordinary coup by bringing in Ty Cobb and Babe Ruth to coach the teams and greet the crowd. Tris Speaker agreed to join in the festivities, bringing together the three greatest outfielders the game had ever seen. Cobb traveled from his summer home in Montana, while Mr. and Mrs. Ruth made the trip from New York.

Rosenblum had started the Cleveland Amateur Baseball and Athletic Association in 1906 to benefit young boys eager to play organized baseball. The association grew by leaps and bounds, serving several thousand boys in the greater Cleveland area. Some of the most talented nonprofessional teams in the country were developed in Cuyahoga County, several of which won national championships.

In the late 1930s the Cleveland Baseball Federation replaced the old association, but Rosenblum continued to work behind the scenes raising money for equipment and medical care for any injured participants. He sold patron tickets to wealthy donors, who paid a premium in advance of the annual CBF Day. Through this outlet, Rosenblum added approximately $5,000–6,000 to the gate receipts, which in 1938 paid for lights at several amateur ball fields. At one of the recent fundraisers, he had brought Father Edward Flanagan of Boys Town fame, in an effort to raise awareness of Amateur Day. Father Flanagan had won many laurels for his foundation, which educated wayward boys and taught them a trade. Now Ruth, Cobb, and Speaker were aboard, ensuring good attendance for the Sunday event.

Even with temperatures soaring near the hundred-degree mark, the three Hall of Fame ballplayers arrived at Municipal Stadium and were driven in an auto around the field while everyone cheered. Within a short time, all three were busy signing scorecards, baseballs, and souvenir tickets. Claire Ruth related to the sportswriters that she and her famous husband rarely attended ball games. "I find myself passing over a steady stream of cards and papers for Babe's signature. We wind up reading about the game in the papers, although we did enjoy a game in Boston when Tom Yawkey placed a couple of guards at our box."

Babe reminisced about a game played in the early 1930s at the stadium. "Mel Harder was pitching for the Indians and I told myself to forget about those stands. So I poked five hits into left field and got me five for five that day. Yes sir, three of them were just inside third base and was Harder burned up!" Babe added that his biggest thrill in baseball came in the 1932 World Series win against the Chicago Cubs.

Ty Cobb reveled in the attention, signing autographs with a small child on each knee and a little one hanging around his neck. Old-timers Elmer Flick and Jim Delahanty (brother of Ed) stopped by to greet Cobb and talk about the early days of the Cleveland Naps and Detroit Tigers. Cobb recounted a story about tricking New York first baseman Hal Chase into throwing to the wrong base. During numerous ball games against the Highlanders, Cobb, advancing from second to third on a ground ball, would round the base, drawing a quick throw from the alert Chase. Each time Cobb would dive back safely under the tag. In one particular game, after rounding third, he hesitated for a second, then dashed for home. Chase, reacting to the movement, could not stop himself from throwing to the third baseman. Cobb romped home, laughing at the ruse he had successfully pulled off.

The smiling Cobb bore little resemblance to the fiery ballplayer of thirty years ago who terrorized clubs around the American League. He signed countless autographs before excusing himself to coach several amateur teams against fellow coaches Ruth and Speaker.

The high point of the day took place when the fans and amateur players clamored for Babe to leave the coaching box and step up to the plate. Although he had not swung a bat in several years, Ruth, wearing his old Yankees uniform, obliged. He took his familiar stance, waving the bat as he had done thousands of times before. The Cleveland Rosenblums, always one of the city's elite amateur outfits, were in the field. The pitcher wound up and threw his best offering towards the plate. Babe took a mighty swing and lined a rope to straightaway center field. Everyone in the stadium rose to their feet, delighted to see the larger-than-life Babe powder the ball one more time.

Cleveland Amateur Day raised between $10,000 and $11,000, a fabulous amount that would buy a ton of equipment and pay all the kids' medical expenses for some time. Ruth and Cobb left together, catching a late train bound for Detroit and a golf exhibition between the two on Monday. All the proceeds from the match were earmarked for the United Service Organizations (USO) to pay for much-needed entertainment and refreshments for the servicemen. The U.S. government paid for the construction of the centers, while donations went toward the free coffee, donuts, movies, and dancing. A total of 186 centers across America would eventually be available for the servicemen to relax and forget about the probability of their serving in Europe.

The 1941 baseball season was filled with exciting play and landmark accomplishments. Ted Williams finished the year batting .406, the highest average since Rogers Hornsby's .424 in 1924. He also led the American League in walks, an indication the pitchers were not giving him many balls in the strike zone. Joe DiMaggio, no thanks to the Cleveland infielders, had his record fifty-six game hitting streak. The Indians claimed no records, finishing below .500 even with most experts picking them to win the pennant. What went wrong? The short answer: A lot of things.

In 1940 Harder, Milnar, and Smith won a total of forty-five games. That number shrank to twenty-nine just a year later. Jim Bagby Jr. contributed an unimpressive nine wins against fifteen losses. Only Bob Feller lived up to expectations, leading all American League pitchers with twenty-five wins. On the hitting side, Hal Trosky could not find a cure for his terrible migraine headaches and spent most of the second half of the season out of the lineup. His absence robbed the team of his usual 100–110 RBIs and 25–30 home runs. The migraines would eventually force a reluctant Trosky to retire from baseball.

Jeff Heath picked up some of the slack, having the best season of his young career. He batted .340, behind only Williams, Cecil Travis of Washington, and DiMaggio. He finished second in RBIs with 123 and hits with 199, and led everyone by bashing 20 triples. In two late-August games against Boston and Philadelphia, Heath whacked three three-run homers and batted in ten. He also stole a career-best eighteen bases, including the steal of home that won a ball game in the bottom of the ninth.

Feller dominated once again, leading all A.L. pitchers in wins, starts, innings pitched, strikeouts (for the fourth year in a row), and shutouts. As of July 18, he owned a record of nineteen wins versus four losses. He seemed a sure bet to win thirty games, but through the rest of the season he won just eight more times while losing nine. It should be noted that his teammates did not help matters by providing mediocre run support and committing untimely errors. He ended the year with another one-hitter, but walked seven batters, leading to two runs being scored. His control for the season took a turn backwards, which was puzzling since he appeared to have conquered his wildness for more than a year. On a July 26 loss at Boston, Feller allowed six base on balls. Eight days later at League Park, Feller lost a thirteen-inning struggle to Detroit, 4–3. He struck out thirteen, yet walked a total of eleven.

The poor late-season performance by most of the Indians gave Manager Peckinpaugh a chance to look over his younger players, such as pitcher Steve Gromek, highly touted catcher Jim Hegan.

and outfielder Hank Edwards. Except for Hegan, who hit .319 in sixteen games, the other guys did little but showed some potential for the years ahead. Slowly the ingredients for another winning ball club were being carefully assembled. Feller was without debate the best pitcher in the Major Leagues, Lou Boudreau was one of the top shortstops around, and Ken Keltner was a steady if not spectacular third baseman. Add Jim Hegan to the mix, another good arm in Gromek, and a young minor league infielder ready to bid for a job in Bob Lemon, and one could notice seeds being planted. It would be a few years before harvest, but sunnier days loomed ahead.

Just days before the end of the campaign, Cy Slapnicka surprised the baseball world when he submitted his resignation to Alva Bradley. For almost twenty years he had been an essential part of the Indians franchise, serving as a scout, then chief scout, and eventually general manager. Slapnicka had spent the majority of his adult life in baseball, starting in 1907 as a twenty-one-year-old minor league pitcher. He broke into the Major Leagues for brief stints with the 1911 Chicago Cubs and seven years later with the Pittsburgh Pirates. In the off-seasons he earned an unusual living as an acrobat, performing balancing stunts on chairs, bottles, books, and all types of strange objects.

In his lengthy career with Cleveland, he personally signed talent including Harder, Trosky, Feller, Weatherly, Heath, and Keltner. On the negative side of the ledger, Slapnicka nearly lost Feller to free agency, did lose the services of Tommy Henrich, and most certainly played a role in Lou Boudreau forfeiting his status as a college amateur. Slapnicka assembled the key elements of the 1940 and 1941 Indians roster, going down with the ship when the Indians failed to capture a pennant. Possibly he grew weary of attempting another rebuild and all the labor that goes along with it.

Alva Bradley accepted the resignation, advising reporters he had talked his general manager out of stepping down at least several times in the past. On this occasion Bradley had no qualms about letting Slapnicka go his own way. The boss seemed upbeat, talking about dividing up the general manager's responsibilities or even moving Roger Peckinpaugh upstairs. There would be no undue haste in reorganizing the Cleveland front office.

At the end of October, Bradley hinted that Peck might become the new general manager. He acknowledged that Roger knew the organization as well as anybody, so why go outside for somebody else? The revelation meant a clandestine search for a new manager had already started or would be starting any moment. Soon names such as Lefty O'Doul, Bill Terry, and Charlie Gehringer were plastered all over the Cleveland sports pages. On November 2 Peck was officially named general manager of the Cleveland Indians, and the field manager rumors continued with the same three names bandied about.

Two weeks later Lou Boudreau arrived in Cleveland for a Friday conference with Bradley. Little news came from the meeting, especially when Boudreau hurriedly left without talking to pick up his pal Ray Mack and drive to Columbus for the Ohio State–Illinois football game. The sportswriters had no inkling that Boudreau had appeared in Cleveland for a singular purpose. He brought along his résumé and was making a strong play to manage the ball club.

The question immediately comes to mind why a ballplayer in his early twenties, with less than three full years of service in the Majors, would desire a manager's job. The answer lies in Boudreau's background and strong personality. He had captained both the Illinois basketball and baseball teams. He was intelligent and mature, earning the respect of his teammates wherever he played. He had probably thought about managing at some point in his career. So why not now? Even if Boudreau failed to get the job, he could earn some points for the future.

While Bradley considered a number of options for a new manager, he grew more and more certain he needed a man who possessed a fresh outlook. The candidates he deliberated on all boasted many years of Major League Baseball experience. Too much experience, to Bradley's thinking. He began to move away, in his mind, from the standard model of managers with twenty or thirty years of know-how who brought the grandchildren to spring training.

The turning point came when George Martin, one of Bradley's shareholders and chairman of the board of Sherwin-Williams, argued for hiring a young man such as Lou Boudreau. Martin, in his eighties, recognized the time had come for a youthful man to take over the reins, and he lobbied Bradley hard. On November 25 an excited Lou Boudreau accepted the job of player-manager of the Cleveland club.

Reaction to the hiring among the local fans was mixed. Many believed it meant the front office had gone on the cheap, in essence hiring two for the price of one. Bringing in a veteran manager might cost the front office $15,000–16,000. Signing Boudreau, they thought, might mean giving him only a small bump in his salary, only a few thousand dollars or so, hardly enough to make a dent in the bottom line.

Of course Bradley denied all the allegations, insisting the choice had nothing to do with money. He told the newspapers, "I don't know of another man of whom I could be so certain that he would be thoroughly respected by players, press and public. Lou is smart, he's a great ball player, a fine young man, a fighter and leader."

Boudreau fielded numerous interview requests from the Cleveland papers. He told one paper, "The first division will be our goal. If we have Bob Feller we'll make it. But if we lose him it will be tough, but we'll be in there hustling that much I can promise."

The new manager disclosed that he would keep Peck's training rules of a midnight curfew and one or two glasses of beer after a game. He planned to extend the Indians dugout at Municipal Stadium farther away from the stands in an effort to keep fans from watching and listening in. Boudreau discussed building a genuine clubhouse for the players with more than just benches, a place where they could come early and relax before workouts and ball games. The enthusiasm and optimism shone through in his remarks.

A week later Bradley felt the need to dispel the talk about all the money savings. He insisted Boudreau had a fair contract to manage the club for two years. He maintained that the salaries of the Cleveland general manager and field manager had gone up significantly with the two new hires. The writers believed Boudreau's contract would pay him $35,000 for the two seasons, not spectacular money but reasonable. Gradually the talk died down as Bradley and his new executives left for the winter meetings.

The league owners played it conservative in the trade market, preferring to hold onto their older players in case the young ones left for the service. The Indians did little to help Boudreau for the upcoming season, keeping the current roster almost intact. They did make one significant move in selling Rollie Hemsley to the St. Louis Cardinals for $12,000. The deal raised some eyebrows, but Rollie had burned a few bridges with management. Bradley said his former catcher played last season like he was on an extended vacation. In addition, Rollie apparently had some designs on becoming a manager, freely second-guessing Peck on his decisions.

The *Cleveland News* reported a disturbing note implicating Hemsley as the man behind the 1940 late-season hotel meeting in Detroit. According to the updated story, the gathering took place in Hemsley's room, where the players either agreed to ignore manager Vitt's signs or simply talked about strategy. It looked like some skulduggery may have indeed occurred, with Hemsley the likely point man.

Combine this with Rollie's participation in the June 1940 rebellion and it becomes clearer why the catcher had to go. The move left Gene Desautels as the only backstop on the club with any real game experience. To complicate matters, Mel Harder had surgery on his ailing elbow, leaving him a question mark for the coming season. New manager Boudreau had a few large rocks in the road ahead of him.

The December meetings would reveal that 277 minor league ballplayers had already been drafted into the army. Owners feared that total would probably double in 1942, given that a large number of players were about to reach draft age. The near future of baseball was uncertain. How much longer would the United States remain neutral in the war against Germany? If the country entered the war, how many players might put their gloves away and immediately enlist? Perhaps night games, a prime moneymaker, should be canceled because of the need to save energy during wartime? There were no answers in the early part of December. But a catastrophic event would change the face of America for years to come.

EPILOGUE

On a tranquil Sunday morning on December 7, 1941, the Japanese navy launched a surprise attack on Pearl Harbor, Hawaii. Two waves of bomber and fighter planes attacked the vital military base, leaving several thousand sailors and soldiers dead or wounded. Many American warships were destroyed beyond repair, along with several hundred warplanes sitting wing-to-wing at their airstrips.

Americans were stunned at the horrible news from the Pacific. The military had not foreseen the possibility of an unprovoked attack and was caught completely unaware. Although the entire assault lasted less than two hours, the destruction of fighter planes, warships, and equipment at the Pearl Harbor Naval Base reached a level never before seen in the Americas.

On December 8, President Roosevelt issued his famous address to a joint session of Congress, beginning, "Yesterday, December 7, 1941, a date which will live in infamy, the United States of America was suddenly and deliberately attacked by naval and air forces of the Empire of Japan." After the speech, it took only one hour for Congress to vote yes on the declaration of war. Several days later Germany declared war on the United States, provoking a similar response. Now the country would be fighting a war on two completely different fronts, one in Europe and the other in the ocean and on the islands of the massive South Pacific.

As the outrage against the Pearl Harbor attack mounted, eligible men flocked to recruiting stations, ready to battle on either front. News developed from Cleveland concerning Bob Feller's major decision to leave baseball behind and enlist in the U.S. Navy. Feller, not waiting to be drafted, had been vacillating for several days on which branch of the military to offer his services to. For several months he had taken flying lessons in Cleveland (unknown to the ball club), and had already logged five hours of solo flight time. Speculation arose that the training indicated Feller had determined to enter the air force as a fighter pilot. In the end Feller announced his plan to join the navy, where he would assist in the physical fitness department.

Gene Tunney, the former heavyweight champion boxer, headed the navy's fitness section, training out-of-condition recruits and building them into fighting shape. Having Bob Feller serving under him immensely helped Tunney in convincing young men the best place in the military was the navy. Commander Tunney moved quickly to enlist other ballplayers, such as outfielder Sam Chapman of the Athletics and Fred Hutchinson, an end-of-the-roster pitcher with Detroit.

Feller signed his papers on December 10 and received a few days off before reporting to the Norfolk, Virginia, training facility. Because of his celebrity status, the ceremony was covered live on radio and recorded in several newsreels. After six weeks of hard work, he would link up with Tunney at the Great Lakes Naval Training Station for assignment as a $99 a month physical fitness instructor. His post would be confined to the United States, far away from the fighting in the Pacific or Europe.

Though Feller wasted no time in enlisting, there were critics who disapproved of his choice of service. Some wrote to the newspapers arguing that the pitcher should have requested active duty rather than remaining in the States. Allegedly the Cleveland draft board had received a letter from Feller's mother, explaining that Bill Feller had an aggressive brain tumor, leaving her son as the breadwinner of the family. She did not specifically ask for a deferment, only provided additional information to the draft file. Nevertheless, a number of people interpreted the letter and the navy assignment as preferential treatment. It seemed to be a case of people resenting a successful person for initially accepting a safe tour of duty.

Several days after the attack on Pearl Harbor, a nervous group of Major League owners met to discuss plans for 1942. Mel Ott, the new manager of the Giants, summed things up. "You can't think in terms of baseball at a time like this. Young men and I mean young ballplayers aren't going to wait for drafting. They're really mad and they're going to be enlisting for this before the season gets here."

There was concern about the teams holding their spring training camps in Southern California, an area possibly vulnerable to the Japanese navy. The owners decided to wait on changing locations until more information came from the military. The commissioner's office raised $25,000 toward buying baseball supplies for army and navy bases, earmarked for soldiers' and sailors' relaxation time.

Clark Griffith wrestled with his fellow owners to make certain the money was set aside for the enlisted men eager to play pickup ball. In the First World War, Griffith had outfitted a ship to take baseball equipment across the Atlantic for homesick soldiers. On the voyage a German U-boat sank the ship with all its contents. Undaunted, Griffith paid for another ship to make a second attempt. This one arrived safely, distributing the baseball supplies all over Europe.

A general consensus of the owners favored donating the proceeds from the July 1942 All-Star game, a sum likely in the neighborhood of $100,000. The magnates were in agreement that servicemen should receive as much support from baseball as possible. To help them stay on track, the Baseball Writers' Association of America pooled their resources for a $1,000 donation to be used toward buying balls, bats, and gloves.

The *Sporting News* initiated a weekly column dedicated to military news, informing readers about the comings and goings of the ballplayers. The names of major and minor league players trickled in, such as Johnny Sturm and backup catcher Ken Silvestri of the Yankees and shortstop Al Brancato of the Athletics. Pitcher Bill Posedel of the Boston Braves traded uniforms, along with Mickey Harris of the Red Sox. Johnny Berardino, infielder for the Browns long before his career as Dr. Steve Hardy on the soap opera *General Hospital*, joined the Naval Reserves.

The minor leaguers outnumbered their counterparts by a fair margin, since many of the players were single and had no dependents. One of the minor league players taken was old-timer Zeke Bonura, who had spent years in the big time, but had chosen to finish his career at the lower level. Bruce Dudley, owner of the Louisville Colonels, donated every foul ball recovered to soldiers at various military bases. His actions opened the door for other owners to do the same or better.

With so much uncertainty surrounding the United States and particularly Major League Baseball, Commissioner Landis penned a handwritten letter to President Roosevelt on January 14. The letter read in part:

> Dear President Roosevelt,
>
> The time is approaching when, in ordinary conditions, our teams would be heading for spring training camps. However, inasmuch as these are not ordinary times, I venture to ask what you have in mind as to whether professional baseball should continue to operate. Of course, my inquiry does not relate at all to individual members of this organization, whose status, in the emergency, is fixed by law operating upon all citizens.

In just one day President Roosevelt replied with instructions to carry on. The March 1942 edition of *Baseball Magazine* printed his response:

> My dear Judge,
>
> Thank you for yours of January fourteenth. As you will, of course, realize the final decision about the baseball season must rest with you and the Baseball Club owners— so what I am going to say is solely a personal and not an official point of view.
>
> I honestly feel that it would be best for the country to keep baseball going. There will be fewer people unemployed and everybody will work longer hours and harder than ever before.
>
> And that means that they ought to have a chance for recreation and for taking their minds off their work even more than before.

The president suggested playing more night games as many workers would be on day shifts and unable to attend afternoon games. He reasoned that there would be 300 major and minor league teams furnishing baseball to at least 20,000,000 Americans, making it worthwhile to continue the game.

Baseball would perform its patriotic duty through the war years ahead. Each season the talent pool was further depleted, but fans in all the Major League cities relied on the game as a welcome diversion from their day-to-day worries. The people of the United States went about their business as routinely as possible, working on the job, then going with their families to see a ball game. The war took a ghastly toll on the men overseas as well as their anxious families left behind. Yet in the end democracy survived the struggle, building an era of renewed hope and prosperity for Americans and of course for the grand old game.

CLEVELAND INDIANS, 1937–41

Year-by-Year Standings

	W–L	PCT	FINISH
1937	83–71	.539	Fourth
1938	86–66	.566	Third
1939	87–67	.565	Third
1940	89–65	.578	Second
1941	75–79	.487	Fifth

Managers

Steve O'Neill	1937
Oscar Vitt	1938–40
Roger Peckinpaugh	1941

Players

Earl Averill OF

YEAR	G	AB	H	R	D	T	HR	RBI	BA
1937	156	609	182	121	33	11	21	92	.299
1938	134	482	159	101	27	15	14	93	.330
1939	24	61	15	8	8	0	1	7	.273

(Traded to Detroit June 14)

Roy "Beau" Bell OF

YEAR	G	AB	H	R	D	T	HR	RBI	BA
1940	120	444	124	55	22	2	4	58	.279
1941	48	104	20	12	4	3	0	9	.192

Lou Boudreau SS

YEAR	G	AB	H	R	D	T	HR	RBI	BA
1938	1	1	0	0	0	0	0	0	.000
1939	53	225	58	42	15	4	0	19	.258
1940	155	627	185	97	46	10	9	101	.295
1941	148	579	149	95	45*	8	10	56	.257

Bruce Campbell OF

YEAR	G	AB	H	R	D	T	HR	RBI	BA
1937	134	448	135	82	42	11	4	61	.301
1938	133	511	148	90	27	12	12	72	.290
1939	130	450	129	84	23	13	8	72	.287

1940 (Traded to Detroit)

Ben Chapman OF

YEAR	G	AB	H	R	D	T	HR	RBI	BA
1939	149	545	158	101	31	9	6	82	.290
1940	143	548	157	82	40	6	4	50	.286

1941 (Traded to Washington)

Sammy "Bad News" Hale 3B-2B

YEAR	G	AB	H	R	D	T	HR	RBI	BA
1937	154	561	150	74	32	4	6	82	.267
1938	130	496	138	69	32	2	8	69	.278
1939	108	253	79	36	16	2	4	48	.312
1940	48	50	11	3	3	1	0	6	.220

1941 (Traded to Boston)

Jeff Heath OF

YEAR	G	AB	H	R	D	T	HR	RBI	BA
1937	20	61	14	8	1	4	0	8	.230
1938	126	502	172	104	31	18*	21	112	.343
1939	121	431	126	64	31	7	14	69	.292
1940	100	356	78	55	16	3	14	50	.219
1941	151	585	199	89	32	20*	24	123	.340

Rollie Hemsley C

YEAR	G	AB	H	R	D	T	HR	RBI	BA
1938	66	203	60	27	11	3	2	28	.296
1939	107	395	104	58	17	4	2	36	.263
1940	119	416	111	46	20	5	4	42	.267
1941	98	288	69	29	10	5	2	24	.240

Roy Hughes 3B-2B

YEAR	G	AB	H	R	D	T	HR	RBI	BA
1937	104	346	96	57	12	6	1	40	.277

1938 (Traded to St. Louis Browns)

Ken Keltner 3B

YEAR	G	AB	H	R	D	T	HR	RBI	BA
1938	149	576	159	86	31	9	26	113	.276
1939	154	587	191	84	35	11	13	97	.325
1940	149	543	138	67	24	10	15	77	.254
1941	149	581	156	83	31	13	23	84	.269

Lyn Lary SS

YEAR	G	AB	H	R	D	T	HR	RBI	BA
1937	156	644	187	110	46	7	8	77	.290
1938	141	568	152	94	36	4	3	51	.268
1939	3	2	0	0	0	0	0	0	.000

(Sold to Brooklyn)

Ray Mack 2B

YEAR	G	AB	H	R	D	T	HR	RBI	BA
1938	2	6	2	2	0	1	0	2	.333
1939	36	112	17	12	4	1	1	6	.152
1940	146	530	150	60	21	5	12	69	.283
1941	145	501	114	54	22	4	9	44	.228

Frankie Pytlak C

YEAR	G	AB	H	R	D	T	HR	RBI	BA
1937	125	397	125	60	15	6	1	44	.315
1938	113	364	112	46	14	7	1	43	.308
1939	63	183	49	20	2	5	0	14	.268
1940	62	149	21	16	2	1	0	16	.141

1941 (Traded to Boston Red Sox)

Julius "Moose" Solters OF

YEAR	G	AB	H	R	D	T	HR	RBI	BA
1937	152	589	190	90	42	11	20	109	.323
1938	67	199	40	30	6	3	2	22	.201
1939	41	102	28	19	7	2	2	19	.275

(Acquired via waivers by St. Louis Browns August 2)

Hal Trosky 1B

YEAR	G	AB	H	R	D	T	HR	RBI	BA
1937	153	601	179	104	36	9	32	128	.298
1938	150	554	185	106	40	9	19	110	.334
1939	122	448	150	89	31	4	25	104	.335
1940	140	522	154	85	39	4	25	93	.295
1941	89	310	91	43	17	0	11	51	.294

Gerry "Gee" Walker OF

YEAR	G	AB	H	R	D	T	HR	RBI	BA
1941	121	445	126	56	26	11	6	48	.283

Roy "Stormy" Weatherly OF

YEAR	G	AB	H	R	D	T	HR	RBI	BA
1937	53	134	27	19	4	0	5	13	.201
1938	83	210	55	32	14	3	2	18	.262
1939	95	323	100	43	16	6	1	32	.310
1940	135	578	175	90	35	11	12	59	.303
1941	102	363	105	59	21	5	3	37	.289

Pitchers

Johnny Allen

YEAR	G	IP	W	L	ERA	BB	SO	PCT
1937	24	173	15	1	2.55	60	87	.938*
1938	30	200	14	8	4.19	81	112	.636
1939	28	175	9	7	4.58	56	79	.563
1940	32	138.2	9	8	3.44	48	62	.529

1941 (Sold to St. Louis Browns)

Jim Bagby Jr.

YEAR	G	IP	W	L	ERA	BB	SO	PCT
1941	33	200.2	9	15	4.04	76	53	.375

Joe Dobson

YEAR	G	IP	W	L	ERA	BB	SO	PCT
1939	35	78	2	3	5.88	51	27	.400
1940	40	100	3	7	4.95	48	57	.300

1941 (Traded to Boston)

Bob Feller

YEAR	G	IP	W	L	ERA	BB	SO	PCT
1937	26	148.2	9	7	3.39	106	150	.563
1938	39	277.2	17	11	4.08	208*	240*	.607
1939	39	296*	24*	9	2.85	142*	246*	.727
1940	43*	320*	27*	11	2.61*	118	261*	.711
1941	44*	343*	25*	13	3.15	194*	260*	.658

Denny Galehouse

YEAR	G	IP	W	L	ERA	BB	SO	PCT
1937	36	200.2	9	14	4.57	83	78	.391
1938	36	114	7	8	4.34	65	66	.467

1939 (Traded to Boston Red Sox)

Mel Harder

YEAR	G	IP	W	L	ERA	BB	SO	PCT
1937	38	233.2	15	12	4.28	86	95	.556
1938	38	240	17	10	3.83	62	102	.630
1939	29	208	15	9	3.50	64	67	.625
1940	31	186	12	11	4.06	59	76	.522
1941	15	68.2	5	4	5.24	37	21	.556

Willis Hudlin

YEAR	G	IP	W	L	ERA	BB	SO	PCT
1937	35	175.2	12	11	4.10	43	31	.522
1938	29	127	8	8	4.89	45	27	.500
1939	27	143	9	10	4.91	42	28	.474
1940	4	23.2	2	1	4.94	2	8	.667

(Signed as free agent with Washington)

Johnny Humphries

YEAR	G	IP	W	L	ERA	BB	SO	PCT
1938	45*	103	9	8	5.23	63	56	.529
1939	15	28	2	4	8.26	32	12	.333
1940	19	33.2	0	2	8.29	29	17	.000

1941 (Traded to Chicago White Sox)

Al Milnar

YEAR	G	IP	W	L	ERA	BB	SO	PCT
1938	23	68	3	1	5.00	26	29	.750
1939	37	209	14	12	3.79	99	76	.538
1940	37	242	18	10	3.27	99	99	.643
1941	35	229	12	19	4.36	116	82	.387

Al Smith

YEAR	G	IP	W	L	ERA	BB	SO	PCT
1940	31	183	15	7	3.44	55	46	.682
1941	29	206.2	12	13	3.83	75	76	.480

Earl Whitehill

YEAR	G	IP	W	L	ERA	BB	SO	PCT
1937	33	147	8	8	6.49	80	53	.500
1938	26	160	9	8	5.56	83	60	.529

1939 (Signed as free agent with Chicago Cubs)

*Led American League

All-Star Selections 1937–41

1937	Earl Averill, Mel Harder
1938	Johnny Allen, Earl Averill, Bob Feller
1939	Bob Feller, Rollie Hemsley
1940	Lou Boudreau, Bob Feller, Rollie Hemsley, Ken Keltner, Ray Mack, Al Milnar
1941	Lou Boudreau, Bob Feller, Jeff Heath, Ken Keltner

SOURCES

Books

Boudreau, Lou, with Russell Schneider. *Lou Boudreau: Covering All the Bases*. Champaign, IL: Sagamore, 1993.

Creamer, Robert. *Baseball in '41*. New York: Viking, 1991.

Feller, Bob. *Strikeout Story*. New York: Grosset and Dunlap, 1947.

Lewis, Franklin. *The Cleveland Indians*. New York: G. P. Putnam's Sons, 1949.

Odenkirk, James E. *Plain Dealing: A Biography of Gordon Cobbledick*. Phoenix, AZ: Spiders-Naps, 1990.

Reichler, Joseph L., ed. *The Baseball Encyclopedia*. New York: Macmillan, 1979.

Rose, William Gansom. *Cleveland: The Making of a City*. Cleveland: World, 1950.

Sickles, John. *Bob Feller: Ace of the Greatest Generation*. Washington, DC: Brassey's, 2004.

Tebbetts, Birdie, with James Morrison. *Birdie*. Chicago: Triumph Books, 2002.

Vaccaro, Mike. *1941: The Greatest Year in Sports*. New York: Broadway Books, 2007.

Periodicals

Baseball Magazine (1936–38, 1940, 1941, 1942)
Cleveland News (1936–41)

Cleveland Plain Dealer (1936–42)
Cleveland Press (1936–42)
Daily Illini (January–February 1938)
Sporting News (1940–42)

Libraries and Archives

Case Western Reserve University Archives (Ray Mack files)
Cleveland Public Library
Cleveland Height–University Heights Public Library
Franklin D. Roosevelt's Papers as President: The President's Personal
    File: PPF 227 (Baseball), Franklin D. Roosevelt to Commissioner
    Landis, January 16, 1942. Franklin D. Roosevelt Presidential Library
    and Museum, Hyde Park, NY
Major League Baseball Properties Inc. (Judge Landis Letter)
Meigs County Historical Society, Pomeroy, OH
National Baseball Hall of Fame Library, Cooperstown, NY (player files,
    Alva Bradley and Cy Slapnicka files)
Society for American Baseball Research
University of Illinois Archives

Audio

Rollie Hemsley, "Alcoholics Anonymous Talk at Cosmopolitan Group,"
    Washington, DC, April 1968.

Personal Communications

Family of Rollie Hemsley
Family of Ray Mack

Internet Sites

http://www.baseball-almanac.com
Baseball Hall of Fame (Inside Pitch), January, March 2017

INDEX

Mills Commission, 113
Milnar, Al, 117, 133, 135, 139, 148, 152, 162,
   169, 172174, 178, 186–87, 190, 198,
   216, 244–45
Milwaukee Brewers, 6, 8
Missouri Pacific Railroad, 143
Mize, Johnny, 151
Monroe, Marilyn, 25
Montana, 226
Moore, Earl, 80
Moore, Terry, 151
Moses, Wally, 124
Mulcahy, Hugh, 221
Mumaw, Lew, 210–11
Mutual Broadcasting Company, 97, 211
Myer, Buddy, 95

Nashville, Tennessee, 92
national anthem, 110, 215
National Association of Professional
   Baseball, 113
National Football League, 126
National League, 2, 38, 41, 53, 72, 81, 110,
   118, 140, 145–46, 151, 165, 173, 207
National Registration Day, 206
Naval Reserves, 236
Naymick, Mike, 150, 186
NBC Radio, 51
Ness, Eliot, 76, 180
Newark Bears, 38, 54–55, 60, 114, 159
New Castle, Pennsylvania, 69
Newhouser, Hal, 176
New Orleans, 5, 7, 52, 56–57, 100, 127, 143,
   149
New Orleans Pelicans, 3–4, 6, 8, 68, 103,
   111, 131, 142–43
Newsom, Buck, 60, 88, 96, 120, 166, 175,
   194–95, 200–201
Newsome, Lamar, 219
New York Daily News, 128
New York Giants, 7, 37, 57–58, 90, 120, 143,
   150, 165
New York Mirror, 167
New York–Pennsylvania League, 28
New York Yankees, 2, 4–5, 8, 20–21, 23–26,
   31, 33, 35–37, 42, 53–54, 69–71, 74–77,
   81–82, 86, 90–96, 104, 108–9, 114–15,
   119, 122, 135, 139, 140, 144–47,
   151–52, 160, 172, 175–76, 179–81, 184,
   186–90, 192, 213, 216–18, 220, 222–24,
   228, 236
Niggeling, Johnny, 220
Norfolk, Virginia, 235
Northern League, 2, 127
North Harvey Merchants, 128
Nunamaker, Les, 54

Oakland Oaks, 23
O'Doul, Lefty, 231

Ohio River, 43
Ohio Unemployment Compensation
   Bureau, 144
Ohio Valley League, 44
Olympics (1936), 67
O'Neill, Steve, 3, 11, 15–16, 18–21, 31, 35,
   38, 103, 127, 166, 239
Ontario Street, 215
Ostermueller, Fritz, 136
Ott, Mel, 81, 117, 151, 236

Pacific Coast League, 23–24, 53
Pacific Ocean, 234–35
Paige, Satchel, 68
Palace Theatre, 51–52
Palmer Memorial Hospital, 31
Parker, Dan, 167
Pearl Harbor, Hawaii, 234–36
Pearson, Monte, 69, 77, 153
Peckinpaugh, Roger, 103, 207, 209–10, 216,
   219, 229–30, 239
Pennock, Herb, 43
Peters, Russ, 174
Philadelphia Athletics, 10, 90, 100, 124,
   134–35, 143, 160, 168, 173, 179–80,
   184, 190–91, 201, 204, 208, 235–36
Philadelphia Record, 212
Phillips High School, 92
Phi Sigma Kappa, 128
Pilsener Brewing Company, 214
Pippen, Henry, 158
Pittsburgh Crawfords, 68
Pittsburgh Pirates, 27, 38, 44, 67, 230
Players' Fraternity, 165
Players' League, 165
Playhouse Square, 13, 110, 159
P.O.C. Beer, 214
Poland, 110, 140
Porter, Mary Nell, 158
Poschke Barbecues, 126
Posedel, Bill, 236
Potter, Nels, 135
Powell, Jake, 95
Public Square, 75, 85, 123, 186, 215
Purdue University, 92
Pytlak, Frankie, 13, 15–16, 21–22, 32, 34, 43,
   50, 55, 63, 71, 78, 85–86, 100–101, 105,
   111–12, 115, 149, 177, 180–81, 183–84,
   189, 198, 205, 209, 242

Quinn, Johnny, 27, 93

Radcliffe, Rip, 199
Reese, Jimmy, 23–24
Reese, Pee Wee, 219
Reninger, Jim, 135
Ribs and Roast Dinner, 98–99
Richmond, Virginia, 105
Rochester, New York, club, 132

254   Index

University of California, 23, 66
University of Illinois, 103, 128–30, 231, 248
University of Oregon, 66
University of Washington, 66, 68

Vander Meer, Johnny, 117
Van Meter, Iowa, 1, 4, 10–11, 17–18, 62, 98,
    154, 156, 206
Vitt, Oscar, 38–40, 50, 52–64, 69, 72–73, 79,
    80–81, 84–85, 96, 100–101, 106, 108,
    111, 113, 115, 117, 123, 132, 134, 136,
    139–40, 149–50, 152, 155, 158–59,
    160–68, 170–71, 174–75, 177–78,
    182–87, 191, 194–95, 197–99, 204–8,
    213, 233, 239
Vosmik, Joe, 5, 14–15, 27, 137, 206

Wade, Jake, 36
Wagner, Honus, 113, 118
Walker, Gerald "Gee," 11, 209, 216, 217,
    223, 242
Walkup, Jim, 16
Walsh, Ed, 80
Wamby, Bill, 80, 125
Waner Paul, 44
Ward, Arch, 131
Ward, John Montgomery, 165
Washington, D.C., 17, 49, 211
Washington Monument, 85
Washington Senators, 18–19, 21, 25–26, 35,
    79, 85, 91, 95–96, 134, 160, 180, 191,
    193, 209, 222, 229, 240, 244
Weatherly, Roy, 8, 13, 18, 21, 33, 79, 84, 87,
    111, 123–24, 133, 162, 168, 174, 176,
    180–81, 191, 194, 196, 198, 202–4, 219,
    223–24, 230, 243
Weaver, Jim, 61
Webb, Jimmy, 111–12, 117, 120, 132
Weisman, Lefty, 16–17, 30, 82, 108, 153, 193

West, Max, 207
West, Sam, 60
Western Reserve University, 126
Westinghouse, 104
Westminster Palace, 52
West 3rd Street, 147, 215
West Virginia, 28, 43, 57
White, Jo-Jo, 31
Whitehill, Earl, 18, 21, 56, 95, 245
Whittier Elementary School, 127
WHK Radio, 9, 20, 60, 75, 109, 126, 187,
    214
Williams, Ted, 92, 96, 138, 151, 169, 190,
    222, 228
Wilson, Bill, 107
Wilson, Hack, 45
Wilson, Jack, 122
Wilson, Wendell, 130
Winegarner, Ralph, 6
Wizard of Oz, 110, 133
WMAL Radio, 17
Wood, Joe, 36, 80, 114
Work or Fight Order, 189
World War I, 189
World War II, 110, 189
Wright, Taffy, 153
WTAM Radio, 51
Wyatt, Whitlow, 18

Yakima Indians club, 67
Yale University, 114–15, 136
"Yankee Doodle," 221
York, Rudy, 32, 176–76, 186, 191, 194–95,
    198, 203, 217
Young, Cy, 80, 118
Young Men's Hebrew Association, 95

Zanesville club, 6, 67–68
Zuber, Bill, 73, 101, 174